The Films of Ingmar Bergman

This volume provides a concise overview of the career of one of the modern masters of world cinema. Jesse Kalin defines Bergman's conception of the human condition as a struggle to find meaning in life as it is played out. For Bergman, meaning is achieved independently of any moral absolute and is the result of a process of self-examination. Six existential themes are explored repeatedly in Bergman's films: judgment, abandonment, suffering, shame, a visionary picture, and above all, turning toward or away from others. Kalin examines how Bergman develops these themes cinematically, through close analysis of eight films: well-known favorites such as *Wild Strawberries, The Seventh Seal, Smiles of a Summer Night,* and *Fanny and Alexander;* and important but lesser-known works, such as *Naked Night, Shame, Cries and Whispers,* and *Scenes from a Marriage.*

Jesse Kalin is Andrew W. Mellon Professor of Humanities and Professor of Philosophy at Vassar College, where he has taught since 1971. He served as the Associate Editor of the journal *Philosophy and Literature,* and has contributed to journals such as *Ethics, American Philosophical Quarterly,* and *Philosophical Studies.*

CAMBRIDGE FILM CLASSICS

General Editor: **Ray Carney, Boston University**

The Cambridge Film Classics series provides a forum for revisionist studies of the classic works of the cinematic canon from the perspective of the "new auterism," which recognizes that films emerge from a complex interaction of bureaucratic, technological, intellectual, cultural, and personal forces. The series consists of concise, cutting-edge reassessments of the canonical works of film study, written by innovative scholars and critics. Each volume provides a general introduction to the life and work of a particular director, followed by critical essays on several of the director's most important films.

Other Books in the Series

Peter Bondanella, *The Films of Roberto Rossellini*
Peter Brunette, *The Films of Michelangelo Antonioni*
Ray Carney, *The Films of John Cassavetes*
Sam B. Girgus, *The Films of Woody Allen*, 2d edition
James Naremore, *The Films of Vincente Minnelli*
James Palmer and Michael Riley, *The Films of Joseph Losey*

The Films of Ingmar Bergman

Jesse Kalin
Vassar College

CAMBRIDGE
UNIVERSITY PRESS

PUBLISHED BY THE PRESS SYNDICATE OF THE UNIVERSITY OF CAMBRIDGE
The Pitt Building, Trumpington Street, Cambridge, United Kingdom

CAMBRIDGE UNIVERSITY PRESS
The Edinburgh Building, Cambridge CB2 RU, UK
40 West 20th Street, New York, NY 10011–4211, USA
477 Williamstown Road, Port Melbourne, VIC 3166, Australia
Ruiz de Alarcón 13, 28014 Madrid, Spain
Dock House, The Waterfront, Cape Town 8001, South Africa

http://www.cambridge.org

First published 2003

Printed in the United States of America

Typeface Sabon 10/13 pt.   *System* Quark XPress™   [MG]

A catalog record for this book is available from the British Library

Library of Congress Cataloging-in-Publication Data is available

Kalin, Jesse, 1940–
The films of Ingmar Bergman / Jesse Kalin.
p.   cm. – (Cambridge film classics)
Contents: Filmography: p.
Includes bibliographical references (p.) and index.
ISBN 0-521-38065-0 (hardback) – ISBN 0-521-38977-1 (pbk.)
1. Bergman, Ingmar, 1918– – Criticism and interpretation.   I. Title.   II. Series.
PN1998.3.B47K35 2003
791.43´0233´092–dc21
2002041549

ISBN 0 521 38065 0 hardback
ISBN 0 521 38977 1 paperback

Thanks

To the many students in classes and seminars over the many years at Vassar and to my colleagues in the Philosophy and Film Departments here, especially Mitchell Miller, Jennifer Church, and Jim Steerman. To Ingmar Bergman for these films and to some of the screen's greatest actors for bringing his vision to life. For the confidence, encouragement, and not least, patience of the many people involved in this project. And to Virginia and Mary.

Contents

Illustrations

Preface

Ingmar Bergman began his film career as a scriptwriter for Svensk Film-industri in March 1943 at age twenty-four. A treatment for a coming-of-age story was referred by the studio's artistic director, Victor Sjöström, one of the founders of Swedish cinema and an internationally acclaimed director, to Alf Sjöberg, who developed it into *Torment*. It premiered on October 2, 1944, and was shot by Sjöberg in a mature expressionist style that conveys its feelings of forbidden love and hopeless entrapment in a way still exciting today. *Torment* caused some controversy in the Swedish press with its attack on a humiliating system of education and its portrayal of a repressive family (and the fact that the models for much of it were easily known). It was a fresh, more serious voice in the cinema, and the debut of a formidable talent.[1]

During production, Bergman worked in the background in charge of continuity, but he was soon given the opportunity to direct on his own. *Crisis,* his adaptation of a current play, was released in February 1946. Since then, Bergman has directed forty films until his "retirement" in 1984 after *Fanny and Alexander* (1982) and its "follow-up," *After the Rehearsal* (1984). Of these forty-one films, Bergman was sole writer of twenty-seven (neither cowritten nor adaptations), including all the films for which he is best known, with the exception of *The Virgin Spring* (1960).[2] This book focuses on that body of work.

The first film Bergman directed using only his own material was *Prison* (1949), a quintessential Bergman work. In it, Paul, a former teacher of the director Martin Grandé, proposes a film in which the Devil is in charge of the world – life is now Hell, and things go on as before with little change:

After life there is only death. That's all you need to know. The sentimental or frightened can turn to the church, the bored and indifferent can
commit suicide. . . . God is dead or defeated or whatever you want to
call it. Life is a cruel but seductive path between life and death. A huge
laughing masterpiece, beautiful and ugly, without mercy or meaning.

In the thirty-six films following *Prison*, this thought is never very far
away.[3]

This does not mean that Bergman himself always believes it. Rather,
this, the meaning of life, is what must always be struggled with, and for.
In this regard, Bergman's work falls into two major parts. The **first period**
is dominated by the "great synoptic" films of the 1950s in which his central filmic images and tropes are formed and life's "huge laughing masterpiece" is in fact portrayed not as merciless but as always offering rebirth
and renewal. This period has three phases: a more austere beginning that
leads to *Naked Night* (1953); its culmination in the mid- and later 1950s
with the poetry of *The Seventh Seal* (1957), the transcendence of *Wild
Strawberries* (1957), and most of all the gentle and knowing laughter of
Smiles of a Summer Night (1955); and then a long struggle from the late
1950s into the 1960s to sustain the heart of this vision, ending with *The
Silence* in 1963.

Though despair and suicide are often central themes, as in *Prison*,
Bergman's earliest films end with a resolve to continue on in the face of
life's adversities of failure, humiliation, abandonment, and death (even
Torment ends with a certain exultation, though this may have been just
Sjöberg's own addition).[4] Characters see who and where they are and
grasp that some measure of life and love is still possible for them. All of
this is hard to discover, harder to sustain, and not ensured to last, but the
hope found, even if muted or only temporary, never seems hollow. This
period of "music in darkness" has its climax in *Naked Night*, which, while
both wildly reviled yet also highly praised at the time, can now be seen
as the first film forming the foundation of Bergman's international reputation and his finest statement of a "gloomy optimism" that trudges res-
olutely onward.

This fragile hopefulness is transformed by the central films of the 1950s
into a more comprehensive and archetypal picture of life that celebrates
the cycles and rhythms of coming to be and perishing; the flourishing and
passing of love; youth and age; the different times, seasons, and smiles of
life; and above all the discovery of a second chance. Each individual story
is part of a great narrative scheme, and our grief and suffering a moment

in a larger grand dance of life. (This is their "synoptic" vision in which the elements and phases of life are tied together.) In these works, there is a joy and lyricism that borders on the rhapsodic. As films, they are in love with life (even in *The Seventh Seal*), accepting it unconditionally with their eyes wide open and celebrating its gift that is too often lost or hidden. In the "great synopsis" there is in fact both mercy and meaning. Its first fully developed expression is *Waiting Women* in 1952, one of Bergman's unknown and neglected masterpieces (along with the preceding *Illicit Interlude* in 1951), and its culmination is *Smiles of a Summer Night*.

Even though the lyrical in Bergman is never positioned apart from the brooding and the ugly, this hopefulness becomes increasingly difficult to maintain and ultimately forced. With *The Magician* in 1958 and *The Virgin Spring* in 1960, the 1960s begin a period of almost vertiginous decline in which Bergman struggles to maintain and reaffirm the basic narrative of second chance and rebirth of the 1950s in the face of growing doubt and despair. The era of the great synopsis, which had occupied him for nearly twenty years, is brought to an end with the "metaphysical" trilogy of *Through a Glass Darkly* (1961), *Winter Light* (1963), and *The Silence* (1963).

Now the joy of the dance of life is gone, and the possibilities of nourishing each other or flourishing in a reclaimed life seem more and more remote. This **second period** in Bergman's films extends from *Persona* in 1966 to *After the Rehearsal* in 1984. During this time Bergman is overcome by a sense that what was once possible has now somehow become even more difficult and perhaps lost. At best, one can only disengage from the turmoil and devastation engulfing everyone and look back in sadness that nothing ever turned out the way it could have (as in *Shame* [1968]) or, if fortunate, find a moment of peace and comfort in the touch of another, alone together and isolated from the rest of the world (*Scenes from a Marriage* [1973]).

What develops during this time is very much a cinema of ruins and remnants, on the one hand, and replacements and substitutions on the other. The films of this period always have in their background those that preceded, and they may often be seen as new versions of these earlier works, now falling short of the old vision and ending in regret. This second period, too, can be divided into three parts.

The five films of the late 1960s (excluding the two documentaries) represent the bottom of the abyss and the point of Bergman's deepest doubt and despair. These are also the films in which he seems most self-conscious about film itself and his own artistry. As a filmmaker, he is like Johan in

Hour of the Wolf (1968), lost and stumbling about in some vast swamp. Yet two of his greatest achievements – *Persona* (1966) and *Shame* – come from this time, as does his darkest and perhaps most hateful film, *The Rite* (1969).

The films of the 1970s – from *The Touch* (1971) to *From the Life of the Marionettes* (1980) – are devoted to coming to terms with this darkening of the world and retrieving as much of the old synthesis as possible. His two finest works of this decade – *Cries and Whispers* and *Scenes from a Marriage* (both 1973) – partially succeed in doing this, yet even their achievement does not survive to its end. *The Serpent's Egg* (1977) projects a social and cultural malaise and grayness of soul that brings either collapse or violence, while *Face to Face* (1976) and *Autumn Sonata* (1978) find a growing internal disturbance and "dis-ease" in the soul that culminates in the psychopathology and murder of *From the Life of the Marionettes*.

If these were to be Bergman's last words, the modern world of *Shame* and *Persona* would have won completely and indeed left us "without mercy or meaning." *Fanny and Alexander* may be regarded as both an epilogue to all this and a valiant attempt to reassert the optimism and essential goodness of the world portrayed in the films of the great synopsis of the 1950s.[5] As such, it is an attempt to reinstitute that vision and insist on the faith and spirit of those films in the face of a contemporary deadliness of spirit. It is also a portrayal of the origins of the artist and of Bergman's own art. Yet, as always before, hope must be qualified, and Bergman tacks on one last final "final" word, *After the Rehearsal,* to keep us honest, as it were. With this rueful story of a director at the end of his career (Alexander in old age, perhaps), Bergman in effect "ends" his film career by giving us a choice for the answer to the original question of "mercy and meaning," a choice between two visions of human life not ultimately compatible: the exuberance and promise of *Fanny and Alexander* (and the films of the 1950s) or the regret of *Shame* and the resignation of the early 1970s.

After 1984, Bergman made a short film about his mother, *Karin's Face* (1986), directed for the stage and television, and wrote memoirs (*The Magic Lantern* [1988]; *Images: My Life in Film* [1994]) and screenplays about his parents (*Best Intentions* [1991], *Sunday's Children* [1992], and *Private Confessions* [1996], filmed respectively by Bille August, his son Daniel Bergman, and Liv Ullmann). He has recently directed his own work again, for Swedish television – *The Last Gasp* (1995) and *In the Presence of a Clown* (1997) – as well as writing *Faithless* (2000), directed by Ullmann, in which Erland Josephson plays Bergman wrestling "with remorse over what he did to the woman he loved."[6] Not all these films are readily available, and an assessment of this last – highly autobiographical – phase of Bergman's career remains to be done.[7]

Bergman throughout his work is concerned with a common set of themes, situations, feelings, and images as he probes this question of whether life offers either mercy or meaning. Indeed, one is startled in looking at his first films at how familiar they already are, and amazed at how the latter ones avoid repeating themselves. It should therefore be possible to give an account of Bergman's work that focuses on these common elements without regard to the films' historical or biographical order, uncovering the essential philosophic, narrative, and filmic foundations of the final choice they offer. This I do in Chapter 1, where I pursue Bergman's idea of a "metaphysical reduction" to arrive at an essential map of our being, what I call a "geography of the soul." This describes the world as a place of possibilities and thus of different spiritual locations in which one can come to reside – some darker, some happier than others, but each part of an overall fabric of human existence. In a particular film, as well as at different times of our lives, one place may be given emphasis or come to be dominant, but it will always be part of a larger whole and derive its ultimate meaning from its place in that picture.

This attempt at a comprehensive overview then informs the six following chapters, which focus on eight films central to Bergman's career as it has been described above – *Naked Night* (or *The Clowns' Evening*), *The Seventh Seal* and *Wild Strawberries, Smiles of a Summer Night, Shame, Cries and Whispers* and *Scenes from a Marriage,* and *Fanny and Alexander.* (A number of other films are discussed in these contexts, including especially *Persona* and the "metaphysical" trilogy of the early 1960s.)

There are many kinds of book that can be written about Bergman. It is beyond the scope of this project to give a detailed account of each film or of Bergman's work in the theater (including the most important matter of his relation to Strindberg), for instance. Much of this has already been done (though with his memoirs and films about his parents, plus the television films in the 1990s, there is a new chapter to be written). Peter Cowie's *Ingmar Bergman: A Critical Biography* is a standard reference for the biographical and historical context of Bergman's work, while Frank Gado's *The Passion of Ingmar Bergman* provides additional detail and an extensively developed psychological (or even psychoanalytic) interpretation that focuses on Bergman's development as an artist and the origin of that art in his personal life, where it stands "as surrogates for conflicts lodged deep in Bergman's personal history" (xv). Hubert Cohen's more recent *Ingmar Bergman: The Art of Confession* provides a more thematic treatment of Bergman's films. All three are extremely valuable works, and the reader should refer to them to gain a more complete understanding of Bergman. (A short "Biographical Note" is included in the Afterwords following Chapter 7.)

However important and illuminating these other approaches may be, the heart of Bergman's achievement is moral and philosophic, and this book is a set of essays that attempts to state that account both systematically and with detailed attention to specific films and their filmic style. As such, I hope it will serve as a fundamental introduction to Bergman as a "filmic thinker" (for he is always that!) addressing what used to be called "the human condition."

Introduction: The Geography of the Soul

Bergman describes the theme of his early 1960s film trilogy as "a 'reduction' – in the metaphysical sense of the word."[1] In the classical conception, a metaphysics was a fundamental examination of all being at its most elemental level, yielding lists of the most basic kinds of thing and of the principles that governed them through change and motion, an ontology that displayed the true structure of the world. These elements were arrived at by stripping away everything that was inessential and thereby reducing the great variety and lushness of creation to its skeleton. It was not that this detail and particularity was worthless or insignificant, but rather that its nature and meaning depended on these deeper elements, which both gave it form and direction and set its limitations. Only if these could be articulated and understood could their filled-out appearances also be comprehended.

Bergman's subject is not being as such but the moral world – ourselves as human beings in the twentieth century: what is deepest and most true and essential about us, and what meaning we can find for our lives in the face of this truth. His goal is an essential portrait, an image of human being with its heart exposed and beating, a picture of what we each look like without our protective illusions, evasions, and lies. Such reduction to essentials provides a mirror in which we can see ourselves as we truly are, face to face.

This essential portrait, however, must show not just what we may be now at this particular moment or in this particular situation but also what we have failed to be and might yet still become. Thus the trilogy, whose announced themes are certainty, doubt, and God's silence,[2] focuses on only part of a more developed and detailed whole. To consider these moments of failure and despair alone is to miss something crucial: It is to place out of sight and thus make inaccessible the joy and nourishment that is equally possible and true of the world.

In this book, I put together an account of Bergman's whole picture in the form of what may be termed a "geography of the soul." Here, *geography* combines the idea of spiritual places and spiritual journey with the more literal sense of physical places and travel between them. Such a fusion of the literal and spiritual is directly suggested by Bergman himself. From his first pictures on, the character of the places in which his subjects and their stories are set is always significant and conveys in its physical features a representation of important elements of their spiritual struggles. What Bergman shows us throughout his films are landscapes in which the moral and the visual are fused into one representation – both something that film does best and the key to the specifically filmic in Bergman's art. What we are given in this new metaphysics is an elemental set of filmic images and places that, when woven into one composite picture, captures the rudiments for understanding who we are.

What, then, is this place that is the human condition? What does this moral landscape look and feel like, what are its most basic features and laws? Bergman's "reduction" reveals our lives as moral and spiritual beings to be constituted by six fundamental kinds of experience and their interrelationships. These occur throughout Bergman's films in many variations and combinations. Sometimes all are present, sometimes only a few. They are the seminal moments of **judgment, abandonment, passion, turning, shame,** and **vision.** Together they delineate the kind of journey life is and the kind of road it must travel. They are the "plot points" through which all of Bergman's stories develop, and they provide the framework for understanding Bergman's films and his achievement as artist and "filmic metaphysician."

1. Judgment

This notion of a metaphysical or moral reduction also, for Bergman, characterizes a central experience that individuals can have when their whole life stands before them as a question and they are judged with respect to its final worth. In biblical terms, it is as though one were before God awaiting final sentence. Indeed, Bergman uses this figure throughout his films. *The Seventh Seal* opens with a white sea bird[3] hovering high in the sky as a chorus sings the foreboding "Dies irae, dies illa" from the Mass for the Dead. A voice reads from the Revelation of St. John the Divine, that is, the Apocalypse. In the world of the film, the "Four Horsemen"

2

of Hunger, War, Disease, and Death in fact ride the land. It is the time of tribulation and last judgment, the "day of wrath, that day . . . when the Judge shall come to try all things truly."

In John's vision this is the time of the final battle between God and Satan fought on the plain of Armageddon. The Book of Life will then be opened, and those whose names are not written within will be cast into the fiery lake with the Devil and Death, to be tortured forever. But for those who have been faithful to Christ, there will be a new Heaven and a new earth. Time will come to an end with the marriage of the Lamb and His bride, those saints who have been saved and whose names are inscribed in the book. They will be united in a marriage feast in a new Jerusalem flowing with the water of life and nourished by the fruit of the tree of life.

As a time of crisis and final **judgment,** the biblical apocalypse is also a time of revelation (literally, of "uncovering" in the original Greek). The truth is necessary, and it is found by removing what hides it. All that is unnecessary is taken away and a person's innermost nature revealed, ready to be seen and judged for what it really is. Indeed, at this point, uncovering the truth and being judged are the same:

Before we saw ourselves as through a glass darkly,
But now, as we are – face to face.[4]

Our illusions are stripped away, and we stand naked before ourselves in an uncompromising mirror. God's probing eye is replaced by our own, and all that remains is for us to acknowledge the verdict. This is the kind of "apocalypse" Bergman is concerned to explore in his films and the moment of judgment we all have to face.

This state of finding oneself judged (and condemned) can occur at any time, but because it confronts us most of all with our failures and limitations (that is, our sins, which we would like to keep hidden), it will be excruciating and a torment in its own right that we will avoid until it is forced upon us. Thus, in Bergman, this crisis is most typically precipitated by an encounter with our own mortality (represented literally by the figure of Death in the *Seventh Seal,* one of Bergman's most famous images, and by Isak's first dream in *Wild Strawberries*). Then, with our lives seemingly complete and thus our future gone, we can stand outside ourselves and see in a more objective fashion, from a viewpoint independent of our own concerns and manipulations [Fig. 1]. In facing our death, we are given the opportunity to look honestly at ourselves, in a clear and unforgiving light, and see who we really are.

3

What we see with this new sight is not just that we have failed at our lives but that in this failure we are already dead: Life has somehow left us long ago, and we have continued with its motions – self-satisfied perhaps but secretly alone and empty – on the edge of loathing and despair. For Bergman, there are two deaths, and the true revelation (and despair) is of the first, the death of the spirit. This is the judgment about ourselves that we must comprehend and accept.

However, its sentence is not final. In Christian theology, one can absolve one's sins through sincere repentance even on one's deathbed; in Bergman's films, actual death is almost always postponed, and one is usually given back one's future.[5] At this moment of judgment, our life as a *kind* of life with its own sense and meaning has been revealed. We see where it is going, how it will be if we continue on as before, and how it *might* be if we act differently. Unlike St. John's revelations, the writing in this book of life has not been completed. We still have a chance, the opportunity to become someone else, someone better. What we now do as a result of this reprieve will determine who we shall finally be when Death returns. And we may never have a "second" second chance.

This time of judgment is often signaled in Bergman's films by the tolling of clocks and the ticking of watches, as well as by images indicating changes in sight, such as mirrors, spectacles, and particularly dreams and visions. Bergman's apocalypses involve removing scales from the eyes of the soul so that its consciousness can change and a true sight be achieved. This change is like waking from a dream or being struck by an epiphany.

Though Bergman draws heavily upon imagery of terror and death in constructing the experience of apocalyptic judgment in his films, this crisis is not an end but a beginning. And it is this possibility of surviving and becoming renewed that underlies the process of self-examination so central to Bergman's films; without it, such self-confrontation would be pointless. What this new life might be and how it might come about we shall see shortly. But there are never any guarantees, and the hope that is present even at the time of judgment is always just that of something better being possible.

2. Abandonment and Our First Death

That one will die is not in itself a source of despair for Bergman, nor is one's mortality the source of inner death. Both of these are grounded in something else – **abandonment.** This experience of having been betrayed and left alone, of having what one relied on taken away or failing, shatters

Figure 1. The moment of judgment. **a.** *The Seventh Seal:* confronting Death. **b.** *Cries and Whispers:* confronting oneself – Karin and Anna.

the security of the world, rendering its given verities remote and untrustworthy. These sources of security – other people, God, or even social institutions such as religion, medicine, the family, or art – are now revealed as inadequate. The love and faith placed in them has been misplaced, and one is left on one's own with only oneself to rely on.

One might call the effect of this abandonment the "destruction of the transcendental." The phrase is particularly appropriate to Bergman's meditations on the eclipse and death of God, where meaning seemed grounded in something beyond this world.[6] But in all cases, it is **that beyond oneself** that collapses, whether it is God, lover, or parent, or even the world itself (as has happened to Jonas in *Winter Light*). Beyond the self there is no longer anything reliable, and meaning in life, our sense of value and purpose, even our delight in being alive, are lost to grief, anger, disappointment, loneliness, hurt. Before, meaning was simply there; now, what we had seems forever irretrievable, we are thrown into despair, and our spirit dies.

As a result, the world becomes silent and the landscape like a desert. In Bergman's films this spiritual starkness is often heightened by the black-and-white cinematography, while the settings themselves often encode its isolation and sense of inner barrenness. *Through a Glass Darkly* takes place on an island surrounded by a sea that blends into the sky, and *Winter Light* occurs at the beginning of winter when everything is gray and about to be surrounded by the snow, which will form a white void. In *The Silence*, the setting is no longer an actual island or one created by the weather, yet it comes to the same thing, for the film takes place for the most part in a train coach or hotel in a foreign country with unknown customs, ominous military activities in the streets, a curfew that enforces inactivity for large parts of the day, and an undeciphered language.

Similar landscapes occur throughout Bergman's films. An island and rocky shore are the settings for *Persona, Shame,* and *Hour of the Wolf,* as well as *The Seventh Seal,* which begins and ends there as it travels through a land devastated by plague. Much of *Wild Strawberries* takes place within the confines of an automobile, and virtually all of *Cries and Whispers* occurs within the several chambers of a single house. Even when the set seems opened up, as in *Waiting Women,* which moves between Paris and Stockholm, events are often narrated from a confined space, here as recollections from a single living room in a summer house itself on an island. Abandonment shrinks the world and constricts one's horizons to what is centered in oneself. Life can go on in such quarters, but it cannot flourish; it loses its pleasure and now must be endured or even suffered.

At its heart, this "destruction of the transcendental" is abandonment by other persons – their failure to love and be faithful, their failure to comfort, protect, support. This may be actual infidelity, where a husband, wife, or lover turns to another person (Isak in *Wild Strawberries*), or something more common, where one is left alone because another is inadequate and unable to give what is needed (Block's wife Karin in *The Seventh Seal*, each of the women in *Waiting Women*). Occasionally, it is life itself that lets us down – a lover dies in a swimming accident (*Illicit Interlude*) or a father is taken by disease, a daughter by madness (Ester's father in *The Silence*, Karin in *Through a Glass Darkly*).

Here one is betrayed by an adult, but one can also be abandoned by a parent. This may simply be a matter of early death (*Fanny and Alexander*) or the problem of a parent having to care for a child without the resources, or wisdom, or even interest to do so – the father in *Through a Glass Darkly*, the mother in *Persona*, Maria and Karin's mother in *Cries and Whispers*. Abandoned children are in fact everywhere in Bergman's films – from Berit as early as *Port of Call* to Henrik in *Smiles of a Summer Night* to the boy in *The Silence* and *Persona*, Maria in *Face to Face*, and Eva in *Autumn Sonata*. This kind of abandonment is perhaps the most destructive of all and the hardest to overcome. Turning away from a child is denying them the very possibility of nourishment, and they can hardly escape undamaged.

Even abandonment by God and the concomitant experiences of religious doubt and loss of faith are analyzed by Bergman as the failure of a person. Tomas in *Winter Light* cannot understand how God could allow the death of his wife. How can this be love by a God who is love, he asks? Such a person can only be a "spider god – a monster" who can neither be loved nor forgiven and hence cannot be believed in. Because He does not care, such a God "does not exist anymore."[7] Töre in *The Virgin Spring* must undergo a similar abandonment when his daughter is raped and murdered on her way to church with candles for the Holy Virgin. There are no justifying reasons for such deaths and the torture they bring, nothing God can say to excuse them. They leave us in a world that is cold, barren, without comfort or meaning. Something in us dies, and we are left to suffer.

3. Passion

We will be abandoned, our worlds will collapse, and then we will suffer. This will happen to each of us, and one can hardly remember a Bergman character who has escaped this fate. Indeed, one might think of Bergman's films as almost systematic explorations of such **suffering,** from the catastrophes of first love in *Illicit Interlude,* to the tortures of marriage in *Wild Strawberries* and *Scenes from a Marriage,* to the terrors of being alone in *The Silence* and of dying in *Cries and Whispers.*

In these depictions Bergman shows himself as the moral psychologist, the pathologist of the soul relentlessly probing its pain, a vivisectionist perhaps too fascinated with the throbbing of the raw nerves of life he has now exposed (a figure not unlike Alman in *Wild Strawberries,* whose examination of Isak is also a dissection). What he reveals is that our suffering does not cease with our initial hurt, humiliation, and loneliness but continues as these transform themselves into new, more general but now enduring and self-perpetuating emotions – into bitterness and spite, sensualism, vanity, and egotism. His almost obsessive focus on these dark times of the soul and their intricate psychology, and the fact that no one seems able to escape their taint, creates a powerful current of pessimism (or even cynicism) in his work, and many have taken this depiction of human relations to be the hallmark of a Bergman film.

Indeed we are like this. It is hard to say that we are ever free of these feelings and emotions and the preoccupation with the self they subtend. But their sense changes when seen as responses to abandonment and the destruction of the transcendental in our lives, and when they are located in the fuller picture that Bergman goes on to draw. For Bergman, this fundamental selfishness with which we must all struggle is much more a response to the abandonment that has befallen us than some innate and fatalistic force of human nature.

Abandonment does not just happen and then pass out of our lives, healing like a fever or cut. Such a deep spiritual wound requires a response not just to its particular cause but to the nature of our lives and the world itself. Thus for some, anger and feelings of injustice turn outward as spite and hatefulness. What has let us down – others, God, ultimately the world – is despicable; the denier of love is itself odious. We hate back and hurt those who have hurt us (as Karin does to her husband, Isak, in *Wild Strawberries,* or Ingeri to the knight's daughter in *The Virgin Spring*) or even take jealous delight in harming the innocent (like Charlotte in *Smiles of a Summer Night*). To strike back, to wound as one was wounded, however, brings little reward and no peace. One sees in these deeds one's own ugliness and inadequacy and so retreats further into self-loathing and a lonely, empty life.

Alternatively, having been abandoned and left alone, we try to fill the silence with distraction – with the sensualism of sex and one-night stands and affairs, for instance (like Anna in *The Silence* or Frans in *Naked Night*). Such promiscuity keeps life going, while the distance kept from others ensures that one is safe from another abandonment. It is this distance that is important, life without contact. This is what David's career as a writer is to him in *Through a Glass Darkly* – a life somewhere else with words and publishers that substitutes for trying to live with a "hopeless" wife and daughter. In these examples, intimacy is deflected, and one becomes preoccupied with something, almost anything, in order to avoid confronting any further the emptiness and loneliness into which one has been plunged.[8]

Perhaps the easiest response, the most normal looking, is to try to turn abandonment on its head and take seriously, as it were, one's independence – to be self-sufficient and to live wrapped up in oneself. This can vary from the prideful self-control of Agda in *Naked Night* to the more pompous, somewhat vain self-satisfaction of Fredrik in *Smiles of a Summer Night*. Such self-centeredness denies any real need for others and keeps human relations again impersonal – matters of business, of use and display, or perhaps dominance and mastery; others are simply parts of one's life, never anything themselves on their own. (Thus Fredrik's view of his young wife in *Smiles* is little different than the more blatant chauvinism of Carl-Magnus, who considers Charlotte and Desirée, his wife and mistress, as kinds of property and ornament.)

That these ways of suffering abandonment are also projects of deceit and flight from oneself suggests that even in daily life people are engaged in a form of theater in which they live through a facade or mask of their real self. This form of theatricality is grounded in the self-estrangement that often ensues from abandonment – the attempt to mask one's loneliness and emptiness by assuming another persona, by acting out a different life, even by pretending that everything is normal. But as a hiding, that face is someone else's, and one is trying to be what one is not – another person. In not being able to be oneself in what one is doing, however ordinary that might otherwise be, a person becomes a theatrical fiction and one's life, rather than being one's own and a genuine expression of self, becomes a performance, an imitation. Such imitation life can continue along smoothly enough, its foreignness put aside, forgotten in habit. But its theatricality remains, and sometimes it breaks through, plunging a person into a gap between who they are and cannot face and who they are not but must appear to be. This is what happens to Elisabet Vogler in *Persona*: She stops in the middle of her performance onstage, unable to go on or even move, broken down, caught in the gap between being herself and being someone else.[9]

This gap between face and mask is a fundamental feature of Bergman's moral universe, and if there is to be any self-knowledge, any possibility of true judgment and meeting oneself face to face, such facades must be seen through and recognized for what they are. As a result, Bergman's characters are frequently placed before a mirror, searching for (or sometimes hiding) their true faces, or confronted by another's gaze (verbal as well as visual) probing for what is behind their appearance. Without this knowledge, there can be no second chance and no change.

Filmically, this moral theatricality and the need for the uncovering of the truth of who we really are grounds Bergman's most characteristic stylistic feature – a frame filled by only a face, or a pair of faces, against an empty, minimal background. Both individually and filmically, the face above all is the arena where the human drama is played out and the key for the presentation of ourselves to ourselves. For Bergman's audiences, the film itself is just that mirror in which their own faces appear and are scrutinized for their underlying truth.

These three central responses of rage, distraction, and self-sufficiency, and the theatricality they encourage are, of course, not mutually exclusive. In whatever way they are assumed and lived through, the original loneliness of abandonment remains, perhaps hidden, perhaps not. The maintenance of such deceit is exhausting, and often the facade cracks, the anguish returns, grows, and the soul seeks escape.

While physical death is usually natural and its inevitability morally neutral, suicide is neither. It is a moral failure, at least in the contexts that Bergman explores, because it renders suffering as only that, as unremitting and without cancellation, and it takes as permanent the deathliness of spirit that settles in after abandonment. To be at the point of suicide is to have moved from the immediacy of one's abandonment and hurt to suffer in a new way. It is to see before one only emptiness and loneliness, only the continuation of spiritual death. There seems no difference between now and real death, except real death is bearable and a relief. So one acts to make true in fact what is true in feeling. In the prolonged despair of abandonment, one is led to kill oneself.[10]

Bergman, however, intervenes and, as noted before, almost always refuses success. Death, spiritual or actual, is not the only future to which our abandonment can lead, and therefore there must be a second chance if our condition is to be portrayed truly. To see only emptiness and torment, as Bergman's characters often do in the midst of their tortures, is to be confined in moral vision and blinded to a larger picture. Abandonment and its ensuing torment is more than suffering alone; it is a passion, like Christ's, that ends in resurrection – or more appropriately, like that of the thieves crucified with Him, one of whom is saved and the other not. Thus, though suffering may be a spiritual desert that seems endless, it is always bounded on its far side by another land, a place of rebirth in which the soul may be nourished again.

This "resurrection" is never suffering's justification, the good that excuses it and gives it a meaning. There is no theodicy in Bergman, and such torment can only be regarded as evil. Rather, healing and nourishment are what suffering **needs**, and they exist as real possibilities in the world, however difficult they may be to reach or to bring about. This is the meaning of describing suffering as a **passion**. If suffering is only suffering and there are no other possibilities, then once we are abandoned, this becomes the whole picture and all that our existence could now be. This would be a truly despairing view of the world. But for Bergman there is something else, and to image suffering as a passion is to keep this possibility open.

4. Turning

The scene of Frost and Alma from *Naked Night* is one of the most remarkable sequences in all cinema. It portrays Frost's abandonment and passion. Alma has been enticed to do a striptease before a group of soldiers, and Frost is taunted and jeered as he tries to cover his wife's nakedness and carry her away. For Bergman, their ordeal is a version of Christ's own Passion, and the image of Frost struggling up the rocky hillside, surrounded by the mob of spectators, is also a picture of Christ carrying His cross toward Golgotha [see Fig. 3b]. Here the cross is Alma and their marriage, and as the two blend and reverse positions so that it is finally Alma supporting Frost, Bergman's image suggests we are both cross and savior to each other, both burden and helpmate. The scene offers no other resources – it is barren of vegetation and shelter; all that it gives people is each other. The ambiguity of this truth is reinforced by the sun overhead – on the one hand a burning heat that exhausts and overpowers, finally effacing them in its searing light, yet on the other, a divine halo signaling a special grace.

Here Frost and Alma revolve around an axis of embrace as the holder becomes the held, each desperately turned toward the other, trying in this moment to be their support and protection. Our need is for each other, to turn toward another and for him or her to turn toward us. Of course, this need itself arises out of another turning, also encoded in this image – that of abandonment, when we have been turned away from and in response turn further away ourselves. Thus, this **axis of turning** defines "geographically" the nature of human relationships for Bergman: On it we perpetually move, turning toward or away, unable to escape our mutual need and involvement. This fundamental image comes to dominate his work in the 1960s and 1970s in an even more reduced form, that of two faces close together, even overlapped, usually looking in different directions [Fig. 2]. So pervasive are such "portraits," they are signatures of Bergman's compositional style.

This concept of turning, and the repeated images of faces in motion toward and away, is the spine of the moral skeleton that Bergman's reduction reveals. It gives shape to Auden's assertion that "we must love each other, or die" or that of Tomas in *Winter Light,* who sees that "the only condition under which men can live" is "to live together" – though he cannot appropriate this knowledge himself, either for Jonas, whom he is unable to comfort, or for Märta, whose love he cannot accept. Such "betrayals" are "why we're so poverty-stricken, joyless and full of fear."[11]

Turning toward another, embracing and supporting him or her, is possible for Bergman, but it is always difficult and has no guarantee of permanence, nor even of acceptance. Why is love so hard? Why do Bergman's characters most often turn away even when turned toward? There are at least three reasons. First, they must respond from a condition of abandonment and hence with a special kind of love and turning toward the other, a love that indelibly bears the mark of the abandonment that precedes it, that remembers yet moves beyond it, that has no illusions about itself, a love "after the fall." This is the moral need to which all of Bergman's drama is addressed and is the spiritual location for this central question of turning. It is a rough, frightening terrain. Romance and young love belong to a different time, to a kind of childhood. That love is sweet and passionate and seems simply to happen, spontaneous and natural (like that of Henrik and Maj in *Waiting Women*). But it is also clear that it will

---

Figure 2 *(facing).* The axis of turning. **a.** *The Magician:* Albert and Manda. **b.** *Persona:* Elisabet and Alma. **c.** *Through a Glass:* David and Karin. **d.** *Winter Light:* Tomas, Jonas, and Karin. **e.** *The Silence:* Anna, Johan, and Ester. **f.** *Face to Face:* Jenny and her grandmother. **g.** *Shame:* Jan and Eva. **h.** *Marionettes:* Peter and Katarina (wife).

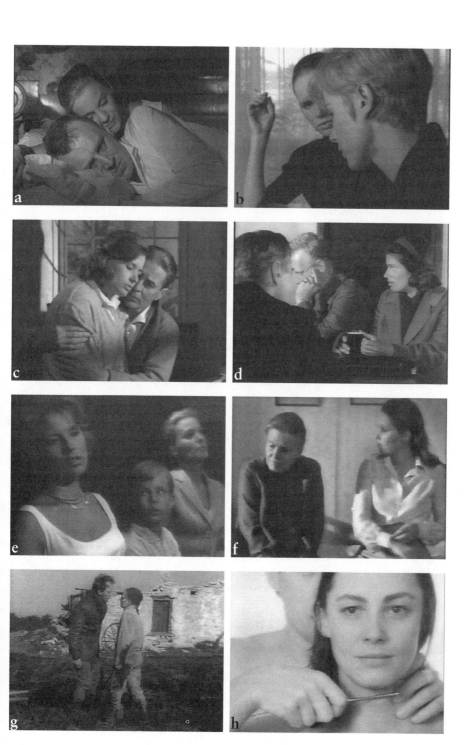

stumble, fail, and be betrayed. Then a different love, one much more difficult and honest, will be necessary, a love for the time we no longer believe in love.

Second, the individuals who make this gesture are ugly and repulsive – sometimes physically, like Märta with her skin disease and bandages; always spiritually. These are people who have failed and caused us harm, who have been self-centered, mean-spirited, cold, who have used us or others. Throughout the trilogy, the outrageousness of this appeal is stressed. Each film includes scenes of accusation in which long-smoldering contempt, disgust, and even hatred for the other is expressed – understandably, justifiably.[12] In turning toward us and asking for our love, these others in addition ask us to overlook not only what they have been but also our own hurt and anger, to be different to them than they have been to us, and to accept them with their regret and new intentions as yet essentially the same people – weak and pitiable. Seeing them as they are exposes them as disgusting and repulsive. How can we live with such creatures?

Third, we see in those turning toward us images of ourselves. They are mirrors that confront us with pictures we do not want to see or face, and in this confrontation it is now ourselves that most repulses and frightens. In Bergman's reduction, we are given no way to distinguish ourselves from others. We are identical in nature and in our need for each other, interdependent, almost one person (captured in Bergman's startling images of two faces as one).[13] As persons, we are fundamentally all the same; therefore, to see others openly in their neediness and dependence asks us to recognize and accept this same fact about ourselves – to expose ourselves too.

These three reasons make any honest response to even feeble and stunted gestures of a genuine turning toward difficult at best. To do so is to return willingly to the condition that betrayed us. It is to put ourselves in the hands of another, to depend again, to be vulnerable where nothing will ever take this vulnerability away. It is not surprising that people refuse and turn away again.[14]

The trilogy makes clear that the result is, if not a deeper despair that leads closer and closer to suicide, then, as already noted, a life that is impersonal. The vulnerability inherent in our dependence on others is avoided or hidden if they are made only "partial" persons, persons who, because their individuality has been given no importance, cannot turn away. They are simply a recurring type. Thus, Martin in *Through a Glass Darkly* has his patients, allowing him to lose himself in his medical practice even though there is no personal involvement or commitment to their lives. Tomas has done much the same with the members of his parish, to whom he now ministers abstractly and out of duty (or desperation) rather than from love or any personal concern. Sensing this, his congregation has dwindled, and he is alone in spite of his efforts. Anna in *The Silence* deals with the silence through a sexual hedonism in which she turns toward other men only in their capacity to provide her with sexual pleasure and diversion. All these protagonists continue to refuse to turn toward others in any fuller sense, and their lives are smothered as a result. In each of these cases, impersonalness is only a minimal affirmation of the world that shuts out any nourishment in return.

We are always placed at this point of turning, always in process, always dependent on others. From early on this is represented in Bergman's films through images of traveling, culminating in the silhouettes of the caravan at the beginning and end of *Naked Night* [Fig. 3a]. In Bergman's reduction, we are essentially itinerant and rootless, tied to neither land nor country for identity or sustenance. Life is arduous, filled with a repetition of the same ordinary things – both good and bad – over and over again. The self-contained mobility of each wagon emphasizes both our mutual dependence and our isolation – our condition of being alone together. They are traveling islands to which we are confined and from which there is no escape. The only resource we have is what we carry with us – our own capacities to love and comfort.

This figure is repeated throughout Bergman's films in many different forms: in *Wild Strawberries* it becomes, of course, Isak's car, whereas in *The Silence* it is the train compartment at the beginning and end of the film. In *Shame*, it is the boat in which they are adrift at the end [Fig. 3f]; in *Waiting Women*, the elevator in which Karin and Fredrik are trapped.

In these vehicles, people are moving either toward or away from each other, and this process is thematized through the various places to which they travel (*The Seventh Seal* and *Wild Strawberries*) or stop to visit (*Naked Night*). These locations take on importance as sites of the various spiritual moments in life to which everyone is vulnerable or even as stages moving from childhood to old age. Here, the temporal image of the journeying caravan becomes spatialized as a set of essential places we inhabit. In *Cries and Whispers* vehicles are abandoned, and we are given a single house with different chambers; in *Fanny and Alexander* it is four interconnected buildings – the family residence (with its summer house), the theater, the bishop's apartments, and Isak's shop. Each of these sites is a portrait of the human soul, with its essential possibilities of abandonment and turning toward always present. Some people are like this, some like that, some living their lives out in this room or place, some in that. But they can also move from one to another; here the axis of turning has been mapped onto the structures of dwelling themselves.

These two similar images of spiritual life – a house with different rooms in and out of which one may move and a set of dwellings that one might progress through – are combined in *Waiting Women* (Bergman's most neglected important film). Physically everything takes place in a large summer house on an island, but the drama in this film unfolds by returning in memory and story to other times and places that mark essential stages of life and reveal its possibilities for love and meaning. What is emphasized here, as in *Smiles of a Summer Night*, is not just that there are many places for the soul to dwell but that life itself has rhythms, that it is framed by the great events of birth, marriage, and death, and that it progresses through stages of growth and understanding, even as people must continually confront the truth of their own lives and their relationships to each other.

Taking these two summary images of "caravan" and "house" together, Bergman portrays our lives as journeys through a landscape of the essential places of the soul. This is our geography. Bergman's metaphysical reduction reveals the axis of turning toward and away as our fundamental spiritual posture within it. Here, abandonment and all its consequent suffering are forms of turning from, and love and its attendant nourishment and flourishing are forms of turning toward. The terms of life and death and the criteria by which we shall each be judged in our apocalyptic moment have been set. Have we loved or not? Do we still remain turned away even though we continue to live, loveless, alone, spiritually dead? Whenever scenes with this axial structure occur in Bergman's films, these questions are at hand, and the choice of turning and exactly how is at issue.

5. Shame

In this apocalyptic moment where we are confronted both by others and by ourselves, what could enable us to turn ourselves significantly around, see our suffering as a passion, and begin to transform it into something else?

There are two essential moments in this reversal of direction: a deep repugnance at our own complicity in such spiritual devastation and the vision of something better. Repugnance is a moral feeling in which a person begins to recognize something as not the way it ought to be through

Figure 3. Life as a journey. **a.** *Naked Night:* the caravan. **b.** *Naked Night:* Frost carrying Alma. **c.** *Wild Strawberries.* **d.** *Winter Light.* **e.** *Shame:* escaping the island. **f.** *Shame:* adrift in the poisoned sea.

the disgust and revulsion it causes. We recoil, draw back, want to be elsewhere. With other people's ugliness this is easy enough to do: We can escape by turning further away and into ourselves. But when we see ourselves as like them, ugly too, equally repulsive, there is no escape, no other place to go; we can only repress this knowledge, lash out at ourselves and others in hatred of what we are, or become ashamed, acknowledge ourselves as responsible, and begin to change.

Repugnance transforms itself into **shame** when it is coupled with the recognition of our own failure. To be ashamed of ourselves is to see that we have behaved poorly and to wish that we had done better. Although we often interchange shame and guilt, and they are closely intertwined in Bergman's films, there is a subtle difference between them.

Guilt is commonly focused on wrongdoing and violation of the law, and insofar as the moral law is chiefly formulated negatively, it arises from doing something forbidden. Moral standing is restored by accepting punishment (and perhaps restitution) and then by not doing what has been prohibited. Understood this way, guilt carries with it the idea of being correct as long as one avoids violation of the law. But this is only a negative picture of the moral – thou shalt not lie, for instance, rather than you must tell the truth as fully as you can – and thus a picture of what we should not do but not yet of anything more.

Shame, by contrast, provides this something more. It is grounded not just in guilt but failure and a sense of being significantly less than we could or should be. Shame moves beyond obligation and law to value, and it includes implicit reference to a standard unattained, a better kind of person. The point, now, is not only not to harm our neighbor but to do something better to help him. Shame thus projects an ideal of what should be, of something to be sought and achieved because it is recognizably better and needed, something always beyond any list of prohibitions. Inherent in shame is a comparison between ourselves now and some picture of ourselves as we ought to be, the positive of guilt's negative picture of what we ought not to do.

For Bergman, guilt and shame are more intimately connected than this account would suggest, and this is because there is no neutral ground (as there is between harming and helping, for example – i.e., neither harming nor helping). The two are sides of the same coin, and the guilt of turning away points to the shame of not turning toward. In the end, the deepest guilt will be the deepest shame, the absence of shame itself.

What is shameful – for us – is not that we have been abandoned but that we have abandoned those who most need us and have not turned toward them. This sense that our behavior is shameful because we treat each other so poorly pervades Bergman's films, and it is just this awareness that compels Marianne in *Wild Strawberries* to expel the spiteful and bickering Almans from the car "for the sake of the children" traveling with them. It is also the reason she finally decides to keep her own child even though it means separating from her husband: The denial of life that she sees all around her must end somewhere. Such death cannot be allowed to continue, and she must do what she can to stop it. Seeing the failure of life as in some way one's own failure awakens one again to those one really cares for and loves. This is what happens to Isak in the film as well.

Although shame can and should function this way, however, such reversals become, after the 1950s, more and more difficult to achieve. In the trilogy, for instance, shame seems to underlie everything and to be everywhere, and it is coupled with love and at least the gestures toward something better.[15] But in the end Tomas remains alone (*Winter Light*), Ester is left dying in a strange hotel (*The Silence*), and the moment of touch between David and his son, Minus (*Through a Glass*), seems forced by Bergman and artificial.[16] Moreover, there is an additional element in these films that makes shame both more palpable and oppressive than before, and more difficult. What is shameful now is not just domestic relations and our own behavior but life itself. This is the effect of the spectacle of Karin's mental deterioration, cringing before her spider-god or seducing her brother (*Through a Glass*), of Märta's skin lesions and bloody sores (*Winter Light*), of Ester's self-pity and terror as she spits up blood, dying of tuberculosis. The ugliness in these conditions is not just our own but the world's, and what arises is no longer shame but humiliation.

Humiliation is a theme that has always concerned Bergman, beginning with his first film script, for Sjöberg's *Torment* in 1944. Indeed, its depiction and exploration is characteristic of his films, adding further evidence to the claim that he takes a particularly morbid and pessimistic view of human nature. But his interest is more than clinical, for humiliation undermines shame's power to reorient and transform, and makes it even more difficult for a person to turn out of themselves and toward others. Humiliation, like shame, is an awareness of one's defects and failures, and thus a condition of self-reproach, but it is also a feeling of being cornered and helpless. Here, we feel our shame as coming from outside, as being caused by other forces and imposed on us, making us victims. It is not our fault. Exposed in our failings, we are despised and hated, even ridiculed and taunted. Our desire is to hide in some way, simply to endure, finally to escape however we can.

As humiliation grows, it focuses more and more on one thing: negating itself, making the humiliation go away. We come to strike back at anyone who seems responsible, anyone who can see or judge us, in an attempt to stop what is happening – their looking at us and laughing. This is what Albert does in the circus ring in *Naked Night*. In this sense, unlike shame, humiliation has no orientation toward a new future, points to no better condition, draws one toward no ideal. Its only direction is away from itself, to get this ordeal over with as soon as possible. Its danger is to send us back deeper into ourselves, turned further away from others and life.

As a consequence, humiliation presents special temptations for Bergman's characters. Even when shame is grounded in an awareness of our own failings, our impulse is to hide and not expose ourselves. It is easier to suffer the private shame of continuing to fail than risk the public humiliation of another's rejection.[17] And when we do try to do better yet still fail, it is tempting to focus on the humiliation that may result rather than on what we might further do; for the other's rejection of our turning toward him or her is something that someone *else* has done, not a failing of our own, and it is now the *other* who has caused our exposure, not ourselves. Focusing on humiliation makes it easier to stop trying and even gives us an excuse for anger and hate. Indeed, it is often more bearable to be openly humiliated than to be openly ashamed; it requires no more than endurance and allows us to continue on essentially as we are. There is thus a delicate balance in Bergman's films between shame and humiliation, and his characters often oscillate between them.

However, as already suggested, there is a second concern, a growing worry in Bergman that existence itself, and not just our behavior as men and women, may be shameful and thus intrinsically humiliating. If so, what failings could we acknowledge or toward what vision of a future could we turn? Disease and its physical and spiritual deformities become central images for this fear in the films of the 1960s and 1970s. Time and again characters speak of their humiliation at its hands and how their bodies have betrayed them.[18] And along with disease, Bergman adds a growing number of references to a mad and uncontrollable political situation, which becomes the focus of *Shame* and *The Serpent's Egg*.[19] Now God appears not silent but monstrous and malicious, no different than the cancer or nuclear weapons He allows.

Such real helplessness, if we do give into it, removes all hope and deprives our physical existence and suffering of any intelligibility, even that of a passion. There is only our humiliation. It is perhaps this feeling that drives Jonas in *Winter Light* to suicide as the only escape as he trembles before the certain but inexplicable fact that the Chinese will soon bring about the world's destruction with their atomic bombs.

Nevertheless, for Bergman it remains necessary to resist the defeat and despair these conditions counsel. Within this helplessness we must find something to offer each other, if only our shared humiliation and the comfort of not being alone. In such desperate conditions it is still possible to be ashamed of how we treat others and to be moved by the thought of something better. In *Shame* (Bergman's most desolate vision of contemporary life),[20] Eva thinks of the events of the nebulous "civil war" that is destroying her island home as a dream so humiliating that its dreamer should wake up ashamed and stop it. She herself tries, though too late, to prevent Jan from killing the young and helpless soldier who has stumbled into their camp. In the end, adrift in a sea filled with dead and bloated soldiers, all she can do is lie in the boat, her arms around her husband, waiting to die. Years later, this scene is echoed in *Cries and Whispers* in the image of Anna holding Agnes after she has died of an excruciating cancer and in Johan and Marianne's embraces at the end of *Scenes from a Marriage* [see Fig. 23a,c].

It should not be forgotten, however, that there is a less grim side to Bergman and that he is responsible for some of the finest comedies, including *Smiles of a Summer Night*. These comedies of the 1950s turn on a gentler form of shame: embarrassment. Their target is most often male vanity and self-importance, and their means a gentle ridicule that punctures the other's exaggerated seriousness, enabling these men to see themselves as they are seen (by women). Moral ugliness is replaced by something more benign – ordinary pomposity and officiousness – which is then deflated by a fall in the mud or a bit of shaving cream behind the ear at a formal ball. The embarrassment that results is a door to an acknowledgment both of the pettiness of the male's pretensions and the fact that he is not really independent, that a man could truly share his life with a woman and be the better for it. In *Waiting Women*, when the disheveled Fredrik and Karin are finally rescued from the elevator (after spending the night in each other's arms), he resolves to include her in the family business and take her on his trips as his secretary (and though this seems never to have fully happened, something important in their relationship does change). And at the end of *Smiles*, another disheveled Fredrik asks Desirée not to leave him and sighs, "That's good," as she puts her hand on his forehead and says, "I'm here" – both settling down to a new marriage.

6. Vision

In addition to a sense of shame or embarrassment with how we are, there must in some way be a **vision** of how we could be. Shame itself points vaguely elsewhere through its sense of loss, but it needs to be given something more concrete to guide aspiration and even perhaps, if we are lucky, provide proof for its faith. We must see where despair can be replaced by joy, fear of life by its celebration, the dance of death by a dance of life.

These experiences are perhaps the most fragile and ephemeral elements in Bergman's films and usually occur in the ambiguous form of recollections, dreams, visions, or stories (ambiguous because they can be rendered suspect as fictionalizations). They are often magical moments, such as Isak's return to his youth and dream of his mother and father welcoming him in *Wild Strawberries*, Jof's vision of the Holy Mother and Infant Jesus in *The Seventh Seal* (replicated in images of his own family), or Agnes's reminiscence of herself in the garden with her sisters, at peace and together, at the end of *Cries and Whispers*. Sometimes they occur as real events: the meal of wild strawberries and milk in *The Seventh Seal*, the picnic in *Shame* that ends with Eva and Jan making love under the table, the dance round the kitchen table in *Waiting Women* celebrating reunion and marriage [Fig. 4b], Frid's exultation and the ecstasy of the dawn in *Smiles of a Summer Night* [see Fig. 16]. Sometimes they are moments that we, as viewers, can notice but whose importance escapes those involved, such as Albert's care for Anne as he covers her in the cold morning at the beginning of *Naked Night* or the enthralled audience during the overture to *The Magic Flute*.

Peter Cowie refers to these scenes as "charmed spaces" but comments that "the yearning for such moments means more than their possession."[21] This might suggest that they are essentially illusory, deceptions of wishful thinking to make life more bearable, or at best always unattainable. This interpretation would render their occurrence either pathetic or ironic, and it is clearly Bergman's view that they are neither.

Such yearning is grounded in the sense of loss experienced in our confrontation with ourselves and our lives. It is the other side of repugnance and part of shame itself. We see the damage we have suffered as the loss of something we could have had (as Karin, the knight's wife, does with respect to their life in *The Seventh Seal*), and in doing so begin to recognize something else that we do not yet have, but need and value. Bergman's moments of vision give this something form and make it palpable as not just something lost but now something imaginable.

To be sure, after the destruction of the transcendental, what is envisioned is remarkably hard to achieve and then always vulnerable, always needing to be redone. But sharing a life in which we support and nourish each other is not a vain hope for Bergman, only a difficult one; if it were out of reach, there would be no place for shame in our lives (since we would be falling short of no standard), our suffering could never be a passion, and the only one to be judged would be God, not ourselves. Humiliated and miserable, eternally doomed, we would nonetheless be off the

Figure 4. Life's dances. a. *The Seventh Seal.* b. *Waiting Women.* c. *Fanny and Alexander.*

hook, and Bergman's films, always ordered about these structures and references, would have to be entirely different.

Yet Bergman's sincerity or even sometimes desperate faith that these images are not false is not proof, nor is it enough to displace an audience's (or character's) doubt. Is there anything in the images themselves that can warrant their acceptance or move a person toward what they represent?

First, there is a deep sense in Bergman in which "possession" of these "charmed spaces" is *repossession* of something we once had. Of the several forms of "vision" that occur, recollection seems the most powerful, for in recalling what had been, one also knows that that kind of state is genuinely possible because it was once actual and true of oneself. This is the insight Isak achieves in *Wild Strawberries* as he returns to those moments in a summer morning by the lake long ago and sees that he both loved and was loved. For him (and perhaps the viewer as well), it comes as an epiphany. Seeing these moments in the lives of others has almost the same force.

We can resist this knowledge only by thinking we have become such different persons that what once could be is no longer possible, or by doubting that what is possible for others is possible for us. And here the second fact about these images shows its force, for we can simply *see in them* that something better *is* possible and that it is for want of trying hard enough that we act so poorly. There is nothing keeping Isak from being a better father to Marianne and Evald than Isak himself – this, after all, is the ground of his growing self-reproach and feeling of shame. This is painfully clear to viewers as, for instance, they watch him be mean and insensitive to Marianne. These images of something better both confront us with this knowledge when we measure ourselves against them and arouse our desire for what they offer.

Nothing is easy, however, and nightmares are as much visions and a part of Bergman's moral reduction as dreams. Alongside the many images of grace and joy are counterimages of damnation and terror – the tortured death at the stake of the young girl in *The Seventh Seal,* the rape of Karin in *The Virgin Spring,* the descent of the spider-god in *Through a Glass Darkly,* Jenny's hallucinations of her grandparents in *Face to Face.* Such scenes increase in ferocity through the 1960s and 1970s, culminating in the amoralism pictured in *The Serpent's Egg* and *From the Life of the Marionettes.* These new counterimages are given a particular horror by their real-world references – a self-immolating monk in Vietnam and the Holocaust in *Persona,* the medical experimentation of Nazi Germany in *The Serpent's Egg,* child abuse in *Face to Face,* and sexual murder in *Mar-*

ionettes. Our own world from the newspapers and television is right there before us, and these victims could just as well be ourselves.

Throughout Bergman's films there is, as it were, a battle waged between images of life and these counterimages of death. This is a battle without victors, for one picture is soon followed by the other, often its direct negation. Thus, the meal of wild strawberries in *The Seventh Seal* is later reenvisioned as Jacobi's proposition to Eva as they sit at the kitchen table in *Shame,* shortly before his death and betrayal, and then as the estranged dinner between Karin and her husband in *Cries and Whispers,* before she mutilates herself as he looks on; yet it returns in the Christmas and christening celebrations of *Fanny and Alexander.* Sometimes, indeed, they occur together, seemingly inseparable, as in this latter film, where the bishop's "palace" is a short walk from the Ekdahl's residence and the theater, or in Eva's last dream where she holds her baby daughter beside the wall of flaming roses.[22]

This battle in addition reflects another, more philosophical conflict that also touches on the relation of life and art. Bergman's "charmed spaces" have a timeless quality, as though one had stepped into a kind of eternity where time no longer matters. In scenes like the sharing of wild strawberries in *The Seventh Seal* or its counterpart, the outdoor lunch by the lake in *Wild Strawberries,* there is a serenity and calmness that suggests both completion and sufficiency. Here, there is enough, and nothing more is wanted (like heaven, that other mysterious place outside of time); here, we can be content with what is offered and do not need more time or other places. Bergman's counterspaces are just the opposite, immersed in time and the immediate, with everything insistent and obtrusive and always too little or too much, filled with desperate longing for another chance and escape to somewhere else (most fully expressed in *The Hour of the Wolf,* a film that is perhaps the record of one long nightmare).

Art, however turbulent within, is essentially contemplative and allows us to stand back and see all our life in its fullness. Life itself is usually immersed in the needs and urgencies of its details. Bergman's moments of special vision bring art and life together, for they provide both an image of what wholeness in our lives could be and refer to actual moments that share its qualities. What happens in these "charmed spaces" is always some form of sharing life together, of supporting and nourishing each other, and they convey contentment in finding this "little" enough. Bergman's visions provide both distance and involvement, both perspective and satisfaction, and thus have some privileged status over their counterimages.

25

Figure 5. *Prison:* Death and the Devil.

7. Between Death and the Devil: The Geography of the Soul

What is life? To recall the words of the film director in *Prison* quoted in the Preface: "After life there is only death. That's all you need to know. . . . Life is a cruel but seductive path between life and death. A huge laughing masterpiece, beautiful and ugly, without mercy or meaning." Tempting as it is to take this as Bergman's own voice, there *is* more to know, and it is the key to both meaning and mercy.

Figure 5 *(cont.)*

The films taken together show our lives to have an essential structure: apocalypse (**judgment**), the crisis of self-confrontation and choice; **abandonment** by others and the collapse of the support and comfort of the "transcendental"; the suffering (**passion**) and crisis of doubt that follows, often marked by humiliation and increasing isolation; the availability of a **vision** of something better, along with the possibility that the new awareness of spiritual death created by seeing ourselves "face to face" will ground a growing sense of **shame**; and the ability to **turn** toward

27

another, as well as turn away from them. These elements give us some direction and allow for something more than being "sentimental," "frightened," or "indifferent," however difficult this "more" may be. Ultimately we are revealed to be deeply damaged in a world that is essentially good, that is, where the possibility of something better is not an illusion.

Some films develop this structure as a whole; others dwell on certain moments, presupposing the rest. Sometimes this picture itself, or the efficacy of the art (film and theater, especially) that portrays it, is called into question. But always, one best understands a Bergman film by seeing it in terms of this "geography of the soul" – that moral landscape in and through which each of our lives must be negotiated. Seen this way, the films will more readily reveal their many riches and their own capacity to nourish the spirit.

An early, haunting, version of this geography is given in *Prison*. In an attempt to reach out to Birgitta and save her from her despair, Thomas screens for her a short silent slapstick comedy packed away with a projector and other childhood toys in his aunt's attic. (References to this film appear again in both *Persona* and *Fanny and Alexander.*) The scene is a single room, sparsely furnished with a bed and a few pieces of furniture [Fig. 5]. A man in a nightshirt and cap tries to settle down for the evening. In the process he starts a fire, fends off a burglar with a skillet, and is joined by a nightstick-wielding policeman. He is even assaulted by a spider coming down from the ceiling. During this general frenzy and chasing back and forth, Death (represented by a man in a skeleton costume) pops up from a trunk at the right side of the room, driving the man to the other end, where he is accosted by a suddenly appearing Devil. Everything that happens is framed by these two limits. There is no other place to go, and the only escape is literally to leave the picture – which the three mortals do at the end by jumping through windows (or the film itself) that now constitute the back wall of the room.

This short comedy provides an image of life that is both naive and sublime. Here the emphasis is not on the journey or the particular sufferings we must survive, but only the "bare bones" of our condition and its mortal dangers: We live between death on the one side (as the story of *Prison* itself makes clear, this is the spiritual death that is the result of despair and the failure to grasp onto life) and wickedness on the other (here stylized as the Devil, standing for our own failure to be better and the temptation to malice, spite, and humiliation). In the face of this threat and terror, there is nothing outside ourselves that is available, no recourse except each other – sharing the same place, the same room, alone together.[23] We can exit this scene only by ceasing to exist – that is, by literally leaving the picture.

Our life and its daily tasks take place between death and the devil, and our goal is to avoid both of these while keeping ourselves warm and safe. In this, we are both hindrance (thief) and helper (policeman) to each other, but whatever happens, we are in it together. Emphasized in this picture is the immanence of "salvation" (or "heaven"). There is no other place for life except this one, under these conditions, and between these two possibilities of failure and defeat. And, as perhaps befits a child's tale, both death and the devil can be kept in their places – at least for a while, allowing for some happiness and joy, as reflected in the laughter and delight of the audience. Stark and promising at the same time, this is a more hopeful vision of our situation than that of Frost and Alma.

The films themselves are the heart of Bergman's art, and the discussions of them that follow are divided into three parts. **Part One** focuses on four seminal films of the 1950s, the period when Bergman established his international reputation and displayed his greatest optimism, when the geography of the soul and its six elements were given their fullest representation – *Naked Night* (1953), *The Seventh Seal* (1957), *Wild Strawberries* (1957), and *Smiles of a Summer Night* (1955). **Part Two** examines the subsequent decades of "second thoughts," of doubt, qualification, and even despair, focusing on three of Bergman's major achievements – *Shame* (1968), *Cries and Whispers* (1973), and *Scenes from a Marriage* (1973). **Part Three** is a "final look" at life as given in his "last" film, *Fanny and Alexander* (1983), both a reaffirmation of life and an impassioned defense of the necessity of art and artists, theater, and film.

PART ONE

THE FILMS OF THE FIFTIES

2

The Primal Seen: *The Clowns' Evening*

Gycklarnas afton (1953) received its American title, *Naked Night*, at a time when European cinema was shown mostly at often seedy "art" theaters and marketed by sensational posters exploiting images of more open and daring, if not explicit, sexuality.[1] Although from this point on I translate Bergman's own title as *The Clowns' Evening*, I have always liked the title *Naked Night* and find it particularly appropriate,[2] even though most critics have deplored it. It emphasizes the notion of a reduction of life to its essentials at a time of self-revelation and judgment. In the course of the film, Anne and Albert are stripped naked, displayed to a leering audience, exposed under glaring lights, and left without illusions. Indeed, *The Clowns' Evening* is the most raw and primal of all of Bergman's films, the one that shows human nature closest to its animal forebears, least qualified and transformed by the artificialities of society. In fact, it is a film directly about the relation of these elements and about the origin of the human from the animal. It is a film of primordial beginnings, spiritual as well as sexual, and is thus a fitting first view of the geography of the soul.

1. Escaping the Circus

It is clear from the first words Jens speaks to Albert as the caravan approaches town in the cold hours before dawn that something broods over the circus and that this day will be different and difficult. "Feel strange about seeing your wife and sons again?" Several years before, Agda left Albert and the "Cirkus Alberti," where he is now manager and ringmaster, to open a small shop in a quiet city and raise their sons safe from its bad influences. The circus has not been doing well since. Will Albert leave Anne, his "circus wife," and join his real wife? Will the troop be disbanded, the equipment sold, and everyone left stranded on their own?

Anne is particularly worried that Albert will abandon her and return to Agda ("How shall I manage without you?") and does not believe his claims to love her. The two quarrel as he prepares for his visit. "You're sick of the circus and me. . . . You don't love me, or you wouldn't go and see your wife. . . . I won't be here when you get back."

There is also something deeper at issue though: the circus itself and the kind of life it represents. To Albert and Anne things seem clear. The circus is an existence of continual travel, one-night stands, little money, begging and stealing, cramped quarters, and long hours of hard work for little return. It is a "world of flight, insecurity, misery, lice, and sickness," as Agda says, and its drudgery has gotten to them. They are tired of it and of each other as well. What kind of life can this be for human beings? The town, with its theater and small businesses, represents their dreams of a better life, and they each try to escape to it but are defeated, forced to return to the wagon and each other – Albert because Agda refuses to have him back, Anne because she has no money and could only become a whore. "Now we're stuck, Anne. Stuck in hell."

As *The Clowns' Evening* shows, however, these dreams are fantasies, and the lives they project outside the circus artificial and hollow. The town and its settled life is the place of illusions and spiritual death. Though the circus remains hard, it is only there that true human life is finally possible. This is what Anne and Albert must come to learn.

2. Anne and Frans

Anne is impelled toward the theater most of all by the repulsiveness of the circus – its mud and crudeness, its sweaty work and smells, its oppressive routineness. She desires in their place finery and elegance, romance and noble feeling, a lover who will praise her beauty and submit to her will – above all, something that will make her special and her life more than ordinary. The theater seems to offer all this. Its appearances fill her with new sensations, arouse her sexually, promise excitement. At last she can have real perfume and no longer smell like an animal – and have security: All she asks is that Frans, a local actor, take care of her; marriage is not necessary.

Yet everything she sees in this theater, and especially Frans, is false and designed not just to deceive but to exploit and manipulate such longings. It is like the play being rehearsed: a romantic melodrama filled with stilted

34

language, conventional sentiment, posturing rather than drama, an image not of life but of how someone might imagine life to be. Anne cannot tell the difference. When Frans "stabs" himself, she is completely taken in.

This difference between images that reflect truth and those that reproduce desire is of central importance throughout Bergman's work. In both the theater and the circus, mirrors are used first of all to confirm that the performer has successfully hidden his or her face behind makeup or a costume and looks the part of someone else. The image actors and clowns seek to reflect is thus not their own but a fiction. This is the key to the composition of the two scenes where Anne encounters Frans, first in the costume room (though Albert secretly watches nearby) and then when she later comes to his dressing room, intending to leave Albert and the circus.

In the first, what Anne begins to see as she tries on fancy dresses is the fulfillment of her desire for escape and a new life; she catches a glimpse of a new person with a new future. The mirror gives her dreams a corroborating image, and she starts to believe it. This is what enables Frans to insert himself into her life and what leads her to return that afternoon after she thinks Albert has abandoned her. As she now admires how she looks, his voice is heard from the side, trying to seduce her with lines from a play. The viewer does not see him, but Anne can as she continues facing herself in the mirror. She thus first sees Frans through the eyes of her image, as part of the picture of herself that she has been composing, perhaps the gentleman that is to go with this new lady escaped from the circus. Although she here resists and even insults him, she is attracted; and the excitement and, finally, momentary seduction she experiences are grounded in both her desire to escape and this mirror vision of another kind of life. For Anne, Frans comes to complete this picture and make it more than fantasy. For the viewer, there is only the reflection of Anne; the rest is an image in her mind.

Here the mirror image represents both Anne's misperception of reality and the falseness that underlies it. When she goes to his dressing room that afternoon, the mirror is used in the same way, first showing Frans and Anne together as he flatters her and gives her some perfume. Even after she realizes his true strength and that he has been toying with her and can now do as he likes, Anne is still taken in by Frans. As she stands to the right of the frame looking toward him, we see his reflection in the mirror as he offers her his "valuable amulet," only an image and still a lie. As she begins to undress, the mirror is empty. The image of desire is canceled by its reality. After Frans has gotten what he's paid for, this shot is repeated, except now Anne is in the mirror, dressed as she entered, returned to where she began. Her dream of escape, her desire for freedom and a new life, remains nothing more than an image in a mirror. She will soon know this completely when she takes her new necklace to the jeweler.

Although Anne does initially offer herself to Frans and finally lets him buy her, her unfaithfulness occurs earlier in the wardrobe, for when she kisses him there she really does give herself to someone else and realizes how deeply she wants something Albert cannot give.[3] Her second visit is after Albert has left to return to Agda, and her intention then is at least to make a bargain of it, to give herself only in return for something to take his place, either Frans himself or his "jewel." And while it may be that Albert ends up being a cuckold, the hurt, as it is with Frost, is in the abandonment and the sense that he cannot satisfy her need, that his love can never be enough, that she does not love him, that he is unlovable.

All this reveals Frans to be an egotist who in becoming enwrapped in himself has shut out any concern for others or for anything else. His world has shrunk, and he has become alone and passionless, someone who can at best divert himself with games offering sensation or conquest but little pleasure beyond the triumph of humiliating someone else. His life is empty; everything about him is artificial and a kind of playacting to substitute for the real thing. The others in the theater seem like him – actors off the stage as well as on. The life *this* theater represents is thus one in which ties with others are severed, people retreat into themselves, and pretense replaces true feeling. It is a desert existence in which one is hardly alive.

3. Albert and Agda

Does Albert find anything different? It might appear so, for certainly Agda has succeeded in maintaining a small business and raising two children, creating what looks to be an island of calm and contentment. She has what Albert longs for – bourgeois respectability, the security of a comfortable home and steady income, a quiet and peaceful life. "I want to be an honest citizen, with money in the bank and a respectable wife," Albert tells her. And so far as they go, these things are neither illusions nor false goods. But here they are bought with a price that is both too dear and out of Albert's reach.

In fact, Agda is as much an egotist as Frans. She rejects Albert's "proposal" to reenter her life not because she has found something to take his place but because her "peace of mind and freedom" is founded on their separation and his absence. It consists in not being disturbed by the wants and needs of a husband, any husband. Her freedom is freedom from having to adjust to a will other than her own. Her peace is that of a person contained in herself, affectively isolated from others and even the world.

Agda's life in the circus, the life she fled, was filled with emotion – she loathed its misery and insecurity, feared that their boy would hurt himself as he learned to perform. "But when you left me, all feeling died – overnight," and she is grateful. She is now someone who has stopped living and retreated to the edge of the world, away from other people and alone. Albert begins to realize this – "How quiet it is, always the same, summer, winter . . . year in, year out, life stands still." "To me it is fulfillment."

It is clear that Albert cannot stand such a life even though he hopes against hope that Agda will agree to change her mind and give him a second chance. But even in the two hours they are together there is a constant bickering and undercurrent of tension between them, and already Albert has begun to indulge the boys with a penny for the organ-grinder, spending more than he can afford. For them to live here together would be no different from before, when they were both in the circus, another hell. Agda understands this clearly and says no: She has found a refuge she will not leave, a kind of lifelessness that passes for life, and she will not sacrifice this peace and freedom to become vulnerable again.[4]

The feel of this world and its anesthetized nature is conveyed by Bergman in the hushed atmosphere of the shop, the unhurried stillness of its back rooms, the ticking of its clocks – here, nothing happens except the passing of time. Everything has a certain remoteness (and indifference) to it – the vague prints of romantic dancers, formal pictures of relatives, traditional furnishings, cut glass, clocks. It is there but lifeless. Here the windows are curtained, and Agda is shown with them behind her. The world where things happen, where life is played and lived, is on the outside. The windows may reveal another place, but they also close it off, keep it out. Perhaps for a moment something stirred, but now Agda is not even looking.

In the geography of *The Clowns' Evening*, a person can exist in a place other than the circus but only if they (emotionally, at least) disconnect themselves from the fundamental nexus of relationships and possibilities that a shared life with others involves. It is this dimension of human being that the circus represents, with its poles of love and humiliation, joy and despair, comfort and dependency. Escape from the insecurity and messiness of life is only apparent and will always involve choosing either death or the devil: withdrawal into a kind of suspended animation like Agda or immersion into a theater of cruelty like Frans and his associates at the playhouse. The price in both cases is a kind of suicide.

Albert, like Anne, is forced outside, into the street and life with all its vulnerabilities, into that world against which Agda shields herself. Dejected because their dreams of escape have been crushed, neither is yet fully aware that these were only places of confinement or that the circus is the only place where their lives have a chance to flourish.[5]

4. Beasts and Other Animals

John Simon notes, as have many others, that much of *The Clowns' Evening* is composed around "a striking set of images compar[ing] men and beasts."[6] The most obvious are between Albert and "the decrepit, emaciated bear" and Anne and her black and white cat, but there is also a costume bull, the organ-grinder's monkey, dogs, cattle, a cock, and most important, perhaps, the circus horses. The key to all this is something on which Simon does not comment: the contrast between the wild and the domestic and the ultimate replacement of the bear by the horse as Albert's emblem and counterpart (an animal also more closely connected with Anne than her cat).

The association of Albert with the bear is made immediately. As the caravan moves toward town, we see the bear pacing in its cage, followed by a cut to Albert's wagon (another cage) and then to Albert inside. In retrospect, this confirms the foreboding everyone has as they sense that Albert, too, feels restless and imprisoned and wants to escape the circus.

Albert even looks like the bear: His undershirt has a gray chevron covering his chest, the exact counterpart of the bear's white breast patch [Fig. 6]. When he is exposed with his coat off – when he promises Anne he will return; at Agda's; in the wagon with Anne and Frost; in the circus ring with Frans – the two are revealed as the same animal with the same primal desire to escape their imprisonment.[7] (A similar undershirt is worn by Frost, extending this desire throughout the circus and suggesting that being a clown is in some way related to it.)[8]

The bear is a beast (like the tiger they no longer have) and can exist in the circus only as long as its wildness is checked and kept under control. It is always dangerous and can never be left free. But now the bear is continually agitated and has become so unruly that Alma can no longer control him in the ring. Albert, too, wants to be free of the circus, and the beast in him, Albert's true identification with the bear, is this desire not to be domesticated or at the mercy of others but to escape the ordinary, gruelling conditions of everyday human life. This is the raw emotion, the almost feral desire that grows in him as the day wears on: It paradoxically

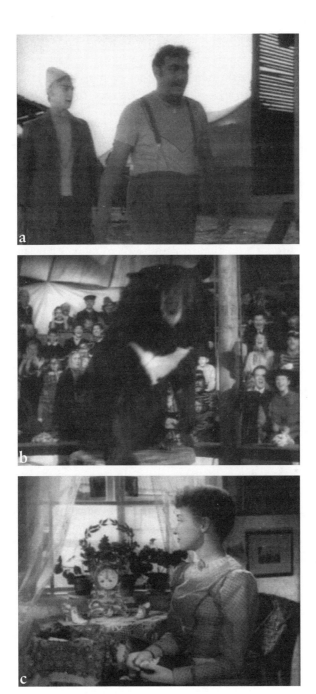

Figure 6. *The Clowns' Evening:* The mark of the bear. **a.** Frost and Albert. **b.** The bear in the circus. **c.** Agda.

sends him to Agda and then desperately into the ring to lash back at his tormentors.

Simon likens the fight with Frans that evening in the circus ring to a bullfight and Albert to a maddened bull, but this seems mistaken. The better reference is the wild-animal act of the circus in which the animal (lion, tiger, bear), not really tame and still dangerous, is made to perform tricks for others' entertainment, tricks that go against its nature (to take a head in its jaws without biting, to balance on a ball, to dance). In Bergman's version, the customary veneer of craft and professionalism is put aside for the overt delight of bear baiting. Frans insults Anne as she rides her "wild Andalusian" and then taunts Albert about "their afternoon together." Frans, having taken on the role of the trainer with whip and pistol, reduces Albert to an animal filled with howls of pain and despair.[9] He has no rights of fair play; he is simply there to give others pleasure with his agony. Bloodied by Frans's fists, Albert's only moment of advantage occurs when, rather than box (like a man), he lurches at Frans and encircles him like a bear, wrestling him to the ground. In an action we do not see, Frans frees himself by grabbing Albert's testicles. His defeat is now total.

Simon is right that there is something primitively, brutally sexual exposed in this scene, but it is not so much sexual desire itself as the parallel sense of becoming alive through the power of violence and humiliation.[10] While for a moment this may attract Albert (and Anne when she scratches Frans's face), it is in Frans and the audience that this desire is enacted and satisfied. In this moment, they are the wild beasts aroused by the blood of their victim. It is true that Frans incapacitates Albert by attacking his sexual organs, rendering him, as it were, no longer a man. But this "castration" follows from the logic of humiliation: to strike at the other's humanity, to make him or her an animate *thing*, a mere *nonhuman* animal who can then be some other animal's prey (as Frans has earlier done to Anne).

Although it may be that Albert has not been a good sexual partner (for the erotic is one of the things that pulls Anne back to the theater), his deepest failure is as a "husband" who cannot care for her or provide comfort and understanding. This is a failure of love not of sex. There are certainly elements of jealousy, but Albert's initial response to Frans's insult to Anne (like Frost earlier) is really an attempt to restore himself as Anne's husband as he tries to defend her from the actor's innuendos and the jeers and attacks of the crowd as they join in. But his struggle soon becomes something more primitive, a fight to free himself from his tormentors, to escape with some shred of human dignity. He is miserably defeated, like

40

Frost and Alma before – and like the bear who earlier refused to perform anymore and was returned to his cage.

For Albert, there is no escape from the circus. Like Alma's bear too weak to break its chain, all that remains is to put him out of his misery. This is the "human deed" Albert felt drawn to that afternoon in the wagon when he and Anne confronted each other with their infidelities. Then he was moved by the shamefulness of their behavior and pitiful condition and first began thinking about ending it all. This thought renews its grip as Albert sits in despair, locked in his wagon after his beating by Frans, ignoring the pleas of Anne and the others outside. Albert now tries to shoot himself; but the first chamber is empty, and as he examines the gun the second shot goes wild, shattering only his image in the mirror. Something happens to him: He has gotten too close to death and its finality, life becomes palpable again, and his suffocating immersion in his own misery is broken. (His tortured image is "killed" instead.) He is saved, given a second chance, not by anything he has done but by accident, or grace.[11]

Reprieved and firm in his resolve as he steps out of the wagon, Albert pushes Alma aside and shoots the bear. In part, this represents giving up for good his own desire to escape the circus and be like a wild animal, free of the cares and travail of ordinary human life. That kind of animal can't live in "captivity." In part, it is moving beyond his self-involvement in his own hurt to turn toward the needs of someone else; it is the human act for which he has longed. The bear, unlike people, has no other possibilities; it cannot change (nor now be let loose), and so death is its only release from suffering. Albert's act is human not because it relieves pain but because it is a return to taking care of what he has rather than wishing for a life somewhere else.

Albert himself doesn't immediately realize this. As he walks toward the stables, gun still in hand, a moment of fear and alarm goes through Frost and the others. Will he shoot the horses too? But at the stalls, Albert throws the gun to the floor, strokes one of the horses along the head, and falls to the ground in sobs. Finally, he calls to Jens. "See to Prince's left foreshoe before we go." What has been stirred in Albert seeks fuller expression – to touch, caress, care for. This is why Albert turns to the stable and the horses. In giving this comfort and affection to a horse, he has himself been comforted and turned further away from his own death. For the moment his suffering has become tolerable and life has begun to renew itself. "We're going?" "Of course we are."

These gestures that well up in Albert have appeared before – at the beginning when he fixes the covers over the sleeping Anne, for instance.

By nature, they lead to others of protection and support and finally to mutual embrace (the same gestures with which Frost tries to cover Alma's nakedness and take her back to the shelter of the circus). This is the mercy that people should show to each other in the face of their suffering. Such knowledge stirs in Albert, but it will do little good if confined to animals. The primal dream has been killed, but can he ever get over it?

The ending of *The Clowns' Evening* is unresolved and open. As one day ends and another begins, Albert joins Anne and they walk toward their wagon, not yet touching. Soon they will go to sleep, in the same bed as before. And when they wake? Will these two become like Frost and Alma – a ruined man, hateful and alcoholic, and a reclusive woman, pitiably clinging to the little she has left? Or can those gestures of touch and embrace with which the film began be retrieved, given new life? Has there been a reconciliation to the circus and its inescapability that provides their second chance a foundation for something more?

In either event, Albert will continue on, in harness, step by step, plodding along – wild no more, domesticated like the horse he has become.[12] This new representation of human life is a more complex figure than the captured bear it replaces. The circus horse is a draft animal, pulling a heavy load through long cold nights, itself half asleep. Yet there are also moments of rest and comfort – shelter out of the rain, hay, Anne's grooming in the morning. And there are moments of exhilaration, for it is the same horse that prances in the ring in the evening as a "wild Andalusian." It is this kind of life that lies before Albert and Anne.[13] It can collapse into a hell of suffering, self-pity, and mutual torment, but can also be filled with tenderness and love, even joy and beauty. These goods may be rare and they are certainly fragile, but they are absent in the lives of others, such as Frans and Agda, whose lives are lived outside the circus.

In Bergman's tale of our origins, the jungle must give way to the barnyard, the spirit of dreams and freedom to the everyday with its many trials and small rewards – bears to horses. Indeed, now the "Cirkus Alberti" has no wild animals at all.[14] But there is another set of comparisons in the film at odds with this one and far darker in its implications. This is the suggestion that we are neither bears nor horses but monkeys dancing at the end of a string to someone else's tune, or else an audience of cattle following the basest instincts of the herd. Both monkeys and cattle are associated with similar kinds of music – the whine of the hand organ and the raucous blare of the circus band.[15] The two are closely interconnected and share the bond of spectacle and spectators, an idea reinforced by the presence of the theater director, Sjuberg, to oversee the fight in the circus arena.

The organ-grinder appears with Albert's and Anne's visits to town, and his music is often heard in the background as a kind of counterpoint (particularly at the end of each episode). During this afternoon as they try to escape the circus, they are each, like the monkey, hoping by their "performance" to move their audience to take notice of them. Also like the monkey, all they get are a few meager coins and then sent away, perhaps used in the process. This kind of humiliation may be something to which we are always vulnerable, but here its source is our dreams of escape. Albert and Anne think that life in the town will be different and that there they can truly get away from the toil of the circus. This is why they plead and beg and submit themselves to the will of others. They are dancing, as it were, to the music of their own hopeless desires. Having foolishly risked their lives in leaving the circus, they are now foolishly disappointed.

Shouldn't things in the circus itself be different? Shouldn't they be in control there, not ruled by the demands and needs of others? But in the circus people also have to perform and dance, now not to escape or secure a vain dream but simply to make a living. Here the monkey chained to the organ-grinder is transformed into the clown, a clown who also has a master – the herd of unruly cattle that is his audience. Once in the arena, the task is not merely to entertain and secure a livelihood but to placate and keep under control the beast that has come for the performance.

5. The Clowns' Evening

R. G. Collingwood notes that what makes a great actress "is not her ability to weep real tears [but] her ability to make it clear to herself and her audience what the tears are about."[16] Bergman does something similar in the circus scene of *The Clowns' Evening*: He shows us what being a clown is about. This is one of the great passages in world cinema.

Here we see that the performance of the clowns that precedes it is a ritualized version of the fight between Frans and Albert. This thought occurs to the viewer during the film and becomes even clearer in retrospect. The circus ring allows the clowns and their audience to engage in a kind of preemptive strike against their lust for humiliation, to transform it into something that is vicarious and only playful fun, something that stops the real thing before it gets out of hand by displacing it somewhere else.

The clowns' act is a comedy of domination in which partners are made awkward and helpless (precariously stranded on ladders), victimized by thoughtless action (struck from behind), reduced to bodily functions (farts), pissed on, beaten (with a noise bladder that's both a heart and a

43

penis), pushed from behind onto the floor, even kicked in the groin – all for the pleasure of a roaring audience delighting in the contest and each new dirty trick. Frans and Albert's performance is simply the real thing and hence the original version of this act, its source. It is not accidental that the same gestures are repeated – that Albert kicks Frans in the buttocks, sending him into the sawdust, or that Frans grabs Albert in the balls. The mad, animal howl that erupts is echoed in the clowns' earlier comic yelps and cries.[17]

Filmically dominating the fight is an extraordinary sequence of close-ups in which we discover what the clown has perhaps known about his art all along. Thus, for example, the clown's eye markings are associated not with tears but with blood, the blood flowing from Albert's beaten and swollen eye [Fig. 7f,g]. They are the physical marks of humiliation and the corresponding desire to destroy the other, to draw blood and take his dignity and power to resist. This sense is reinforced when we later see Anne claw at Frans's face, marring his good looks to wound his vanity. What for Albert and Frans are marks of humiliation are transformed in the clown to stylized decorations, identifying signs of the clown itself, with their real meaning safely hidden.

The other revelation concerns the clown's grin, painted on so that it can remain always the same. This paint hides the true expressions such humiliations call for, transforming them into something safer and less vulnerable. At the same time, through its unalterability, the clown's visage encourages the audience to keep a similar face, to take everything as a goodhearted joke and laugh back, to keep themselves in check and not go too far. What the clown's grin masks is also shown [Fig. 7g]. As Frans throws his first punch, Jens knows what will happen and how it will end. He is stunned and then desolate, defeated in his knowledge that there is no escape, that the suffering and humiliation that will ensue can only be endured. This is a knowledge that Jens the clown must hide, in part because it is so painful to bear, in part because it is this suffering the crowd most eagerly desires. Its acknowledgment would turn comedy into tragedy and put the clown out of business.

Thus, in hiding the reality of the torment their act ritualizes, clowns also try to keep the crowd in check and its deepest desires appeased but hidden, and to work out a compromise in which the victims can retain some dignity – if nothing more, at least that of their art. Their painted faces are the site of a dual struggle: one within, in which the feelings of the human being resist the clown's displacement of them and threaten to erupt untransformed, and one without, in which the audience's desire is

Figure 7. *The Clowns' Evening.* **a–d.** The clowns' entertainment. **e–h.** Albert's entertainment.

to be aroused and satisfied but kept from demanding its true object. In this regard, the clown's face corresponds to and elicits the wide grins and guffaws of the crowd [Fig. 7d], expressions not so innocent, pointing to something primal and reminiscent of a human beast, which shows itself first as leers and eager smiles that urge the fighters on and finally sadistic satisfaction bordering on the obscene [see also Fig. 8].[18]

These gazes and the laughter that accompanies them permeate *The Clowns' Evening*. They seek to strip their targets of all dignity and render them mere playthings to satisfy a selfish passion. In these scenes Bergman provides an essay on the power of the look that rivals Sartre's and is more disturbing, for what is revealed is a deep sadism that revels in others' destruction and gloats in seeing them beaten to a pulp. Rather than seeking acknowledgment of the victor's power and position (as Sartre argues), this desire, which is common and ubiquitous, wants the other sightless and prone on the floor, completely helpless, a dumb animal.[19]

Thus the real beast to be tamed in the circus, the true wild animal, is outside the ring – the crowd itself. In *The Clowns' Evening* Bergman gives us little clue as to the source of such a lust to command others totally. Everyone is vulnerable to it – townsmen, theater people, soldiers, circus folk, women as equally as men, children – and it feeds on itself: Inflamed by the laughter and leers of others, a boy hides Frost's suit, someone throws a firecracker under Anne's horse, spectators push Albert back into the ring. Yet perhaps a clue can be found in *The Seventh Seal*, in the scene where Raval threatens Jof with a knife and makes him take the part of a dancing bear.[20] There is no pity at all in the faces of the crowd at the inn, and they soon join in the torment with pounding mugs and jeering laughter. For them, it is a time of plague and evil omens – "people are going mad with fear . . . judgment day. . . . It will be terrible to see." But for now Jof is at their mercy; they are in control, and the impending evil can be deflected onto someone else.

Here the desire to humiliate springs from fear and hate: fear that one will soon die and that nothing can help, along with a deep hatred for having been made so vulnerable, a hatred that finds its target wherever it can. Such lust is founded above all on an inner terror and sense of powerlessness, of life draining away completely beyond one's control. Perhaps this momentary dominance over another creates a feeling of mastery and self-worth and a temporary sense of escape.[21] "If I can make it happen to someone *else*, it won't happen to me." "Let *them* be the one who is humiliated, life's loser." The other becomes both scapegoat and a vehicle for retaliation, attacked and clawed by a wounded animal.

46

The darkest feature of this portrait is the absence of shame. The circus audience cheers as Albert is beaten again and again. His own friends push him back into the ring. Only when it is finished is there silence and a hint of unease, but this is mostly chagrin at having been caught in the act. There is no regret, no acknowledgment of responsibility for having encouraged such humiliation, no sense they should have behaved differently, no rejection of their enjoyment. Only the victims feel such shame.

This is perhaps the final key to the clown's performance: to hide the shamefulness of the scenes enacted and the guilt everyone shares – not that this is a guilt the crowd will accept.[22] But the enactors must also hide this shame from themselves and forget that what's being mimed has its origin in shameful acts to satisfy shameful desires if they are to join in the joke and play their part.[23] The circus act is possible only if everyone is freed of shame, which is precisely what happens; for although the performance is mean, vulgar, and sexually charged, it is merely the antics of clowns, "fit for women and children." In being freed from shame, everyone is kept safe from the humiliation they desire for others yet fear for themselves. Spectators can indulge in it free from rebuke and actors offer it free from the guilt of complicity. Everyone can have what they long for if everyone keeps the disguise. A shameless performance for a shameless audience, the clowns' evening is a time where anything goes so long as it does not go too far.

However, when the clown frees the world of shame, he makes a bargain with the devil. In appeasing our fear of humiliation and death and the hatred of life it engenders, the clown gives in to and accepts the base desires of the herd at its most vulgar level. In so doing, he turns life into a kind of obscene joke. Everything becomes dirty and squalid, something to mock and deride, with nothing worthy of respect. Thus, Jens is ready to leer with the others at the spectacle of Frost and Alma, and he tells their story not to warn but as salacious gossip to pass the time. Frost himself regales Albert and Anne with off-color remarks when he enters their wagon. In rendering the world a realm where everything is sordid and shame does not apply, the clown degrades it so that it becomes ugly and unlovable, now seeming to deserve the hatred and contempt felt for it. No longer able to find something or someone in the world to turn toward and care for as a way of overcoming the damage suffered, the clown turns away, more and more lost in his separation and despair, neither bear nor horse nor monkey but a willing member of the herd.

6. The Clown's Afternoon

The sense of Bergman's title is finally ironic and cautionary. If the clown's strategy is to protect himself – not by literal escape to another place or an egotistic retreat from a world of genuine emotion but by a balancing act of involvement and comedic distance – then it too must fail. Furthermore, no one will keep the unspoken agreements on which such acrobatics rest, as the evening itself makes clear. It is the clown's "afternoon" as told by Jens as the films opens that shows both the ultimate landscape that we inhabit and the possibility that we may finally become something more than animals.

The story of Frost and Alma is among Bergman's finest achievements and remains unique in its rawness and yet lyrical evocation of elemental forces. Bordering on a lurid nightmare, it is, as noted in Chapter 1 (section 4) an unmatched expression of Bergman's central themes of abandonment, passion, and turning, and from the very beginning of the film sets a tone of brutishness, coarse sexuality, humiliation, and searing pain.[24]

Besides presenting a parallel story that foreshadows that of Anne and Albert (as well as a master image of our fate that reverberates throughout all his work), this short, silent-film-within-a-film provides a visual catalog of essential human expressions as we face each other. People are presented above all in terms of their faces and gestures. What Bergman shows is how close these expressions are to each other and how easily they can change (all this made even clearer by the omission of speech and Blomdahl's modernist music). Thus, smiles and laughter slide toward sexual innuendo and anticipation, and this to ribald (unheard) shouts and cheers, reaching finally rapacious leers and then silent shrieks of pain. It is one continuum. Without sound, one can hardly tell the difference between Frost's cries and the crowd's convulsions of enjoyment, and at bottom they share an animal unity and a common fate. Bergman's genius is to fill the sound in later when these events repeat themselves in the circus ring that evening. It is an uncanny effect. Frost's cry here is not heard until Albert's howl later, after Frans gets him in the balls – the same wound, the same suffering. It is as though this silent drama is both the mold from which all life will be cast and an image of the ghosts that will haunt us as long as we breathe.

As for gestures, Bergman dwells particularly on those involving clothes and touching one another. With respect to their appearance, for instance, Anne and Alma are revealed as identical, in some sense the same person. They both display themselves with a kind of enticing bravado in similar dresses as they leave the circus, Anne with an umbrella, Alma with her sun hat and basket. We know why Anne has gone back to the theater; is this a clue to Alma's motives as well? Is there something of the same longing, the same neglect and need? What responsibility does Frost bear for her actions? When Alma begins to remove her outer garments in her striptease for the gathered soldiers, the pose and action are almost identical to Anna's later undressing. The same mold, the same repetitions leading to the same sufferings and trials. Is this always our fate?

Undressing, of course, removes restraints on sexuality. This is an element intruding everywhere. Many of the soldiers are without shirts, and Alma is finally naked. But while sexuality gives us needs and desires that will always deeply shape our lives, this nakedness is most of all a sign of our embodiment and vulnerability to the look of others. Undressing is thus used throughout the film to indicate something more than sexual desire; it is a spiritual exposure and nakedness, a time of crisis when one is put before the truth and judged. Thus, Frost, too, removes his clothes (his clown costume) and strips to his underwear to go to Alma in the sea, actions reenacted by Albert later in the circus ring.[25]

In the sea, Frost tries both to cover Alma's nakedness with his arms and to lift and carry her away. This gesture is continued as he struggles up the rocky shore [see Fig. 3b]. The image created embodies all the ambiguity Bergman finds in human relationships. Frost both holds and fights with Alma, caresses and forces her, and she both resists and gives in. He has locked her in his arms to prevent her escape and save his ego but also to protect her and hide her shame – all at the same time. It is an embrace in which they are intertwined, clinging fast to each other yet the source of each other's misery. As Frost begins to stumble, their roles reverse, and for a moment one can no longer tell who is carrying whom – they are mutual burden and mutual support [see Fig. 9a,b]. From a distance it even looks as though they are copulating, making love. And perhaps this is the image of love we should have – as all these things. At the end, this picture of Alma and Frost stands ahead of Albert and Anne as their future (and not just their present ordeal), to be endured in a mutual torment of turning away or nourished in a genuine caring for each other.

These faces and gestures are located in a setting – half symbolic, half vivid image – that reinforces their character as the elemental material on which ordinary life rests: a stark landscape with a rocky path and boulder-strewn shore, devoid of shelter and exposed to the merciless sun. Here, Bergman has found for the first time that complete match between visual image and spiritual condition that will become the hallmark of his films in the 1960s and 1970s – an often excruciating examination of faces as people confront each other and themselves in a barren landscape.

The regiment's cannons are emblems not just of sexual desire but of conquest, of a lust to have pleasure at another's expense, and thus of the fundamental force that energizes this place and the "herd" of soldiers and circus folk gathered there. As weapons of war designed to destroy and obliterate, they suggest a sadism unredeemed by any countervailing urge to feel pain or sympathy. The hurt of the other is to be enjoyed, not shared and certainly not apologized for. All this is the stage setting for a spectacle of humiliation accompanied by its soundtrack brass band and musical strutting and laughter, raucous taunts, and animal cries of pain and delight, a primal scene also to be reenacted later in the circus arena [Fig. 8].

What happens to Frost in such a setting can hardly be surprising. Alma betrays him, though we do not know why. On the one hand, such things happen, and for Bergman this may be all that is important: It is something on which we may rely – sooner or later we will be betrayed, and then we will suffer. Yet Bergman also suggests we are never innocent victims without responsibility for what happens to us. When told that Alma is bathing for the soldiers, Frost seems to approach it as a joke in which he too will share. He is still a clown (and still in costume) and doesn't yet take the matter seriously. Perhaps this emotional distance was characteristic of their marriage – perhaps he had always been the clown with her.[26] In this sense, Albert too begins as a clown, not because he takes life as a joke, but because he is preoccupied with himself and his own longings and fails to attend to Anne and what they have together.

The suffering that ensues is that of humiliation before a jeering crowd and the despair of having been forsaken and left alone. As noted, Bergman directly likens it to the passion of Christ carrying His cross toward Golgotha, at the same time suggesting that Christ's suffering and human suffering are one. Bergman's image shows we are both cross and savior to each other, both burden and helpmate. The scene offers no other resources. Frost collapses, and the circus people carry him off toward his wagon. He thus returns to where he began – his shared life with Alma. If there is to be a resurrection, it must be here, in this world, among these people; and it is only through this possibility that Frost's (and Alma's) pain and humiliation can genuinely escape being meaningless. Yet all Bergman provides in this scene is the idea of turning toward another as the source of renewal and healing and the suggestion of its possibility. Their future is open.

This unwritten narrative space is the ground for hope, though often it leads only to further despair. For Bergman, all life stories are essentially

Figure 8. *The Clowns' Evening:* Seashore and circus a–d. The seashore. e–h. The circus.

open. As actors, what gets written will be through our choices, and the meaning of our lives is not a fate that overtakes us but something we must take up for ourselves. The story of Frost and Alma expresses the core of Bergman's vision in which our most basic weaknesses and vulnerabilities are portrayed in a master narrative of abandonment, passion, and return,[27] and at one level, everything else he has done is a variation on this quintessential minifilm.

7. Life and Art

The Clowns' Evening is an intricately structured film combining both linearly developed and formally repetitive elements. Its beginning scenes – the wagons traveling, Albert and Anne, Frost's story – are recapitulated at its end – Frost's dream, Albert and Anne, the wagons leaving. These elements set the story within a particular frame and are each important to the film's interpretation.

Thus, while the story of abandonment and passion is central to *The Clowns' Evening,* and both the seaside and arena scenes give essential images, the dominate metaphor of the film is the caravan: life as a continuing journey through the same terrain with the same people, ever repeating itself. It is in this context that all these other events are located. Along this road there are many ways to get lost but no real escape. The trick is to find that space between death (self-isolation, egotism, loneliness, despair) and the devil (the desire to humiliate and strike back, the fear and hatred of others and of the world) where one can endure such trials and manage to move on, sing and dance a little, and touch and hold one another.

A small vision of such a place is in fact given in the scene where the circus is resting before the evening performance – a second "clowns' afternoon," as it were. Indeed, this scene is preceded by another version of Frost and Alma's story but with a different ending. Albert has seen Anne leave the theater and confronts her in their wagon, but he does not believe her story that Frans forced her to sleep with him. "Want to know what I think? You're sick of the circus and me. And I'm sick of the circus and you – now we're stuck, Anne. Stuck in hell."

Frost enters, with his clown's face on and half-drunk. Albert drinks more and more; as his despair grows, he picks up the gun left by the tiger tamer. "You ought to shoot the bear. He's in a bad way," Frost remarks. "Don't forget to shoot my wife, too." "Yes," replies Albert," shoot everyone you're sorry for. Shoot you too, Frosty." As Albert points the cocked gun to Frost's head, the clown immediately sobers. Albert turns the gun toward himself. The pressure of death is palpable in that small cabin, and suddenly the two tumble out of the wagon as if thrown by an explosion, out into the open air amid the bustling sounds of the circus as people relax or prepare for the evening, relieved to have escaped still alive. "What a life, look at all the life around us – I love you."

Everything has become alive again – children play and shout, some performers are practicing and others just playing music and dancing, animals are grazing quietly while others are being shod and taken care of, some eat and some take a nap. People are together enjoying life and one another. Albert and Frost themselves start singing, and Albert gives instructions for the evening's show, returning to his responsibilities of caring for the circus. It is a brief moment but one never lost, never impossible to find again; and it is a time and place found within the caravan, always traveling with it.

The life of the caravan is the most encompassing framework given by the film, its version of the metaphysical reduction described in Chapter 1. The story of Anne and Albert is located within in it, and it sets the horizons and possibilities for their lives. By placing their first and last appearances in this formal and symmetrical position as the middle "ring" of the film's frame, Bergman loosens the first scene from its strict temporal occurrence and changes its modality. Is this first scene – that moment of tenderness and affection when Albert puts the covers over Anne in the cold morning – past or future? Only fact or also possibility? Does it precede this last scene of Albert and Anne together or follow it, or both? As the wagons begin to move out, completing one day and one cycle in the caravan's perpetual journey, Albert is left alone in the cold dawn, stolidly looking ahead. Anne comes toward him, and there is finally the faintest smile. She turns, joining Albert as they walk toward their wagon, side by side – the two not yet touching [Fig. 9c–e]. And how will they do this, what will happen? Is the first scene still possible?

Are they left to fumble through their lives, groping, guessing, hoping, fearing? They have been given a second chance, and thus a little mercy, but how much do they understand, how much of the larger picture have they seen, and what good can it do them? This is the question posed by the third and inner ring of the film's frame – the ring that directly encircles the action and the events in the lives of Anne and Albert that day. It is the question of the power of art, and Bergman's answer is qualified at best.

Bergman in his films almost always, though usually indirectly, makes clear that they are stories and thus a form of theater and art. Exploring them, one can usually find a metatheme about film/art itself. Thus, in *The*

Clowns' Evening Bergman contrasts his form of theater with that of Sju-berg and his theater company's plays of melodramatic distraction. "It was terrible," as Sjuberg says. The clowns' art is also deficient since it lacks shame and panders to people's basest feelings. Rather than distract or pan-der, true art should give us insight and enable us to aspire to something better and to see the whole of which our lives are a part. But can even this kind of art do any good? Can it ever be of actual help, or does it always come too late, comprehended only after we need it? Are audiences ever ready?

The film's "third ring" is formed by two stories told to Albert, both par-ticularly intended for him. The first, by Jens about Frost and Alma, warns him about what will happen to him and Anne, yet Albert quickly falls asleep and never hears it. Even if he had heard it, he may have made no connection nor seen anything universal in the specific events of their story. But without it, Albert also cannot properly appreciate its conclusion in Frost's retelling of his dream and Alma's midnight call to rest and obliv-ion. Albert hears this second story but does not know where it comes from, does not know that it is also about what can happen to him after he returns to Anne. The first story was a warning Albert never heard, and the second is a warning he cannot recognize.

Frost's story is one of escape founded on his original abandonment and humiliation, an escape not unlike Agda's, where there is no longer any emotion, only the stillness of sleep, and thus little life as well. That after-noon Frost dreamed that Alma came to him: "Poor Frost, you look tired and sad. Wouldn't you like to rest a while? Then you shall, darling, like an unborn child. You can creep into my womb." "I did as told. I slept so beautifully, so peacefully. . . . Then I got smaller and smaller until I was a little seed and then I vanished." As he and Albert walk in the night, Al-ma calls to him from their wagon. "You see, she cannot sleep if I am not there." Frost's dream of escape is a dream of death. Still beaten down and defeated, this will be Albert's greatest temptation, to simply give up and anesthetize himself – with drink perhaps, like Frost – and retreat into the silent corners of life, not quite alone, but suspended from life, coming out only to do that minimum needed to keep the wagons moving. Albert has been warned, but what can he hear?

We, the film audience, can of course see everything, the "whole picture" as Bergman has drawn it. But are we any better off than Albert? For Berg-man, what is most problematic about audiences is their lack of interest in having self-portraits in the first place and their unwillingness to take art for what it is – a picture with a place in it somewhere for themselves, a

Figure 9. *The Clowns' Evening:* Alone together. a. Frost takes Alma from the sea. b. Alma supports Frost. c, d. Anne and Albert face each other after everything is over. e. Anne and Albert go to their wagon as the circus leaves town.

picture that also shows the central places that define life and sets the terms of our being. Without such pictures, we may never be able to construct enough of this "geography" on our own. It would then be only chance and fortune that would allow us to escape being lost. That such pictures may be before our eyes yet unseen is the final irony and the part of *The Clowns' Evening*, rather than its gloomy and brutal portrayal of human misery and passion, that constitutes its deepest pessimism.[28]

3

The Journey: *The Seventh Seal* and *Wild Strawberries*

Wild Strawberries and *The Seventh Seal* both recount a "final" journey by their central characters. It is a trip from one place to another, occupying a single very long day (approximately dawn to dawn). But in fact what appears to be linear is part of a more complicated journey that in essence starts at home, wanders far away, and finally returns to where it began. It is this last stage that we see. For Bergman, this represents a central task of adult life to return to one's past and in some way retrieve something essential in life that has been lost. It is in this return that we find our second chance.

For knight Antonius Block in *The Seventh Seal* this would be to restore his marriage, but his time is up, and he can only rejoin his wife to await their end together. Still, he can save someone else (the juggler Jof and his wife, Mia) and thus replace his own salvation with that of another, a partial fulfillment of this essential project of return and reappropriation. Aged physician-professor Isak Borg in *Wild Strawberries* cannot save his marriage, since his wife has been long dead and their rupture is thus irreparable. But he can substitute his son's marriage and home for his own, becoming a true father again to his children (and grandchild). Moreover, in returning to his childhood home, he comes to feel once more alive so that at least he won't die dead. *Wild Strawberries,* then, is a drama of rebirth (mercy and meaning) through both reappropriation and replacement of what has been lost, whereas *The Seventh Seal* achieves only the latter. Both are variations of the same journey.[1]

Interwoven in these stories of departure and return is the theme of two deaths. The first is of the spirit, occurring after abandonment and the destruction of the transcendental, and it is the more deadly. In Isak's case, this happens with first-love Sara's rejection of him in favor of his brother

Sigfrid, and then with his wife's betrayal. For daughter-in-law Marianne, it perhaps begins when husband Evald turns away from her caress as they stand outside their car in the rain by the sea. For Evald, it is the absence of his father, Isak. As for Block, we never really know. He seeks with God the kind of relationship he could have had with Karin, his wife, and it is God's silence that he takes as abandonment and betrayal.

This identity between Borg and the knight is conveyed even at the level of their names. A *borg* is a castle, a home made of rock or boulders (*block* in Swedish), *blocks* of stone for building an impregnable barrier, a defense to *block out* all invaders. The knight and the physician are fortresses, as it were, dedicated to such exclusion and to evading true involvement with others. It is appropriate that chess shows up in both films, for it is a game about trying to ensure that one's walls are not breeched by an outsider.[2]

Still, inside these strongholds that turn others away, something of life survives. It is this deeper awareness of what is missing that emerges into consciousness in Borg's first dream, still darkly clothed and obscure, calling him to the journey that follows. And it is something similar that impels Antonius Block to forestall Death until he has reached God and heard Him speak.

THE SEVENTH SEAL

The Seventh Seal is filled with remarkable images: death itself, the chess game, Mia and Mikael, the vision of the Virgin, pilgrim flagellants, the supper of wild strawberries and milk, the burning of the witch, the dance of death at the end, Jof's radiant face. The film's power is their memorability, their capacity to stay in our imaginations, playing themselves over and over again, no longer bound to that particular story. Perhaps they balance each other out as they haunt us, no one displacing another. The emptiness of death remains side by side with the serenity of an evening meal of wild strawberries. They endure as images of realities always possible for everyone.

However, the film also has a discursive character that invites both reflection and analysis. It is, for instance, framed by quotations from two liturgical forms: the Requiem Mass and the Gloria, the first a prayer for the dead, the second praise of God as merciful creator. This change from threat of impending judgment to celebration of God's glory and the world He has given us is already encompassed in the mass itself, which begins and ends with an appeal to Christ for mercy and peace, that the souls of the dead be delivered and "pass from death to that life which Thou didst promise." This structure of rebirth, of a salvation that goes from earthly death to spiritual life, is further echoed in the film's many references to St. John's Apocalypse, which itself ends in a holy marriage in the new Jerusalem. All of this suggests that the narrative of *The Seventh Seal* is meant to trace this progress and show where God's mercy truly lies.

1. A Silent God

God's mercy and a transformation from death to life is what Antonius Block seeks. We do not know why he studied theology at the seminary in Roskilde or left his young bride for ten years to find answers in Palestine. For Block, God is silent and absent. He cannot be seen, He does not talk. People imagine Him, but that is not the same thing. That is the product of their fear. There is something literal about the knight's need "to grasp God with the senses." God must be palpable, definite, knowable like another person, someone who answers questions and can prove Himself. Perhaps Block is too scientific, or perhaps simply educated and modern.

Alternatively, perhaps it is because he can see no intermediate option between pure faith and absolute knowledge. Block lives in their gap, repelled by one, desperate for the other. He cannot give himself to the unconditional faith of the flagellants, which asks for no evidence and is capable of making a fourteen-year-old child a witch and the cause of a terrible, but natural, disease. But he also cannot accept the cynical secularism of his squire, Jöns, who sees God as just an image made to mask the emptiness of life and our fear of death, love as merely sex, and our helplessness as our one consolation. A world where these are the only alternatives is indeed inhuman and unlivable – Godless – so Block pursues his quest, playing chess to gain more time, to find his answers.

Are these answers given to him? Yes, though he perhaps never truly believes them. They occur in two forms, the negative and the positive. In the forest, Block presses Tyan, the witch-girl, to tell him of the Devil, as she is about to be burned; he – the Devil – must know about God if anyone does. "You can see him anytime," she says: "Look into my eyes." "I see fear in your eyes, an empty, numb fear, but nothing else." "But he is with me everywhere. I only have to stretch out my hand and I can feel his hand. He is with me now too. The fire won't hurt me. He will protect me from everything evil." "Has he told you this?" "I know it." Tyan, too, like all the others, has only a desperate faith. In his anger, Block turns on the presiding monk only to be confronted by Death himself. "Don't you ever stop asking questions?" The fire is lit. As they give her a drug for the pain,

Jöns presses the knight: "You don't answer my question. Who watches over that child? Is it the angels, or God, or the Devil, or only the emptiness? Emptiness, my lord! . . . Look at her eyes, my lord. Her poor brain has just made a discovery. Emptiness under the moon."

A bit later when the travelers have stopped in the forest, after the chess game is lost, Block questions Death for the last time: When you come to take us "you will divulge your secrets?" "I have no secrets." "So you know nothing?" "I have nothing to tell." And, indeed, when he does come again Death does not say a word.

Nonetheless, as Jöns notes after asking for directions from a plague-stricken corpse, Death in fact "speaks most eloquently." He tells us all there is to say about an afterlife, all that we can know: nothing. Death promises only an end to life, only darkness. To understand this is to turn our attention from what is beyond life to what is within it. This is the true realm of the spirit and where God's answers can be seen and heard. Death's silence is not God's silence, and this is the first – negative – answer Block is given.

Who does watch over this child? Is it really only emptiness? What of Jöns and the knight themselves? They give her some comfort and mercy, some release from pain and terror. They are all she has, which in this case is not very much but not nothing. This is the positive answer that is hard for Block to see. In sharing the wild strawberries with Mia and Jof, he is for the moment content, and all else seems no longer important. In viewing Mia and Mikael he is struck by their beauty and recognizes the love and affection that blesses Jof and Mia's marriage. His "one meaningful deed" is to save their lives. But though he has been given a picture of the divine, has partaken in a moment of communion and epiphany, and done his meaningful deed (more than one, in fact), he still does not find the peace he seeks. As Death comes for him, he falls abjectly to his knees in urgent, desperate prayer: "From our darkness, we call out to Thee, Lord. Have mercy on us because we are small and frightened and ignorant. . . . God, you who are somewhere, who *must* be somewhere, have mercy upon us." In the end, he sees no more than did Tyan.

Unlike Isak Borg's, Block's return home does not bring him the mercy and meaning he seeks. As with his initial departure, we never really know why. In the end, it comes down to this inability to see – the absence of a different, transforming vision, in which ordinary things can appear as also something else, something spiritual. If God appeared directly, as Block demands, what would He look like? Would the Devil have horns and a tail? Or would each look like just some other person, or natural object, or malformed creature? If God exists and there are assurances to our doubts, then He will be palpable in some other way.

In fact, God and the Devil are everywhere and as real as other people. The Devil is the wickedness present in Tyan's suffering and torture, the evil in ex-priest Raval's thievery and lust for rape and murder, the humiliation in the sport made of Jof at the inn, the shame and despair felt by blacksmith Plog as he is cuckolded, the loneliness of Block's solitude. God is in Jöns's protecting of Jof and the girl, the relief given to Tyan, the joy and love of Jof and Mia's family, the sharing of the wild strawberries, the knight's meaningful deed, even Karin's calm at the end. These are the only answers that can be found, the only evidence of God or the divine that can be given us.

2. God's Immanence

The response given in *Prison* to this quest for answers is that "God is dead or defeated or whatever you want to call it." This seems sometimes Bergman's view, as in *The Silence,* and his portrayal of ministers is usually as dead, pitiable souls (*Winter Light, Cries and Whispers, Fanny and Alexander*), or in the case of Raval – a former doctor of theology – worse. One could leave it at that; but often, and in a profounder way, Bergman counterposes this dismissal with an account of God as immanent and identical with the spiritual in man. This is not institutional religion nor a matter of doctrine, but it is, for Bergman, the inherent truth of both (at least of Christianity). Block wants God to touch him through his senses yet does not realize that this has happened. He has so displaced the real with the transcendental that he takes what is at best a symbol to be the actual thing, even though he is separated from it. As a consequence, hunger for certain contact with a perfect God comes to replace the love felt for Karin and the desire for her companionship.

As a theological position and interpretation of the nature of God, such immanentism is not unlike Jöns's view that God is an image projected by humans to enable them to live with their fear. As figures of thought, God, the Devil, and Jesus are indeed representations of human truths and a kind of mirror in which we can see ourselves and see what we most need to know played out in their images and narratives. Religion at this level becomes art.

It is through such art that the truths of both religion and life are conveyed in the film. In *The Seventh Seal* this representation of the real in pictures and words is a primary form of knowledge. The walls of the church visited by the knight and his squire are covered with paintings of the dance of death, sinners and penitents, and the plague itself, while the crucial fact that Death plays chess, the information that allows Block to stall for time (so that "the soul of man" can be saved),[3] is known from paintings and ballads.

However, it is also necessary that these images not misrepresent the reality on which they are grounded. For Bergman, this is a matter of having a fuller picture and knowing which representations are primary. Thus, Christ appears in *The Seventh Seal* three times as a wooden statue – in the church and among the penitents He is on the cross crucified, whereas in the knight's castle he stands beside the entrance to the main chamber. Both are representations of human passion and suffering. This is fixed as the moment after Christ's cry of despair, "My God, My God, Why hast Thou forsaken me?" He, like Block, is frozen, overwhelmed by a feeling of being utterly alone and abandoned, waiting for God's voice to say it isn't so, a voice that never comes (not even in the Gospels; see Matthew and Mark).

Perhaps it is this image and its eternal cry to God that keeps Block from looking elsewhere. In his search, he is imitating Christ on the cross, alone, waiting for some transcendental reply. But in seeing Christ's abandonment and suffering as that of real people – Jof tormented by the crowd at the inn and Tyan tortured on her cross, but also Plog's jealousy and Block's loneliness and self-loathing – we also see that the response they each need is the help or comfort of someone else. After the cross is the tenderness of Mary and the three women at the tomb, not a voice from the heavens.

As noted before, suffering for Bergman is the need, and hence the invitation, for a response of compassion, of turning toward. This is God's mercy (and His reply), found in our becoming better persons, fulfilling our best possibilities. Christ on the cross alone, divorced from other images, leads us to forget this, to fail to see that the failure represented by such a figure in pain is not God's but our own.

In such acts, we respond to others in terms of their need, not our desire, and give freely of what we have. In turn, we are touched and share something together. This occurs in the evening with the sharing of wild strawberries and milk, and is also what is symbolized by Jof's vision of Mary and Infant Jesus, made immanent in Jof, Mia, and Mikael themselves. They are the true holy family and have all the divinity that Mary and Jesus do.

As the travelers rest and eat together, they have entered a state of grace and for the moment experience the world as a gift. It is a place of calm and satisfaction, where people are generous and share what they can. Here

Block receives the gift of hospitality and rest for his weary and troubled soul; Jof, a gift of milk from strangers;[4] and everyone, a gift from creation itself since the strawberries are wild and discovered by chance. Altogether, it is the presence of God, Bergman's version of holy communion, in which Christ's body and blood become literally present [Fig. 10]. The personal contact that constitutes the sharing of the wild strawberries and milk is the spiritual nourishment (and mercy) the knight so desperately seeks, but it seems finally not enough.

The story of the suffering Christ on the cross is to be completed by the story of the Infant Jesus. This reverses the Gospels, which begin with the Nativity, yet, in a deeper sense, completes them by its insistence on the possibility of moving through our suffering and returning to a new beginning, a place where life can offer more than fear, selfishness, blind faith, or cynicism, a place where the "soul of man" can be nourished. It is this grace – which is both this generosity of nature and the human heart, as well as the fortune to find them – that the final Gloria celebrates.

3. Final Judgments

The Seventh Seal is a morality play, and its figures serve as exemplars of human types and possibilities. Character, therefore, derives more from the kind of person the drama requires than from personal history or individual psychology, and this may in part explain the difficulty in fully understanding the origins of Block's "crusade" or his final persistence in his quest to contact God directly. The story is about what happens to people of this *type* who must have "knowledge, not faith or suppositions," and how because of this they are ultimately closed off from God, even though He is all around them, not as a matter of faith, but as an object of a different kind of sight. Such a story makes its point not by having Block change (and "repent," as happens to Borg), but by having him remain the same, intransigent in this demand, and thereby condemned to his life of "emptiness . . . filled with fear and disgust" and to a pitiless death.

Here, the knight is not alone, for fear and disgust are everywhere in *The Seventh Seal*. They are what drives the flagellants on in their desperate attempts to appease God's wrath, impels the villagers and Plog in the inn as they humiliate Jof, spurs the soldiers as they transform a child into a witch. All are afraid to lose the little they have and grasp at anything that will give them even a small bit of control over their fate. And it is such fear that finally consumes Raval, as he dies alone and in terror, unable to be helped by anyone.[5]

This fear is, most literally, that we will lose our lives, lose them before we are ready to give them up, and then that we will be punished for our sins. This fear is set up by the very beginning of *The Seventh Seal,* which is itself the beginning of God's final judgment of mankind: "When the seventh seal was opened . . . there was a great silence upon the land. . . . And then the angel took the censer . . . filled with fire . . . and threw it on the earth."[6] After this last tribulation, our present world will be destroyed and all the dead brought before the throne of God to be seen as they really are. But for Bergman, this final judgment is to be made ultimately by ourselves. Death is not a judge, and God is not something apart from His creation. Accordingly, when Death does come to the knight's castle, he does not speak. We see what he sees: each person as they stand before him giving their own verdict (see Fig. 1a).

In fact, what they say is correct, as we can plainly see. They know who they are and what they have made of their lives. The smith speaks first: "I am a smith by profession and rather good at my trade, if I say so myself. My wife Lisa. . . . She's a little difficult to handle once in a while and we had a little spat, . . . but no worse than most people." The knight, Antonius Block, falls to his knees and prays: "From our darkness, we call out to Thee, Lord." He remains what he has been, lost in his loneliness, while Jöns in his diffident cynicism castigates Christ for this hoax on his master and relishes one last sensation of life. He will be silent only under protest as Karin, dutiful as wife and mistress of the household, seeks to calm him with a gentle shush, as though to a child or crying baby. The girl rescued by Jöns quietly accepts what has happened and that her life is over.

What is their punishment or reward? They have already had it. What we see at the end is not Death leading his subjects to another life in Heaven or Hell, but simply death leading them away from this one, to its own "dark land" of nonexistence. Death truly has no secrets. Its peace and relief – "while the rain washes their faces and cleans the salt of the tears from their cheeks" – is that of oblivion. The only place of light (and of spiritual radiance)[7] is that associated with Jof and Mia, and that is in this life. The sufferers are released from their suffering, no more.[8]

It is noticeable, nonetheless, that not everyone who has died that night, nor even those in the castle, are on Jof's list or a part of Death's dance. Where are Karin and the girl, and Tyan, who was also taken by Death? Most likely their omission is just an accident of filmmaking and nothing more should be made of it.[9] But it is worth noting that these three constitute a special class – they are innocent and seem victims to a degree the

Figure 10. Wild strawberries – communion. **a.** *The Seventh Seal:* "wild strawberries." **b.** *Wild Strawberries:* lunch by the lake. **c.** *Winter Light:* Sunday communion.

65

others do not. Furthermore, Karin and the girl have a quietness and peace of soul about them that relates them to Mia and marks them as special. Perhaps they already have that for which the knight and Jöns have longed? While Karin and the girl, and certainly Tyan, don't deserve the suffering they endure, the others do, at least insofar as they are responsible for what they have made of their lives. The flagellant monks lead a group of penitents behind a huge cross as they whip themselves in hope of achieving a grace that will evade God's punishment – and thus do God's work for Him. Raval's own spiritual nihilism and hatred condemns him to a terrifying death bereft of any comfort or inner strength. Block's self-loathing and Jöns's cynicism each paints an exaggerated picture of the world that imprisons its subject in a way the world itself never does, reducing God to the nothingness of death and humans to base and selfish creatures.[10] Block, in particular, has had the greatest opportunities but has shut others out of his life and in abandoning Karin has abandoned himself. The punishment for this, as noted in *Wild Strawberries,* is the usual one: loneliness.

Block and Jöns are both soldiers; hence the appropriateness of chess and its place as the knight's emblem. Chess is a game (and a mode of thinking) for adversaries and, if one's opponent is stronger, its strategy is keeping one's distance until one can be sure, just like the knight with life. This is also Block's bargain with Death: "I may live as long as I hold out against you. If I win, you will release me." It is not, however, a way to reach God. God is not an opponent. Thus, such a strategy is also a refusal, or at least a delay, of life. Only if Block wins, and can banish Death from the board, can he be released from the grip of its final nothingness. But no human can do this. Life is not won as a prize for conquering death. It is rather accepted, as a gift always there, like the wild strawberries. For Block, Gods' gift and mercy was Karin's love and youth, which he could not see as enough or take for what it simply was. His journey back to his home and starting place finally accomplishes very little for himself. Although he achieves the replacement of his (and Karin's) life with that of Jof and his family, this doesn't lead to his own rebirth or even calm his soul. Isak Borg will be more fortunate.

Yet this judgment may be too harsh and fail to appreciate fully the kind of story Bergman has told. His morality tale is also a version of *Everyman* in which each person represents some aspect of human being – greed, sexual desire, egotism, patience, tenderness, generosity. In this sense, Block and Jöns, as well as Raval and Skat, Karin and the girl, Tyan, the crowd in the tavern, and even the flagellants, are aspects of one person, of the "soul of man," of ourselves. They are ways and possibilities of our lives, particularly as we come to face our own deaths. But if so, the journey does achieve a retrieval and rebirth of life, not just a replacement of one life with another. For in saving Jof and his family by diverting Death and sacrificing himself, Block saves life itself – that spirit of joy and exuberance Albert finds for a moment in the afternoon of the circus (and that the servants Frid and Petra celebrate in *Smiles of a Summer Night*),[11] that communion at a feast of wild strawberries, that love and companionship shared by Mia and Jof. At this decisive moment, Block's sight too is transformed, and he turns away from the transcendental and acts upon the truth he sees before him. Life escapes Death, and will always escape death, for it is something that is always possible in life itself.

WILD STRAWBERRIES

Wild Strawberries (literally, "The Wild Strawberry Patch [or Place]") is one of Bergman's most sophisticated films. Its overall structure is in many ways another version of *The Seventh Seal*. Often appearing to be a record of events as they occur, it is in fact a retelling of what happened to Isak Borg on his "special" day of judgment, focused on his growing awareness that he had been someone else most of his life.[12] Its fabric consists of dreams and visions and other people's stories, as well as poems and songs. This allows him to attain the kind of perspective closed to the characters in *The Seventh Seal* and ignored or not grasped by Albert or Frost in *The Clowns' Evening*. By the end, Borg is able to see who and where he is and achieves the capacity to be both actor and audience at the same time. For Bergman, this is the closest to wisdom we can achieve.

4. Nightmares

Like Antonius Block, Isak Borg has a deadline and within that time must outwit death. But Borg initially is only dimly aware of his situation. Indeed, it appears that everything is settled, his life near completion, and congratulations about to be rendered. The University of Lund is to award him the "Jubilee Doctor" degree commemorating his fifty years as a general practitioner and county health officer, followed by a career of teaching and medical research.[13] All he must do is travel to the university (for it then to be proclaimed with trumpet and cannon, as though the judgment of heaven itself). But will this public verdict of respect and honor be true? Is it deserved? These judgments can properly rest only on a thorough examination of his life, conducted finally by the doctor himself. Borg must experience an apocalypse and come to see himself as he really is. Then he will be ready to accept his award in Lund.

This self-confrontation is centered in Borg's two nightmares.[14] In them, his awareness grows from vague feelings of unease and apprehension to explicit speech. The first nightmare is suffused with silence. The commentary (and the music) are external, given in retrospect by Borg as he retells his experience. But as his dreams progress, speech moves from dialogue to more discursive analysis and explanation, until Borg at the end of the second nightmare can finally speak out loud to Marianne: "It's as if I'm trying to say something to myself which I don't want to hear when I'm awake." "And what would that be?" "That I'm dead, although I live." The nightmares develop this theme of death in life and present the evidence against him. It looks as though the special degree will go to a corpse.

In these scenes, Bergman has created some of the most powerful and mysterious sequences in world cinema. They are composed of poetic images that dance and play throughout the film, tapping elemental forces of understanding and feeling that go far beyond this particular drama. In his first dream, Borg finds that his usual morning walk has taken him to a strange and unfamiliar street. Everything is deserted and silent. At the far end stands a church, flanked on each side by dead trees with limbs and branches mostly cut off. These stark trunks are vaguely like human stick figures; looked at more carefully, perhaps they remain alive, at least barely so, for a branch can be made out here and there. It is odd, of course, that they have not simply been dug out and removed.

This motif of the dead tree recurs throughout the film and is associated with both Isak and Evald, as a figure of their own shriveled and emotionless lives. One stands behind Evald as he listens to Marianne's "dire" news. And a similar tree is in the wild strawberry patch where Borg falls asleep (identified as an old apple tree); we see only its forking branches, so that it appears to have no leaves. Such silhouettes are a foreboding presence in Borg's second nightmare and are echoed in the burned framing of the abandoned house in which Borg and Sten Alman stand to view his wife's betrayal. The image of the stunted tree serves as both a representation and a warning of what they will be if they continue as they are. (Its real occurrence is more hopeful, for the old apple tree has a strawberry plant at its roots and the young, present-day Sara in its branches.)

Walking along the street, Isak passes a clock without hands. The image is ambiguous. It is not just that time has stopped; it has run out and reached the point "when time shall be no more." But this image can also mean that Isak does not know what time it really is or recognize what time is truly for. (He checks his own watch and sees the same thing – its face has no hands.) Time is not easy any more and cannot be taken for granted. The same holds true for sight. The bleeding eye in the glasses below the clock suggests that his ability to see is also defective. For both senses, something beyond the ordinary aids is needed: a new sense of time and a new way to see.

The clock and watch in Isak's dream are just like that of his father, which his mother intends to give to his nephew, who will soon be fifty. Perhaps this "dead man's" watch will not be Isak's inheritance after all, perhaps he can escape what seems to wait for him. This tension between still having time and its already being too late pervades *Wild Strawberries*. Isak must get to Lund by five o'clock (and see himself clearly in the process if he is to escape death), while Marianne and Evald must decide about their pregnancy before it is too advanced. The first thing Isak does when he awakens is pick up his bedside clock. It works. There is time after all. There is still time. He decides to change his plans and so undertakes a journey of return to his home and his beginning.

This new time he has discovered is the time needed to see himself for the first time. In his second nightmare, the Sara of his youth holds a mirror for Isak and forces him to look, and Borg fails Alman's examination because he can find only his own eye in the microscope: He does not know how to focus his sight correctly or where really to look. (Marianne provides a different kind of mirror when she reminds Isak of what he said when he rejected her plea for help,[15] as do the Almans as they present a picture of his own marriage.)

As this (first) nightmare continues, Isak walks up and back along the street. There is nothing. Then, with some relief, he sees a figure standing where he had been. As the man turns, he reveals only the puffed outlines of a face, bloated and almost unrecognizable as a human. He collapses, deflating like a balloon, a puffed-up man who is really nothing inside but air and a dark, bloodlike liquid. Here is someone who was once a man, human at a distance but not close up, face to face. That squished face indeed resembles Isak's own when he frowns at his housekeeper, Agda, or scolds Marianne. He does not recognize it here anymore than he can tell the dead from the living in Alman's examination.

As the puffed-up man falls, the church bell begins to toll. A hearse passes, catches its wheel on a lamppost, and discharges its coffin. Isak is almost hit by the loose wheel – a close call, like the accident with Alman's car. As the hearse rocks, struggling to free itself, it has the uncanny sound of a baby crying. This strange place to which Borg has summoned himself is revealed to be the site of a funeral, a burial now interrupted and postponed. Borg is being offered a second chance. Can it also be the site of a new birth?

The coffin falls on its side. An outstretched arm leans against the lid. As Isak moves closer to see who it is, the corpse grasps his wrist. It is himself. Is Isak trying to pull himself into his coffin, where he really belongs, or is he asking himself to help pull himself out before it is too late? As they struggle together, the one trying to escape, the other refusing to let go, the faces of the two Isaks begin to merge, then blur. The nightmare is over; he is in bed about to waken.[16]

During this scene, we see the dead Isak's hand from several angles. For a brief moment, it is like Christ's hand on the cross, ready for the nail (recalling Tyan's hands in the *Seventh Seal*). The image is completed in the second nightmare when Isak cuts his palm on a nail after he has observed Sigfrid, his brother, sweeping cousin Sara off into their romance. It represents a suffering he must acknowledge and no longer suppress and try to escape. There are other resonances as well. The hand moves, as though it waves or beckons, to lead him somewhere. But there is also a hint of farewell, for there is no assurance that he will understand the call or change his course. Each gesture is filled with this ambiguity: a beckoning to his grave or to overcoming his death? Is it a farewell to what could have been or to a moribund self?

It would be a mistake to think of these images of barren trees, handless clocks, animate corpses, and bleeding eyes as just obvious symbols. Even with such familiarity, they retain their power in the viewer's imagination, and we can think of Isak as also being haunted by them and puzzling about what they might mean (and thus setting out on his journey to discover their truth). Indeed, this is a way of understanding the second nightmare, as a more explicit commentary on and interpretation of the first. For us, these images make Isak's inner feelings externally visible, and they gain their full sense by association and accumulation. And although their meanings can be articulated, their most basic way of functioning is affectively. We see them, and they come to inhabit our consciousness with all their suggestions and reverberations.

5. Parents and Children

These images in Isak's nightmares and dreams form a subtle web of connections extending throughout the film. When he and his daughter-in-law visit Isak's mother, Marianne is virtually ignored by the old woman, who does not recognize her and hardly cares who she is as she remains standing in the background. The focus of attention would seem to be Mrs. Borg and her relation to Isak, but in fact this entire scene, in terms of the drama, is for Marianne. We learn this only later when Marianne confesses to Isak that seeing them together gripped her with "a strange fear." Mother Borg, "completely ice cold . . . more frightening than death itself" is like Isak, "light-years of distance" from anyone, and "Evald is on the verge of becoming just as lonely and cold – and dead." This is her own future, too, if she continues on their terms. "I thought there is only coldness and death, and death and loneliness, all the way. Somewhere it must end."[17]

At the time, however, all this is conveyed to us pictorially. Bergman's camera suggests this inner reflection when it shows Marianne listening to Mrs. Borg talk about her children. She is holding the doll that belonged to Isak's sister Sigbritt, while over her right shoulder we see an old clock. We are apt to forget that there are two protagonists in *Wild Strawberries* and that Marianne undergoes a journey of recognition and transformation parallel to Isak's and equally as important. The stakes are as high for her, and she too is up against the clock. And this is what we see: Marianne caught between time and something that could be someone's baby. What is she to do with it – keep it or let it go?

The resonances of this moment as Marianne examines the doll and adjusts its clothes go beyond external signs of an internal struggle to one of the central themes of the film. The doll, though belonging to Sigbritt, was abandoned ("She never liked it much") and then adopted by another sister, Charlotta. While paternity and maternity may be automatic as natural states (the doll is still Sigbritt's), as spiritual relationships they are not. (Indeed, it is Sigbritt's real child for whom we see the dream-Sara caring in the film.) Spiritually, our most elemental condition is as orphans, and we must all be adopted. What is central is not the having of children but the acceptance of them as ours whoever they might be. Even as adults, we are subject to this same condition.

This theme is played out in many combinations in the film. Evald believes that Isak doubts his own paternity and that this accounts for his father's coldness to him. Perhaps so, but Isak must put this aside and take Evald as a real son if he is to relate to him as other than his banker. He himself is adopted as Father Isak, first by present-day Sara and the two young men with whom she is traveling (but by Sara especially) and then by Marianne as she kisses him good night. Indeed, in formal terms the film ends by attempting to reconstitute the family that has been shattered by the course of Isak's life (and a form of which we see in his dream in the old strawberry patch by their summer home). Isak in effect recognizes Agda as his wife (as more than a housekeeper), Evald and Marianne become children in more than name, Sara and her friends become grandchildren, with the possibility of another grandchild from Marianne and Evald, and his own father and mother are brought back. The continuity of life, of generations and generation itself, must be restored or at least reclaimed, in an attempt to annul "the light-years of distance" that has beset it. What was isolated and separate must be threaded back together so that the stunted tree might again foliate and flower. Here, *Wild Strawberries* is like *The Seventh Seal*, and each ends with images of "holy families," either as rescued (Jof, Mia, and Mikael) or as retrieved and reconstituted (Isak with his new "family" and his mother and father fishing).

This theme is also the ground for the film's allusion to the biblical Sarah and Isaac, and in some ways *Wild Strawberries* might be thought of as Bergman's meditation on this story. Isaac is God's promise to Abraham of future generations more numerous than "the stars of heaven and the sands of the seashore" (Genesis 22:17), yet at the same time he is a sacrifice commanded by God that his father will attempt to carry out. All of the future – all continuity of life and the fulfillment of all God's promises – depends on some miracle, that there be mercy and Isaac escape death. Bergman finds this mercy and rebirth in the figure of Sarah, Isaac's mother (herself once barren); and indeed the contemporary Sara in the film first appears as though from the "heavens," coming down into the wild strawberry patch from her perch above in the apple tree.[18]

In the film, Bergman splits this Sarah into two (both played by Bibi Andersson). The first, his cousin Sara, brings him into adulthood (in the same strawberry patch). As a birth, it is both an awakening of desire and an opening to abandonment and suffering. This Sara, as first love, occasions both (just as Sarah brings Isaac both to life and to the suffering of his father's sacrificial pyre), but she can do little more – her strawberries are not for him.[19] It is the second Sara, herself a pure gift as wild and free as the strawberry patch itself, who begins to reawaken through her own vitality a liveliness of feeling within him leading to his second birth. And as child, she begins to restore him as parent, not biologically but in the sense of his caring for a life other than his own, prodding the desire to live his life as something that can continue and be passed on to heirs. The promise to Abraham is thus resumed and thereby reaffirmed.

There is, of course, something Platonic, or better archetypal and ideal, in all this (Jung rather than Freud). This is a story that thematizes a set of relations that closely interweave the natural and spiritual senses of its terms. At the same time, it is clearly part of its picture that these senses may disastrously fail to coincide. Marriage may be hell, and children may be orphans and abused victims. The ideal is at best a picture of the possible that can sometimes be actual. Our finding it as actual even just once – whether in memory (as Isaac does his past) or in present fact (as both Marianne and Isak can see with respect to Sara and her friends) – in turn shows us that it is *still* possible, keeping its hope in place. But both the biblical story and Bergman's variation acknowledge that the other possibilities will be actual, too, and the "murder" of one's children is as much a theme of *Wild Strawberries* as anything else. This is Evald's experience of the world and Marianne's deepest fear.[20]

There are few clues to its avoidance and no assurances of escape from such disaster. It is another area of grace, and the terror is made all the more palpable by the fact that Isak is (was) a good man, both in contrast to his brother Sigfrid ("that no-good") and by the testimony of his patients from his first practice. Still, he is not yet a good father, and the testimony that will finally count must be that of Evald and Marianne.

6. On the Axis of Turning

In his depiction of the relationship between Isak and Marianne, Bergman provides in *Wild Strawberries* a visual "essay" on what is described in Chapter 1 as the "axis of turning." In scene after scene they are shown together, side by side, vacillating between turning toward each other and turning away.

This mode of composition reflects and choreographs the drama at the heart of their relationship. Marianne is a daughter whom Isak refuses to adopt. As they begin their trip to Lund in Isak's car, his first words to her are "Please, don't smoke." This insensitivity to her distress and insistence on his own interests (with further remarks about the "place" of women) in effect replays his cold reception to her visit and brutal refusal to become involved with her marital problems: "I don't give a damn about them, and everyone has his own troubles." He is intractable about the loan to his son, even patronizing: "And I know that Evald understands and respects me." "That may be true, but he also hates you." Isak is startled, and Marianne's matter-of-fact tone begins to stir some of the same feelings he had had just hours earlier in his first nightmare. But when he finally begins to mention this experience, she cuts him short – in retaliation, as it were, for his own egotism. "I'm not very interested in dreams." She is now like Isak and does not, or will not, recognize what has really been offered.

Figure 11. *Wild Strawberries:* Marianne and Isak's first conversation.

This scene begins with a shot of the two of them from his side [Fig. 11a]. Marianne is looking down and slightly away, about to light a cigarette; Isak is looking forward, with his head tilted up. The scene ends with the same shot: Isak remains in about the same position, his expression softened, but Marianne is turned even farther away. The distance between them has increased.

Between these shots the same composition is shown from reverse angles and is further developed in a series of alternating close-ups of each

Figure 11 *(cont.)*

character alone. Each almost never looks at the other while talking, and never directly at each other. Their sight lines always go off in different directions. Throughout, they continually turn on the vertical axes of their bodies, sometimes turning toward the other, sometimes away, as they thrust and parry, attack and defend, as well as grope for something more. The scene ends as it began, but now their rupture is out in the open.

In framing this scene as he does and enclosing it within the front seat of a car, Bergman creates a dynamic tension that demands resolution, some state of rest that will dissipate the conflict and achieve stability. Viscerally, this resolution goes inward or outward. Outward motion is escape from the other – opening the door, turning one's back, and running away. Inward motion is reaching to the other, coming finally to touch and hold him or her. But neither will really bring rest.

Keeping turned away is always a temptation in *Wild Strawberries*, but it is hard to forget others and the hurt and sorrow they have caused, or to escape their demands. To achieve this is to become dead like Isak. Leaving and refusing to picture oneself in relation to others is a kind of suicide. People may try it for a moment but they also return, as does Evald after his quarrel with Marianne. A suggestion of its terror is given by the image of Sten and Berit Alman standing forlorn by the road as Borg's car pulls away. Though their own car has broken down and they are too poisonous to be allowed to ride with others, they still prefer to be together and consume each other in their suffering than to be utterly alone.

Turning toward moves through looking and hearing finally to touch, from separation to reciprocation and reconciliation.[21] But even here there are two possibilities: The first is to strike out at and push away the other, as Berit strikes her husband out of humiliation and despair; the second is to caress and hold them, as Marianne finally does with Isak. Perhaps an agon of hatred and bruising touch has a peculiar stability that enables it to endure, almost endlessly repeating its oscillation of contact and distance (its alternative of true isolation always preventing any final separation), but it cannot be desirable and remains only the shadow of a true and enduring embrace.

At the elemental cinematic level, these scenes exhibit a **rhythm of alternation** that permeates the film. The camera cuts from person A to person B, back to A, back to B; it shifts angles, from A's side, to B's side, from A's side again, back to B's side; it includes people together, it sets them apart; it starts with one person, pulling out to show a pair together, or starts with them together and zooms in to isolate a single one. These alternations between "me and you" and "me and us," between us apart and us together, reflect the same ontology as the "axis of turning," with people perpetually moving between turning away and turning toward. Neither position is more stable than the other; each represents a perpetual possibility latent in the other. This is the heart of Bergman's "metaphysical reduction." It is the possibilities of all these, this axis itself, that is the site of human life: We are alone together with only each other as resource, both blessing and curse.

7. Becoming Awake

Marianne and Isak's last encounter before they reach Lund is both a repetition and a continuation of their first. But while it is composed in the same way, it is also a second chance. Will either Isak or Marianne be able to change?

This scene begins with a shot reprising both the beginning and end of the earlier conversation [Fig. 12c]. The angle is reversed because Marianne is now driving; her head is turned down and away, the window open. Things are the same between them, yet they have also deteriorated a step or two. Marianne is in fact smoking (before she had only gotten her cigarettes out), her window is fully open, her head turned further away. Her escape, from both Isak and Evald, is imminent. The threat is that Marianne will not just lean out the window but will open the door and leave – that when she gets out of the car in Lund, she will also permanently depart from his and Evald's lives. This is a realization that grows on Isak and begins to replace his concern for himself and preoccupation with his dreams.

Within this frame is Marianne's confession of her own troubles. Her scene with Evald both parallels and replicates her relationship with Isak and it is composed in the same visual terms, emphasizing Evald's identity with his father (whom we now see as occupying the same place in similar pictures). Yet it also suggests that Evald's future is fundamentally in Isak's hands (for it is included in *his* picture) and that it is not merely his own life for which he will be held accountable. The sequence as a whole starts and ends with the camera searching Isak's face as he begins finally to understand.

Marianne begins her story looking toward Isak (whom we do not see). There is a cut, and in the place where Isak should be we see Evald, looking ahead and away. As Evald turns, the camera pulls back, showing him to be next to Marianne [frames f1,2]. The scene ends virtually as it begins, with Evald and Marianne apart, looking ahead as the camera moves in on Evald alone [frame f9]. There is a cut to Marianne, then the camera pulls back to include Isak [frames g,h], sitting where Evald was, reminding us again that Evald and Isak are one in their response to life and the needs of those they love, and that their futures are deeply intertwined, both for themselves and for Marianne.

As Marianne and Evald talk, they are quickly (and often) shown turning toward each other, coming face to face. These confrontations remain

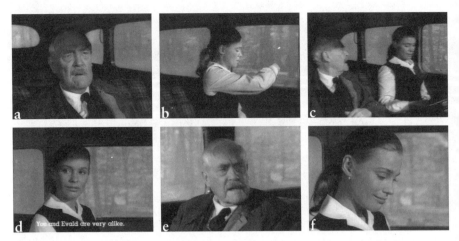

Figure 12. *Wild Strawberries:* Marianne and Isak's second conversation.

just that, however, and the two fall back into avoidance and separation. Outside in the rain (beside a barren, dead tree as warning), their relationship is expressed in the image of two persons close together looking (and ready to go) in opposite directions [frame f4]. They could as well walk past each other as embrace. When Marianne touches Evald, wanting to comfort him and be his lover, he moves away. "You have a damned need to live, to exist and create life. . . . My need is to be dead. Absolutely, totally dead." They will be forever caught between these two poles, like the Almans, unless something decisive is done. Here is Marianne's decision to leave Evald and have her child anyway, even though he is "the person I love more than anyone else."[22]

The symmetry in this inset scene – beginning and ending with a shot of Evald alone, looking off in his own direction – parallels that of the conversation as a whole. Isak's and Evald's are identical stories, and the impending disaster of the one can be avoided only if the other can end in a different way. In the final shot of Marianne and Isak, she is looking down, on the verge of tears, and he is facing toward her. The camera moves in to focus on Isak, as it had on Evald, reversing the opening shot (in which Isak awoke from his second nightmare) and bringing the scene to a formal completion. Everything is knitted together, and Isak is brought back to himself and where he began – at the point of waking up from a nightmare. This is precisely the issue before him: Will the nightmare really be over, or will his life continue on as before? Has he really understood what his dreams, his other self, have been trying to show him? Has he seen what

Figure 12 *(cont.)*

we have seen? This is the point of judgment, and it is Isak himself who must decide the final verdict.

At this moment, the young travelers are heard singing "Long live Uncle Isak." As he turns, the camera follows, and we see them outside the window with their gift of flowers [frame j]. This is a picture that finally gains force within Isak. It is a different future, a different possibility than the bleak and dreary landscape shown behind Marianne or Evald. The youngsters have in effect adopted him as their uncle (or even grandfather) and are celebrating that union. Isak at last becomes clear: He must adopt Evald and Marianne as son and daughter. The journey home must be completed by this retrieval and replacement. Now we can understand Alman's verdict that Borg is "incompetent" and "guilty of guilt." His guilt is this lack of responsibility for this fundamental interconnectedness of lives that must be nourished rather than stifled. His deepest guilt is not recognizing this. Now, as his journey nears its end, Borg understands and looks at his watch. "We better get going. It's already late."

8. Portraits

In *Wild Strawberries*, the ferociously symmetrical ontology of alternation on the axis of turning is balanced (and resisted) by its narrative structures of trial and journey, which emphasize *embedment,* the interpolation of one event, story, or life *into* another. Once put in, such "parts" cannot be taken out, and the histories thus constituted provide the substance – the true base – from which our turnings take their shape. The confrontation between Evald and his wife is, in part, a drama in which such incorporation is the issue: Will another person's story be written into one's own? Marianne has inserted a new event – "I'm pregnant, Evald"; "I shall have this child" – while Evald hopes desperately to remove it – "You'll have to choose between me and the child." But once there, as it now is, how can that child not always be a part of their lives, an unavoidable "story thread"? It is something with which they must deal and a permanent part of their own stories from now on. They may accept it, as Marianne craves; exclude it, as Evald desires; or even try to forget it. But even then, it will be a defining part of who they are (and always available as a ground for future regret, recrimination, guilt).

We are histories in which the parts accumulate, even though we can live the relationships they establish in isolation and separation, turning away from them. Mrs. Borg gives her mementos away, divesting them of any value – "Yes, of course you can have it. It's only trash," she says of Sigbritt's doll. Yet they are still parts of her life, and she remains answerable for them as part of her responsibility for herself. We may live alone, but we do not exist alone. This is what Isak realizes in his final conversation with Marianne: He cannot answer questions about his own identity and life without interpolating into his story the lives and stories of over a dozen others. Who he is is determined by who he has helped them to be. This is a fact that cannot be avoided; it can only be forgotten.

It is in virtue of this that a genuinely asymmetrical element arises, for forgetting (and its cognate forms: ignoring, not noticing, not attending to, being preoccupied, and so on) is epistemologically defective. It puts the truth out of sight. Incorporation, because it is a more complete and thereby more truthful structure, is a figure with a normative weight. It is the structural form of the perspective and the kind of sight that can finally become understanding and perhaps wisdom.

This means that our portraits as human beings cannot be drawn without also including portraits of the others with whom our lives are shared. This is indicated at the film's very beginning, the "Prologue" in which we see Isak in his study and hear him describe his life on the day before his trip. Central to this portrait are the family photographs, literally present as pictures within a picture (his own).[23]

The film, as a revision of this initial "sketch," brings these "other" pictures to life for Isak and restores them to their true importance in his life. Is this, then, the completed picture, the true portrait of Isak Borg, now worthy of the ceremony and honor bestowed upon him? *Wild Strawberries* ends with a shot of Isak's head on his pillow (still in Lund with Marianne and Evald), gently smiling at having just been led by his first Sara to his father and mother by the sea. Is this who Isak is, what he really looks like?

When we examine the overall structure of the film given in Table 1, we see that this image does not yet show us what we need to see. Thus, this analysis of *Wild Strawberries* reveals a marvelous formal unity to the film. Episodes in the first half are balanced by counterparts in the second that develop and advance what was earlier introduced and bring both Isak's trial and his journey to completion. Yet there is no "Epilogue"; the film is missing its final balancing episode. Like *The Clowns' Evening*, its ending is open: Everything is left dangling, filled with question marks. Will Agda respond to Isak? Can Evald ever allow his father to forgive his debt? Will he really accept a child or Marianne give one up? Will Isak himself persist and genuinely live by the truth he has uncovered? The asymmetrical structures of trial and journey, though leading Isak to a new picture of a better person, cannot ensure its choice. The final form of the film, in recognizing and even insisting on this limitation, weakens the force of his revelation against the rhythms of alternation and turning.

Who then is Borg at the film's end? (The image we see is of Borg in Lund, but the voice we hear is from Borg back in his study in Stockholm.)

Table 1. _Wild Strawberries:_ Formal and Dramatic Structure

PROLOGUE: Isak's study Title/credits	[EPILOGUE: ???] Title/"The End"
(1) _Stockholm_ – Isak nightmare (ISAK'S starting events HOUSE)	(11) _Lund_ – Isak reverie (EVALD'S concluding events HOUSE)
(2) _Road_ – in car Isak & Marianne	(10) _Road_ – in car Isak & Marianne (+ Evald)
(3) _Summer house_ 1st dream Sara joins Isak	(9) _"Summer house"_ 2d dream "Sara" leaves Isak
(4) _Road_ Almans quarrel Marianne intervenes	(8) _Road_ Anders, Viktor quarrel Marianne intervenes
(5) _Service station_ Isak's past	(7) _Mother Borg_ Marianne's future
(6) _Lunch_	

Neither we nor Borg know. Perhaps he is not who he was, but if so, he is not yet someone else. He must make himself in a new image, and though he has taken a few steps in that direction, he may not succeed, and the original portrait may suffice after all. It is for this reason that there can be no filmed "Epilogue," no final, fixed picture of Isak Borg to balance the first and temporary sketch. If there were, it would not catch him; he would be somewhere else, somewhere between the two, at best trying to resemble the one and revise the other. Life is choice and struggle, the continuing need to turn toward others and include their lives in our own, along with the temptation (or even provocation) to fall back into an isolated self. _Wild Strawberries_ most deeply embodies this fact in its insistence on openness and its final refusal of closure.[24]

9. Wild Strawberries

At Lund Isak makes an effort to leave his isolation and turn toward the people in his life. He suggests to Agda that they be less formal with each other (not entirely dismissed by her) and tries to approach Evald about easing up on or even forgiving the loan. Evald assures him he will get his money. "I didn't mean that." But Evald is preoccupied with Marianne and their future, and the subject is dropped. Isak and Marianne say a few words as she changes her shoes for the ball, and she gives him a kiss good night. "I like you, Marianne." "I like you too, Father Isak." He is left alone, "restless and sad."

Isak's journey and trial have opened old wounds and aroused the desire to regain what he had lost, even to return to those earlier times. This is perhaps his final choice as he nears his real death: to live more and more in that past or to commit himself to a new, still difficult future. Is it true as long-ago Sara tells him, when he drifts off in a reverie of his childhood (to "calm" himself before sleep), that "There are no wild strawberries left" and that he should find his father and mother again, returning to a time when he was loved and losing himself in its memories (like Frost wanting to vanish away into Alma's womb/embrace)?

Wild strawberries have a place in other Bergman films. One of their first occurrences is in *Illicit Interlude* where the young lovers, Henrik and Marie, picnic near a strawberry patch by the sea. Their summer of first love ends with Henrik's death in a swimming accident, a death that drives her into spiritual numbness and isolation. In *Wild Strawberries* itself, they are most associated with his cousin Sara, who returns in Isak's dreams as he rests in their midst. For Isak, they are both the promise of first love and the place of its loss, for it is in that patch that Sigfrid kisses her and she betrays Isak. For Sara herself, the patch provides a moment of seduction and sexual excitement, a place where her honor is stained, or "at least nearly." *Her* strawberries are in fact for someone else (sexually, for his brother; literally for Uncle Aron – "I forgot to prepare a present. . . . So, he gets a basket of wild strawberries"). None of this can be retrieved, and *these* strawberries *are* gone (though the caring underlying his relationship with Agda might be able to develop more openly into love between companions).

Still, as the film makes clear, such strawberries can be replaced by new ones; they are not the only ones life has to offer, not its only gift. In the present, this same strawberry patch is the source of a new Sara and something that can finally annul the old desires and heal their wounds with a rebirth – if given the chance. Here, wild strawberries are associated with the promise of life, with that which nurtures and satisfies in human relationships, with the sufficiency of people themselves for their own deepest needs of affection and friendship (something present earlier in Isak's life as country doctor when he was so deeply loved by his patients).[25]

In the *Seventh Seal,* it is these wild strawberries that are shared by Jof and Mia with Block and the others in a meal of peace and contentment. In *Wild Strawberries,* this scene is repeated at the inn by the lake as Isak and Marianne lunch together with their young hitchhiking companions –

Sara, Anders, and Viktor – simply enjoying each other's company (it, too, a version of the sacrament of communion) [see Fig. 10b]. The scene celebrates such moments and in that way is a vision of what is better in life.

Isak tells stories of his early days as a doctor, and then Anders recites a poem about how the beauty of creation shows the even greater beauty of its Creator, violating his bargain with Viktor not to discuss "God or science" on the trip. Their ensuing quarrel recalls Block and his squire:

> VIKTOR: In my opinion a modern man looks his insignificance straight in the eye and believes in himself and his biological death. Everything else is nonsense.
> ANDERS: And in my opinion modern man exists only in your imagination. Because man looks at his death with horror and can't bear his own insignificance.
> VIKTOR: All right. Religion for the people. Opium for the aching limb. Is that what you want?[26]

When asked what he thinks, Isak begins another poem, "Where is the friend I seek everywhere?" with lines soon added by Marianne and Anders. Isak ends with this: "I see his trace of glory and power, In an ear of grain and the fragrance of flower," followed by Marianne: "In every sign and breath of air. His love is there. His voice whispers in the summer breeze. . . ." Swedish audiences of the time would have recognized this as "one of the most familiar selections in the *Swedish Hymnal*,"[27] as does Sara, who remarks: "You're religious, aren't you, Professor?" Isak's reply reflects the immanentism in *The Seventh Seal* discussed earlier – "As a love poem, it isn't too bad."[28] This friend for Isak's "loneliness and care" can only be those people in his life now and the love he can find to renew and repair such relationships. What the new strawberries offer is not a retrieval of his old romance or marriage, but their reworking and replacement in the lives of Evald and Marianne, Agda, and the others. This is the gift that lies at the foot of the old tree (that emblem of his deadened and lonely existence) against which Isak falls asleep at the start of his trip to Lund.

In *Wild Strawberries*, the representative and even symbolic persons of *The Seventh Seal* have become internal to the consciousness and drama of Isak Borg. All the earlier characters are now his own possibilities, and if there is to be mercy or salvation, it must occur as growth in his own understanding and change in his own actions. His sight must be altered so that he comes to see both the spiritual in the ordinary and a larger picture that includes the pictures of others in the picture of himself. For this to happen and for him to overcome his first, spiritual death, Isak is given a second chance, one that will leave him essentially unfinished but turned in the right direction. This is played out in a drama of trial and journey in which his first home and relationships can now (in part, at least) be both reappropriated and replaced.

Perhaps Isak's last smile as he goes to sleep is an awareness of this, a smile of affirmation and hope. In this sense, his finally finding his father and mother and returning to them is a figure of rebirth, of his becoming like a child again with a second chance to start over, his smile echoing theirs as they, and even nature itself, greet his return on this bright and exuberant morning.[29] Or perhaps it is simply the smile of sleep and the comfort of an imagined return to his childhood where his parents call and wave to him and he can retreat from the world of real needs and cares before he dies.[30]

4

The Great Dance: *Smiles of a Summer Night*

Smiles of a Summer Night (1955) begins with the world in disorder. Each person is out of place, paired in a wrong coupling that nonetheless seems desirable. Such mismatches must be seen through and undone: False pairs must be separated and each person joined with his or her proper partner. For some this will be a matter of "remarriage," of annulling a divorce that has occurred earlier or restoring a union that has come apart; for others, it will be marriage itself and the creation of union for the first time. The current couplings – Fredrik with Anne, Carl-Magnus with Desirée, and Henrik with Petra – must be undone and rearranged. What makes matters difficult is that these reallocations of commitment and desire can occur only if accompanied by each person's discovery that such changes will put them where they belong and satisfy their heart's true desire. For Fredrik in particular, real marriage will require both self-knowledge and the humility to accept a perspective broader than his own. The order that results is a gift of life, at least for the moment, and a wisdom that recognizes life's seasons of growth and decay, youth and age.

The other great theme of the film, set within its mythic rhythms and providing its dramatic energy, is the struggle between the sexes, and in particular, the taming of male pride and puffery with its egotism and self-seriousness. Relationships between men and women must be readjusted to mitigate the excesses of this exaggerated masculinity and its accompanying femininity that typifies all the characters, except Desirée, and in fact binds them together in their original pairings. True marriages can occur only if there is some real change in what gender comes to. What ensues is a comedy of gentle deflation and ridicule shattering these facades of posturing. Men and women become more than players in a game, able finally, perhaps, to be friends and share their lives.

1. Looking the Part

"It is a late spring day in 1901." Summer has arrived. Advocate Fredrik Egerman sits at his desk, groomed in the sharpest style, smoking a fine cigar, writing in his records. The clock strikes four – time to close up for the day. As he finishes his entry, a clerk brings tickets for the evening's theater. "Desirée Armfeldt is acting tonight, sir." Egerman pretends not to have known nor to particularly care, but already there is gossip: a widower with a grown son and a new wife half his age, and a former mistress back in town![1]

Fredrik and Anne are married. Yet, when we first see Anne with her "stepson," Henrik, in the sitting room, sewing while he reads from Luther, we might think it a scene of courtship in which the young man has made a call on the daughter of the house. Fredrik himself greets them with "Good day, my children," and Anne jumps up to throw her arms around him as though she were a girl hugging her father on his return home. Even though we have just seen photographs of Fredrik with his "young wife," his subsequent address to her as "Mrs. Egerman" still comes as a shock, and our initial impression continues to seem right and closer to the truth. Thus, almost from the beginning, the film makes clear that this is a mismatch and the world is in disorder.

Though we do not yet know it, Anne is still a virgin, not truly a wife. Fredrik is still lonely, more a father than a husband, and now "she" has returned, unsettling things even more. Not entirely unaware of Henrik's feelings for Anne, Fredrik suggests "a nap for a few hours. . . . To be able to really enjoy the performance." Asleep, he begins to caress his beautiful wife and she begins to respond, moving his hand toward her breast, as they embrace in a passionate kiss. But to her dismay, Fredrik dreams of someone else: "Desirée, how I longed for you."[2]

At the theater Anne is both curious and upset as she watches the actress's entrance. "She is so beautiful." "It is only makeup." "How do you know? Have you seen her offstage?" Her husband is surely hiding some deeper relationship with this woman. Troubled and hurt, Anne cannot hold back the tears and asks to be taken home. When she calls him to her room to say good night, she is full of unsettling questions. "Would you be jealous – if Henrik started paying me attention? Or if I fell in love with him?" And why did you marry me? – "So the wolf thought: 'I wonder how it would taste with a really young girl?'" And why did I marry you? – "You were sad and lonely that summer. I was so sorry for you. So we got engaged. I suggested it, silly goose, have you forgotten?" He must be

87

patient. "One day I'll become your wife really, and then we'll have a child" (pp. 49–51).

Thus Fredrik goes back to Desirée for advice: "I want you to tell me it's hopeless with Anne. Or the contrary. Or anything else. . . . You're my only friend in the world. The only one to whom I've dared show myself in all my terrible nakedness." Fredrik's dreams and miseries stir those of Desirée herself and reawaken old feelings and hopes for a relationship she broke off four years before, as well as a longing for a father for a young son also named Fredrik. The intrusion of Count Carl-Magnus Malcolm, Desirée's current lover, and his attempt to humiliate the stranger he finds in his robe confirms her instinct and settles her mind. She will help, but far more will be at stake than Fredrik suspects, as she intimates in the message she sends with Malla, her housekeeper: "She said she was sorry there were obstacles. . . . She said that she expected a lot from the reconciliation."[3]

Desirée had left Fredrik because he would not take their relationship seriously: He had seemed content with seeing other women while keeping her around as "headquarters." Her return to town and his arrival in the audience that night, and then backstage, puts him back in her life. They have both been given a second chance.

Desirée's son seems clearly to have Fredrik as father. Desirée left him before the child was born not due to his philandering but because, being pregnant, she did not want Fredrik to agree to marriage out of obligation or as a result of being forced into fatherhood (and to have to fight over keeping her independence as an actress). By raising little Fredrik herself alone for four years, she has demonstrated that the two of them can get along without him and that he therefore doesn't have to accept the role of husband/father unless he genuinely desires it (and accepts her terms). Fredrik's failure to appreciate this fact immediately is why Desirée, in genuine anger, slaps him when he blurts out that she is not fit to be a mother [Fig. 13f].

If from this disorder something better is to emerge, people must change and their desires and relationships be transformed. Throughout *Smiles of a Summer Night,* this idea is presented through figures involving clothes and stages of undress, a common device in comedy and farce. Thus, Fredrik, soon after seeing Desirée for the first time in several years, is "bathed" in (a puddle of) water and then stripped of his clothes and made naked. What he has been wearing – the garb of the successful advocate and proud husband – no longer suits him, and he must be reclothed. The garments that finally do fit are not those of his philandering rival (Malcolm's robe

Figure 13. *Smiles of a Summer Night:* a–d. Anne and Henrik. e–h. Fredrik and Desirée.

and nightshirt), nor even the somber attire of the tormented sufferer,[4] but the disheveled shirt of a humbled man with a headache and dirty face.

Anne and Desirée must also change what they are wearing. When they first "meet" at the theater, they are dressed very nearly alike, a sign that they both lay claim to the same role (Fredrik's "wife"), as well as of Fredrik's own confused desires. (Which does he want, the wife-daughter or the wife-companion?) Later, alone with Fredrick, Desirée takes off her theater costume to erase the confusion and clearly distinguish herself from Anne. As they talk, Fredrik's situation becomes more and more clear, including the fact that Anne probably knows of his dream, that she is still a virgin, and that she likes him "as if I were her father!" Before donning a gay red dress for her "party with Fredrik Egerman to awaken old memories," she shows herself naked in her bath, thus offering to replace Anne's body with her own (which would make whole his erotic dream of that afternoon, itself divided between the feel of his wife's body and the desire for another woman). Here, Desirée is clearly not a girl but a women – someone both more his age and more suited to him. As naked and cleansed, both Fredrik and Desirée are ready to accept the truth about their situation and themselves and to become someone new.

Anne also feels the need to address Fredrik's (and her own) confusion of desire and to find out who she really is. The next morning she rejects her maid Petra's choice, picking another dress and deliberately keeping her hair down, precisely to remain a girl rather than imitate a sophisticated woman (like Desirée in the theater the night before or Charlotte, Malcolm's wife, a little while later). Much of our sense of Anne is in fact given by her clothes. Throughout, her dresses are frilly and flowered, youthful, not tailored to fashion. Standing next to Charlotte and Desirée, and especially Fredrik, she looks too young and out of place – a childish girl among adults. Only when she is with her true equals, Henrik or the teenage Petra, does she seem to belong and begin to look a young woman.

Though neither Anne nor Henrik is stripped of their clothes as completely as Fredrik and Desirée, Anne appears in her nightgown in this scene with Petra. She does so again later, during the Egermans' visit to Desirée's mother's country estate, when Henrik first kisses her in the king's mistress's bed (which has surprisingly come rolling into his room with the sleeping Anne on it) [Fig. 13c] – a state soon followed by a radically new appearance as Henrik's "wife."[5] Anne's frustration and desire for a change in their roles comes to the surface when she divests Henrik of his pipe, robe, and slippers [Fig. 13b], clothes all too reminiscent of Fredrik and his masculine world of sexual adventures and trophies (and the events of the night before). One feels that if she could, or if Bergman could have found some excuse for it, she would have taken away all his clothes and given him a bath then and there. Symbolically, this "cleansing" instead occurs after his failed suicide, when he sees Anne coming toward him on the "magic" bed and douses himself with a pitcher of water.

Anne is also jealous of Henrik's attention to Petra the night before (when he "fell off his horse"), just as she is hurt by Fredrik's interest in Desirée. She does not want Henrik to be like his father; nor does she want someone like that as her husband. Anne gives Henrik a slap for his dalliance with her chambermaid, just like an outraged wife. Uncomfortable with the situation yet trapped within it, she throws the clothes she has collected to the floor and storms from the room. She follows this abortive attempt to re-dress Henrik into a husband with a visit to Fredrik in his study, where she sits on his knee like a little girl. Fredrik would rather read his law book. She now finds herself as neither proper daughter nor proper wife and is convinced she must soon become one or the other (or both).

2. Family Portraits

This wife/daughter dilemma has already been indicated in the photographs Fredrik picked up on his way home that first afternoon – half show them together, half show Anne alone. They have their origin both in his pride at having a young and sexually attractive wife whom he can display as evidence of his own virility and success (as in the theater box that evening)[6] and in his desire for a woman who will be a real wife. But what the pictures try to offer as fact is not true: Anne is not his wife, emotionally or physically, and he remains a lonesome widower.

Indeed, they hint at their own falsity. The portraits are stiff and posed, and – as they are laid out on the table – finally exclude Fredrik from the scene. It is there, when she is alone, that Anne is most striking, most beautiful. These photographs thus picture not only Fredrik's pride and desire but his folly as well. At the end of the film, they are removed by Desirée and tucked into her pocket; Fredrik must give them up and recognize them for what they were – impostures. Yet she doesn't destroy them. Why? Perhaps because, like all pictures, they also have their truth, which must also be accepted: They are portraits not of husband and wife but of father and daughter, and of a young woman ready to be given away in marriage to another man.

What the plot (both Desirée's and Bergman's) must accomplish, if right order is to triumph, is a new "family portrait." And indeed, Bergman constructs a rather remarkable sequence based on this idea, located at the pivotal point when the film's action shifts permanently from the town and Fredrik's house (where he is master and his identity most secure) to Madame Armfeldt's villa (where other forces – and women – are in control).

The sequence begins with Fredrik alone in his study examining his pictures of Anne (a paper wife) and worrying over her casual yet knowing inquiry about his health [Fig. 14b]. It ends with Fredrik and Madame Armfeldt watching Anne and Henrik boat on the pond, while Malla tends the young Fredrik nearby, an alternative picture of grandmother, son-in-law, and three grandchildren. All that is missing is the true daughter and wife – Desirée – and it is precisely her plan to complete *this* picture by winning Fredrik's acceptance of it. This can happen only if he opens his eyes, looks, and at last sees what is so clear to others.

The transition between these two scenes shows this discovery as it begins to take shape in Fredrik's mind. He has taken his pictures – those of Anne alone – and laid them out on his desk as though reading Tarot cards. Her portrait does not include him. "I don't understand," he mutters. As factual records, these photographs should prove that this woman is his wife – yet they reveal only a beautiful and distant girl, embroidered with flowers, but with no sign of being married to him.[7] As Fredrik sits there puzzling this out, the scene slowly fades to Anne and Henrik boating [Fig. 14d,e]. Is this Fredrik's imagination filled with premonition and foreboding? Or his dawning realization of why Anne remains unmarried to him – of even why, perhaps, she was really attracted to him to begin with? Has he begun to accept what he "cannot understand"? Or is this simply what he should finally recognize, what is in open sight yet something he continues to avoid?

As audience, we cannot decide which of these applies, and our indecisiveness can be said to mirror Fredrik's own. Just for a moment, the viewer does not know whether what is shown is real or just in Fredrik's imagination, another version of the many times he has seen his son and bride together. This "ontological indefiniteness" keeps all these questions and feelings in play, and it is these thoughts that continue to torment him as he sits there with Madame Armfeldt.

If there is to be a real family portrait, this romance on the lake must be allowed to come true, and Fredrik must accept this as both appropriate and best. Now he stands between Madame Armfeldt's report of the obvious – "Your children are lovely, especially the girl" – and his own desperate resistance – "She's my wife." He must accept one and reject the

Figure 14. *Smiles of a Summer Night:* Fredrik bewildered.

other. If he clings to his own fond desire, he will in effect remain where this sequence began – miserable, lonely, mourning for a dream now clearly unrealizable, a true fool.

There is never a doubt for the viewer as to what Fredrik should do or why. Bergman continually draws attention to how incongruent Fredrik's desires are to the world in which he lives. This is never more apparent than when Desirée, a few moments later, welcomes her guests to her mother's estate. We see the four "Egermans" together for the first time, in their first attempt, as it were, at this new family portrait [Fig. 15a]. Though, strictly speaking, there is only one couple there – Fredrik and Anne – the composition and balance of figures suggests that there are really two. Fredrik and Desirée are in the foreground, matched for size as well as being larger and facing away, as though they were coming from the house to receive their visitors, Anne and Henrik. This other couple, too, is matched for size, but smaller and facing forward, as though they had just arrived. Although we know the relationships at this moment are different, and hear Fredrik introduce Anne as his wife, we are visually convinced it is all a mistake.

3. Men and Women

Fredrik, however, is reluctant to give up Anne and stubbornly puts aside these other possibilities. After Madame Armfeldt's invocation of the wine with the "mysterious, stimulating power," where each drinks "at his own risk" and thinks his most secret desire, Fredrik's wish is "Anne" (while hers is the more ambiguous, "I drink to my love"). Only when he comes upon the two eloping is the truth unavoidable, and crushing.

Egerman takes it very hard yet is let down very easy, because, it seems, he is in a society of women (in contrast to Frost and Albert in *The Clowns' Evening*, and the groups of men that surround them). In a scene written but not shown in the film, Charlotte, on her way to winning her bet in the pavilion, gently laughs at him and giggles as he tries to be serious in his misery: "Poor, poor Fredrik.... Poor, poor, poor, poor Fredrik." "There he sits, the wise lawyer amidst his little catastrophe, like a child in a puddle" (112–14). (Later, of course, he is comforted in much the same way by Desirée, and with more than a hint that he deserved it. Even Malcolm doesn't take him seriously, for his dueling pistol is not loaded.)

The goal of this kind of laughter is not humiliation but putting things in their right perspective and showing that there is still hope, still someone who cares or can at least share that misery. After laughing, Charlotte says, "Now you know how it feels," and Desirée must think the same. In fact, both Fredrik and Malcolm have been made the fool and treated by women the way they have treated them. Now they are equal, men and women both, and this is perhaps the basis for a new kind of relationship between them.

Fredrik and Malcolm are quite alike. Each is especially self-confident and smug about his own virility and his competence to run things, and each is focused on himself and on his own plans, accomplishments, and

94

Figure 15. *Smiles of a Summer Night:* **a.** Mixed signals: "Fredrik and Desirée" greet "Anne and Henrik." **b,c.** Charlotte and Count Malcolm.

pleasures.[8] As a result, neither is particularly sensitive to others. When Anne comes to sit on Fredrik's lap in his study, he cannot see that she is troubled or even that she very much dislikes his cigar. He is relieved that she soon goes away so that he can get back to his books and his smoking – and to his own problems. Earlier, though he in fact might be giving good advice to Henrik in urging him to "mount his horse again," his manner is uncaring, and he cannot grasp the real issue. Malcolm is similarly

95

obtuse to Charlotte's distress at his behavior and takes her pistol shot toward him as feminine pique only rather than a message about who they really are.

Most of all, both regard love as a kind of game and women themselves as objects for display or status or self-assurance. Women may require special care and attention ("Fifty red roses for Mademoiselle Armfeldt and fifty-five yellow roses for my wife"), but they are not equals or partners, persons with whom a life is to be shared. They are seen only in their role as wife, mistress, daughter, maid, conquest – always as some kind of actual or possible possession ("She is my wife") and thus, in the strict sense, as some sort of plaything.

These conceptions of masculinity and femininity must be broken down if a true reordering of relationships is to be achieved. If Fredrik is to move from one picture to another, he must recognize more to love than gamesmanship and just his own desires: He must see and accept that it asks for reciprocity and shared feeling, mutual giving and taking (and even loss of control) that goes beyond any kind of game; and he must accept that love cannot be a matter of possession or a special kind of ownership. For him to do this is for him not to be the man he was, and it is very hard. ("Fredrik Egerman loves! It isn't possible.") To love Anne in actuality, Fredrik must recognize her feeling for Henrik and, out of his own feeling for her, give her up: Instead of wife, he must take her as daughter (and be "cuckolded" by his son in the bargain). Fredrik resists even as he changes and grows toward such an acknowledgment, until he finally acts, more out of some new sense or instinct than thought or deliberation, to let Anne go and to let go of her. Allowing her to be a person, and himself genuinely to love her, hurts very much.[9]

Henrik and Malcolm also change and move away from the extreme masculinity with which they begin. This seems easiest for Henrik, who is never comfortable in the role of wolf or playboy and is embarrassed by both the urgency of his own desire and Petra's superior knowledge and ease in sex, while throughout doubly guilty over his desire for his father's wife and his attempt to make Petra a substitute for Anne. Giving all this up to finally take Anne as his wife is a great relief (and "heaven," too). But it is also a moment of assertion, of standing up to his father, saying what he believes, and finally taking charge – sweeping Anne off her feet and running away with her – of finally being a man. He is a romantic hero, no longer the bedraggled puppy dog so appealing to Petra who lets others push him around and tell him what to do. What will he be like five or ten years from now when the honeymoon is truly over?[10]

And Count Carl-Magnus Malcolm? How can he ever change? Still, something in him softens toward Charlotte and toward Egerman. Why duel with Fredrik at all, even if it is not a real duel? He could simply rough him up and throw him out, as he does when they first meet at Desirée's apartment. As a nobleman he has no obligation to duel with a commoner, particularly a "shyster" lawyer. Is it because his feelings for Charlotte have been genuinely aroused, or some begrudged respect because Fredrik has in fact bested him over Desirée? Fighting even a quasi-duel has its risks. The count could lose, and how would he ever live that down? Or it could be a tie, as it very nearly is, which would make Fredrik his equal, or even his better, since Fredrik believes the gun is loaded. Carl-Magnus is doing nothing manly at all; the real game (of love or of honor) is not worth it to him here, for whatever reason. What is clear is that the comedy can proceed, and its realignments achieved, only if he does back down, if again the extreme masculinity of the beginning is mitigated.

These "retreats," in addition to allowing the male characters to accept something better, open the space for something similar for *Smile*'s female characters: They are not so hemmed in by the femininity that is correlative to this masculinity. Petra is a tease and perhaps a gold digger; Anne, often a little girl. They are playing their side of the game, taking up the appropriate role of object or plaything – to be pursued, or flattered, or kept happy with theater tickets and new dresses, to display themselves in the right kind of way (whether with open bodice or upswept hair) that befits their femininity. The danger for Petra is that she will be used up and cast away, and for Anne, that she will suffocate. No one – except Henrik – takes her seriously, as more than a girl, as someone who can be mature and have responsibility (she can't even water the plants). For Fredrik she is not yet more than a beautiful ornament or a perhaps delicious morsel for the wolf; for the household cook, not her mistress but simply underfoot and a nuisance.

Charlotte is the most constrained, and perhaps the most damaged. She responds to her husband's extreme code of male behavior and egotism by, as it were, internalizing its denial in her own bitchiness and sexual torment. Here she retains something of herself, though only in its power of negation. (Her other choice is to become, in effect, like him and be the seductress with as many affairs as he; perhaps what Madame Armfeldt was, and what Charlotte toys with being at the villa.)

One can imagine what sex between them is like and why she hates both it and him for it. It is what he does as a right, as a duty, as expected, for his own pleasure. She is his wife; when he returns they sleep together.

Passion, ardor, attraction? – only pro forma roses. She is not a mistress, not even cause enough for jealousy ("I can tolerate my wife's infidelity, but if anyone touches my mistress, I become a tiger. Good morning!" p. 80); *she* is not even there, only a proper appearance, a possession in the true sense. No wonder she is so bitter. Is Carl-Magnus's change enough? Even though he has been bested by a woman and in fact found himself jealous because of his wife, his concessions and promises hardly sound adequate. Only time will tell.

4. The Juggler's Art

Is Desirée any different than Fredrik or even Carl-Magnus, any less constructed by gender and by an equally strong notion of the female? Is the world she projects any better, any more equal than theirs? On first view, *Smiles of a Summer Night* suggest it's not.

Desirée is introduced onstage with a speech from a French comedy, *A Woman of the World*. A woman can, and may, she says, get away with anything as long as she keeps her man's "dignity" intact – his sense of self-importance, control, masculinity. "Then he is in our hands, at our feet, or anywhere else. . . ." This is clearly just the feminine side of love and sex as a game (or even a military campaign – the view so offensive to Anne and Henrik and their ideal of romantic love). What Desirée does in staging a party at her mother's villa seems precisely a move in such a game, calculated all the way. Women should join together, she tells Charlotte, even if sometimes enemies. "Men can never see what's good for them. We have to help them find their way. Isn't it so?"

Here, men are to be manipulated by women so that everyone can be better off. Rather than the playthings women are to men, men are a kind of selfish and spoiled child, to be humored or gently chided and kept out of trouble, and finally to be mothered.[11] Near the end, after Fredrik makes sure Desirée will not leave him, he asks: "But why did you name him 'Fredrik'?" Her reply: "'Fredrik' is such a nice name for a boy." Does she now have two?

These gender differences need not be as extreme as the machismo of Carl-Magnus, the self-centeredness of Fredrik, Petra's sexual tease, Charlotte's vixen, or Anne's doll-wife. Each of these can be toned down, and they can finally mix and share some of each other's traits. This is perhaps the meaning to be taken from Madame Armfeldt's fabulous wine, each cask mixed with "a drop of milk from the swelling breasts of a woman who has just given birth to her first child and a drop of seed from a young stallion" – the masculine and the feminine, the wild and the domestic tempered together, indeed married into one mysterious, stimulating, even dangerous thing. Moreover, as a result of drinking this wine, such changes occur, and four marriages or remarriages come about.

Fredrik allows the feelings of consideration, tenderness, and love he has gotten from Anne to grow and finally acts on them. Carl-Magnus sees that a woman can do what he does, besting him in the process, and promises to be different, better, less what he was. Frid, Madame Armfeldt's groom, swears on his manhood to marry Petra and so gives up his bachelorhood and his roving eye (and wandering hands), perhaps still a stallion, but now broken to the saddle and bridle.

Two images help reinforce this more moderate sense of gender, in which relations are less a game, less like combat. When we first and last encounter them, Carl-Magnus and Charlotte are seen with a gun [see Fig. 15b]. At their manor it is a target pistol, loaded by Malcolm and lethal. Perhaps for both, but certainly for her, it is the sublimation of a deep domestic anger and bitterness. She could indeed kill him with his own weapon (because of who he is and how he treats her, sexually and simply as a wife). At the end, at Madame Armfeldt's villa, the weapon is more modern, a revolver, and loaded with blanks; in fact, at the moment they embrace, with the gun beside her head, it is not loaded at all. Something has changed, something poisonous and lethal has been removed from their relationship.

The relationship between Fredrik and Desirée is figured in a similar way. What we see first in the film is Fredrik contented and self-assured in his office chair with a cigar and a great puff of smoke. (A cigar he knows his wife does not like.) What we see last is him lying in a chair, his face covered with soot, the worse for wear – and Desirée taking a cigar and lighting it as she sits there taking care of him. The cigar has moved from the one to the other – the male to the female (just as earlier the female moved to the male when Anne's sweetness and affection touched Fredrik). What has saved the day is his tenderness and her strength.[12]

What out of all this change, this softening and blurring of gender, will endure? *Smiles of a Summer Night* begins realistically but ends as a kind of fairy tale in an enchanted garden and finally as a cosmic myth. Taken out and away from their proper homes and ordinary world with its ordinary business, these men and women have been freed to transform themselves. What happens when they go home? Can they continue to be what they have begun to become when they must live a daily life? Something may now be possible, but nothing is assured.

Is this equality? Equality with a difference? Men and women on an equal footing, as partners? Has Desirée really changed? When she sees Charlotte enter the pavilion with Fredrik, she remarks, "How stupid I've been." Is this because she trusted Charlotte and her plan is going awry? Calling on Malcolm, with his unpredictable "duel," is even less reliable. Has she, too, learned a lesson? When the gunshot is heard outside the pavilion, no one – neither audience nor Desirée nor Charlotte – knows that it is not real. There is a moment of shock at the thought that Bergman has changed the rules and turned comedy into tragedy. What Desirée goes through is not that different from Fredrik – a moment of death, of utter seriousness beside which, finding themselves still alive, everything else – all their games and fond hopes – pales. Here's a second chance, and life's not a game.

In the French play, a lady responds to Desirée's speech: "Do you think this can be combined with real and sincere love?" Desirée's reply changes her first figure, and with it the basic conception of love, to something no longer advice for the fashionable world of sophisticated strategy and maneuvering but for the genuine article. "Love is a perpetual juggling of three balls . . . heart, word, and sex. How easily these three balls can be juggled, and how easily one of them can be dropped."

Love – and likewise an enduring and stable relationship – requires a special attention from both partners with respect to its elements of emotion, sex, and what one says, any one of which may be gotten wrong and unbalance the relationship if not corrected. Then, men and women can be genuine friends, a kind of friendship we've seen emerge and begin to blossom between Fredrik and Desirée.[13]

5. The Smiles of the Summer Night

Smiles of a Summer Night is also about mortality and the unforgiving passage of time. Life proceeds, time passes, people grow old, they die.[14] But it is also always the same, a pattern of cosmic rhythms in which individual stories play themselves out. This is the theme of the three smiles of the summer night and the final image of the stationary but ever-turning windmill.

Smiles is filled with signs of mortality and death, from the continual punctuation of chimes and bells to the wooden figure of Death with its scythe in Madame Armfeldt's ancient clock. Here the dance of death is presided over by its master, time. Indeed, Madame Armfeldt herself is such a figure of death (as well as an ancient goddess of love) as she orchestrates the reception and entertainment of her guests, her life finished, her body shrunken and confined to bed and chair. As cynical and detached as her counterpart in *The Seventh Seal* (both accomplished players of military games), she is more beneficent and will wait, allowing the players to escape for the time being and for a moment dance a different dance.

At the root of Fredrik's behavior is the fact that, like Antonius Block and Isak Borg, he has been disturbed by his own mortality. Everything is precipitated by a death – that of his wife of twenty years or more, a death that opens a void in his life and tells him of his own age. Fredrik tries first to fill this void with youth and a renewed sexual virility to certify his own escape from what awaits. But such measures do not work, and the unavoidable sense of their failure is what makes Fredrik's gaze at the pictures of his beautiful wife so perplexed and sad. In his heart he knows that this attempt to be young again (in effect, to be his own son) has failed. He fears he will die alone and thus desperately wants to keep the bride who is not his bride.

Fredrik cannot escape death, but he need not die alone. He, like others in the film, is given a second chance. The outcome is a set of marriages and remarriages, each of which is associated with one of the smiles of the summer night. The first, between midnight and daybreak, is for young lovers, when they "open their hearts and bodies . . . a smile so soft that one has to be very quiet and watchful to see it" – Anne and Henrik (p. 109); the second, just before the dawn, is for "the clowns, the fools, the unredeemable" – Frid and Petra (p. 121); and the third, in the light of the next day when "everything takes on its true color in the warm sunlight" of the newly risen sun, is for "the sad and the sleepless, the confused, the deceived, the frightened, the lonely," all those who need that second chance – Fredrik and Desirée, as well as Carl-Magnus and Charlotte (p. 124).

For John Simon, the final question of the film is

> whether the three general conditions to which the three smiles address themselves are to be taken as simultaneous but separate, or, as stages of the dawn follow one another, as successive phases like the seven ages of man. Are some people happy lovers, others insouciant buffoons, and still others sad, abandoned, and lost? Or are these merely three consecutive stages of the brief summer's night and day that are human life?[15]

The answer is something of both. Petra and Frid and Anne and Henrik, as couples, each represent ways that relationships can begin as well as forms of love that continually shape people's shared lives – physical desire and sensual pleasure, on the one hand (the "profane"), and romantic love with its mixture of emotional passion and spiritual aspiration on the other (the "sacred"). And though these two forms may be genuinely independent beginnings of desire, they are usually intertwined. There is a great deal of lust and physical passion between Anne and Henrik (and in their worldly innocence and idealism they are also one kind of fool),[16] while for all Petra's delight in sexual play and its heady hedonism, she has a sexual realism that insists on marriage, on something that binds more than their bodies together, and that is a sign of more than convenience or pleasure.

These two couples represent sides of essentially one thing: the foundations of human love, with its dual basis in biology and spirit. Frid and Petra chase and run about like birds courting in an ancient (and genetically determined) mating dance, whereas Henrik and Anne tenderly touch and kiss, melting into one. Together they are Tamino–Pamina and Papageno–Papagena, and the film as a whole has more than a passing connection with Bergman's later production of Mozart's *Magic Flute*. (In both films, these elements are inscribed in distinctions of class.)

Sexual attraction and romantic ardor are both chemistries that can bring people together and something all of us experience and long for, especially in our youth. But the fate of both is to wear out and to lose their charm and all consuming self-sufficiency. Each of these relationships has its illusions. For the first smile, love is eternal, a union of souls who share an ecstatic space and cannot exist apart from each other. Their pain is separation, but their punishment will be the drudgery and disappointment of ordinary life. For the second smile, the illusion is perhaps not as deep, but it is a fleshly optimism that play and pleasure, and the standard social forms to contain them, are enough and that they will thus continue to be satisfied with each other. They are married now, and so each of these couples will have to return home after their midsummer night's adventure – Anne and Henrik to find their own house (or are they to live with Fredrik and Desirée?), while Frid and Petra are already on the way to the kitchen. There they must work, earn a living, get pregnant and have children, get sick, become tired and bored and dispirited – and suffer loss, betrayal, abandonment, like everyone before them.

This "third" stage and its perils – what is perpetually after love's beginnings – is represented by Carl-Magnus and Charlotte, and, if one is fortunate, finally by Fredrik and Desirée. It is a stage that can still include in some form the earlier romance and sexual exuberance but not in their innocence, not as they first occurred in the summer night. To endure, these relationships must grow to something more, to where lovers (of the spirit and the body) become friends and companions.

These pairings and their corresponding smiles represent, therefore, stages of love, as Simon suggests, but also each stage's other possibilities. Relationships can always have their passion and romance renewed (as Desirée seeks to do with Fredrik), and romance (or passion) with someone else can always be sought to replace a relationship that is dying or dead (as Fredrik hopes of Anne and Malcolm seeks in his mistresses). Yet there is both a natural and normative order to the third stage. What is suggested by *Smiles of a Summer Night* is stated most overtly in *Waiting Women* and most mythically in Bergman's *Magic Flute*.

In *Waiting Women* there are two sets of young lovers. The youngest, Henrik and Maj, pledge eternal love to each other and at the end of the film set off for Italy in a kind of romantic elopement, boating across the water into the sunrise, just as Henrik and Anne race away through the trees into the distant dawn. (This Henrik, too, is at odds with his father.) They think nothing can happen to them as they begin their life together – in part because they have not paid attention to the stories of other young lovers, and in part because, like Henrik and Anne, they believe that, because they are true lovers for whom love is not a game, they are different.

However, the companion story of the older Märta and Martin, also initially a romance but more sensual and erotic, makes it clear they are not. These two fall in love in Paris in the spring, as deeply and spiritually as Maj and Henrik, but ultimately Märta is left pregnant and alone when Martin returns to Sweden without her, as demanded by his brothers, rather than forgo his share of the family inheritance.

This – abandonment – is the fate of all young lovers, as well as of fools and clowns like Petra and Frid (or Frost and Alma). It will perhaps hit the first harder, since they are more certain they are different. But any union of lovers – any marriage – must have its trials. There will be loneliness, fear, infidelity – always turning away in one form or another. Frid is not really joking when, having given in and promised, he says, "The fun is over. Now I'm on my way to hell." When it is indeed hell, it is the marriage of the Almans in *Wild Strawberries,* or the marriage that looms over Albert and Anne, and Marianne and Evald. (In *Waiting Women,* it is that of Rakel and Eugen.)

It is also the marriage of Carl-Magnus and Charlotte as we first see them.[17] The Malcolms represent both a real moment of trial that any marriage (or joining into a shared life) may become lost in and have to suffer through if it is to survive, as well as a perpetual possibility that, even when overcome once, may always reoccur. Charlotte and Carl-Magnus are an always possible future for every couple, something latent in any relationship at any stage.

Nonetheless, it is also possible that a "disillusioned" love can arise, a mature love for adults who must continue to live in the face of death and after their own betrayals and sufferings, in the full light of day. As Charlotte says to Fredrik, "Now you know how it feels. . . . We deceived, we betrayed, we deserted. We who are *really* ridiculous" (p. 114). This is love as mutual comfort and caring, as companionship – lovers as friends.[18] When Fredrik asks Desirée not to leave him, she says only, "I promise nothing." She will stay, without illusions or inflated expectations, and they will try to make it work together. And it is possible that some of the romance and even the sexual excitement of the beginnings of love can be rekindled, as happens for Martin's older brother, another Fredrik, and his wife, Karin, in *Waiting Women* (acted also by Gunnar Björnstrand and Eva Dahlbeck – an earlier version of Fredrik and Desirée). This, too, is an always possible future for every couple.[19]

Simon is misleading in suggesting that the film gives a complete picture of life as a "brief summer's night and day." As Petra hints, the film leaves out autumn, the time when the flourishing of spring–summer bears its full harvest, and then dies away; and it leaves out the winter that follows, with its muted light and long, despairing nights. The summer night, as a time of flourishing and renewal (and truth and illusion), is one moment of an ever-recurring cycle, like the passage of the day itself. And *Smiles,* like *The Clowns' Evening* and *Wild Strawberries,* leaves the essential next scene of its action unspoken and yet to happen. Will in fact these couples make it home? And what will that home be like?

6. The Great Dance

Comedy transforms humiliation into simple ridiculousness and shame into embarrassment. What we see is not the spite and meanness of people (though both Charlotte and Malcolm push this border) but their foibles. In all his trials – falling into a puddle, being thrown out in his nightshirt, being seduced or losing a sham duel, even having his son and wife run away together – Fredrik never seems humiliated but, at most, defeated, tired, humbled. He does not have the experience of Frost or Albert in *The Clowns' Evening.* There is no terror, no feeling of horror that rises in the viewer. Instead, his helpless (and hapless) state brings out a gentle laughter and sympathy – and a smile.

This is because the viewer can see how things should be and knows that such defeats bring Fredrik closer to what is best. The element of vision in *Smiles* (or the comedies in general) is not the "magic moments" of wild strawberries in *The Seventh Seal* or the lunch by the lake in *Wild Strawberries*. Rather, it is the "picture" of Anne and Henrik together, of Fredrik and Desirée sparking, indeed, of the "family portrait" itself. This is what *should be*. In these pictures, we see the characters' potential; we see them as more and better than they now are. Knowing that this is a comedy, we know that these setbacks are not real and that neither Fredrik nor we need really worry.

Fredrik, too, begins to see this. What is ridiculous is not being wet or in a nightshirt, but being an advocate in a top hat sitting in a puddle or walking the street at midnight. The ridiculous is not a son eloping with his father's wife when the two are deeply in love but the attempt to regain one's manhood by marrying an inexperienced girl better suited as a daughter. What begins as embarrassment yields to the recognition that one didn't really know their proper place and had puffed themselves up to be more than they really were. Comedy, like tragedy, is about hubris and thinking too much of oneself. This is the real embarrassment, and seeing it is to understand that the cause of woe is not from others (as in humiliation) but in the situation and oneself. It is something in Fredrik's own control, and it gives him a way out. The laughter here is laughter that Fredrik can finally share and to which he can say, Yes, you're right.

While *Smiles of a Summer Night* moves from home lost to that same home regained, it is the theater (including the country villa, the photography shop, and even Desirée's apartment) that enables this to happen. One can understand one's life and see what is ridiculous and what needs to be taken seriously only by seeing oneself as another person on a stage. A person must find the right perspective – essentially, that of an audience. This is what Fredrik is finally able to do, and it is the achievement of theater at its best as an essential place in *Smiles*'s (and Bergman's) geography.

Such theatricality is the goal of Desirée's plot and her weekend gathering at Madame Armfeldt's country estate. This retreat, where the film ends and we last see its characters, is a place of enchantment, a kind of twilight between being awake and being asleep, a sort of waking dream. It is not unlike the semiconsciousness of Fredrik's afternoon nap with Anne, where the true desires of both begin to reveal themselves, or the rapturous joining of Anne and Henrik in the king's moonlit chambers: "I love you." "I love you." They kiss again. "I've loved you all the time." "I've loved you all the time" (p. 108).

The same sort of awareness is precipitated by Madame Armfeldt's story and the wine that is drunk by each of them. The night for everyone is a moment of honesty, of the release of desires and dreams, and the beginning of lucidity. Everyone has put themselves onstage as they really are and will soon be able to see, if they choose to, who that is and what they need to do. They are like the knight's family and companions as they stand exposed before Death in the castle, asked to give one final account of themselves.

As they wake and the spell of the villa fades, the morning light reveals something more. There is apparent now not just buildings like theaters, shops, and mansions but the world itself that contains and supports them. The final image of the film shows this world in its essential nature – as earth and sky and the mortals who dwell between them. What fills the screen is the great mill amid the vast field of wheat with Frid and Petra dancing in joy and celebration, silhouetted against the horizon [Fig. 16]. "There isn't a better life than this," Frid exclaims. The scene is an exact counterpart to the dance of death at the end of *The Seventh Seal* and is in fact its replacement. Here and now, in this time and place, there is the dance of life that Jof and Mia and their son Mikael represent.[20]

As Frid and Petra leave the frame, the mill amid the wheat remains, its blades continuing to turn in the wind, taking the grain from the field and making it into flour for bread. The world is thus not merely a place where we are born in order to die but also our provider. Existence is more than the "cruel but seductive path between life and death . . . [a] huge laughing masterpiece, beautiful and ugly, without mercy or meaning" that *Prison* originally declares. From out of itself, the world sustains us, and our time here is a gift, a gift of life and nourishment, of the possibilities of joy and celebration that we must grasp and take for ourselves. It is a place where, though mortal, we can still flourish. In this comic drama between death and the devil, death may have the last word, but neither it nor the devil is our master.

Figure 16. *Smiles of a Summer Night:* Frid and Petra – the dance of life.

PART TWO

SECOND THOUGHTS

Bergman has often been criticized as apolitical, producing chamber dramas of the soul detached from any larger sociopolitical context. Though this view omits the social realism and working-class settings of his early films, especially *Port of Call* (1948), *Prison* (1949), and *Summer with Monika* (1953),[1] it is by and large correct, particularly in reference to the films of "metaphysical reduction" on which his international reputation was made – *The Clowns' Evening, Smiles of a Summer Night, The Seventh Seal, Wild Strawberries, The Virgin Spring,* and *Through a Glass Darkly.* In this regard, *Shame* in 1968 is a film radically different from any of its predecessors,[2] both in its political awareness and unremitting focus on political events and forces, and in its dramatic resolution. It marks most clearly a crisis in Bergman's thought that had been developing throughout the 1960s and a nadir of depression and despair in which even the most restrained hopefulness of his earlier films is lost.

This does not come without some warning, as the earlier discussion of the trilogy suggests. There, Jonas in *Winter Light* (1963) fears the Chinese will start an all-out nuclear war, while tanks and other military vehicles (like those in *Shame,* in fact) patrol the streets during curfew outside the hotel in *The Silence* (1963). Elisabet, in *Persona* (1966), is both transfixed and terrorized by images of a street execution and a monk's self-immolation from the U.S. war in Vietnam, while later her apprehension and foreboding crystallize in the famous picture that she finds in a book of a small boy in the Warsaw ghetto with raised arms in front of a German soldier. The world, and Europe in particular, has already suffered one Holocaust, and there is a growing sense that a similar catastrophe is imminent, one from which no one will survive. These images, and the political noise that pervades the radio and television, are deep in people's minds, and they belie the political words extolling peace, democracy, and security that accompany them. This anxiety that will not go away is both the subject and the world of *Shame,* and it is the real world, not just of 1968 but of now as well: the world of Chechnya, Bosnia, Kosovo . . . central Africa, Palestine, Israel, Chiapas, Afghanistan, Iraq. . . .[3]

The brooding that grows within Bergman's creative heart during this time takes its toll on film style and form. An earlier lightness and recourse to comedy, as well as expansiveness in story line and construction, vanish. Except for the ill-fated (but droll and amusing) *All These Women* in 1964, Bergman's last film in which comedy is significant or even present until *Fanny and Alexander* in 1982 is *The Devil's Eye* in 1960 (and his 1975 version of *The Magic Flute*). This follows on *The Magician* (1958) and *The Virgin Spring* (1960) in which this dramatic chilling has already taken hold. In *The Seventh Seal,* the harshness of the plague-ridden medieval world is mitigated – rape is only threatened, and the young witch's sufferings are cut short by the knight's drug. In *The Virgin Spring,* there is no relief, no mercy: Karin is brutally raped and murdered, and the little boy cruelly slaughtered for his brothers' crimes.

There seems no place left in the two decades after the "golden age of the 1950s" for laughter or amusement at human foibles. Bergman's canvas displays a new somberness and restriction in range that comes now to typify his work. It is at its most concentrated in the films that end the 1960s: *Persona* (1966), *Hour of the Wolf* (1968), *Shame* (1968), *The Rite* (1969), and *The Passion of Anna* (1969). These are all in black and white except for the last, and in each of them the world has become particularly ugly, and even the films themselves look ragged and crude. *Shame* provides the essential clue to what has happened.

5

A Dream Play: *Shame*

In *Shame*, civilization itself has become threatened and is at the brink of extinction. The global destruction of the biblical apocalypse is no longer a dramatic figure or the framework for a medieval morality play. What was feared by Jonas comes to pass, and what appears to be some sort of civil war or intra-European conflict brings about the end of the world. The geopolitical terror that invaded an otherwise secure national life through the newspapers in *Winter Light* and through television in *Persona* has become real and at hand.

That modernity is an attack on civilization itself and not just stressful to this or that individual is marked throughout the film on three levels. Most obvious, of course, is the dominance and ubiquity of the military (and of whatever the military is fronting, which goes unanalyzed). Tanks, soldiers, personnel carriers, planes are everywhere. Persons – people living ordinary lives – are first transformed into citizens and civilians, and then into enemies or patriots. Everything is a proper target of destruction – farms and churches, refugees, children, animals, prisoners of war, unarmed boys, former friends and associates – even wives and husbands. There remain no ties that bind.

When this occurs, when anyone and everyone becomes an acceptable object of violent force, social relationships and human intercourse itself become transformed into something inhuman, brutal, and equally deadly. This is the second level of ruin. Words can no longer mean what they say, and all discourse is governed by ulterior ends and meanings: All speaking is constrained, and so undermined, by ideology. You say what you think the other wants to hear, and if not, your words are rearranged to form the other's meaning anyway. This is the lesson of the filmed interview of Eva in which someone else's voice and words are used. Nonetheless, she is charged with treason. Under these conditions, there is no public space where one can both survive and be one's own author. All public and social relationships become controlled by this humiliating force that continually robs individuals of their own will and agency, rendering them more and more some sort of conscious, feeling, *human thing*. They can exist as persons only in private, and this is a privacy that, excluding others more and more, ends up solipsistically buried deep within an outer shell.

Both following on and preceding this rubble of social and political life is the ruin of culture itself. This third level of deterioration is both effect and cause in the collapse of civilization, and *Shame* is strewn with its traces and remnants, now mere shards of something that once nourished and preserved life, whose sight becomes increasingly unbearable. The orchestra in which Jan and Eva Rosenberg performed has been long disbanded, hands roughened or damaged so that they can no longer play, the instruments themselves broken. Music is replaced by "news" and the cacophonous noise of the radio and the political rhetoric it broadcasts (the very first sounds we hear, during the opening credits). The fine wine shared with friends or between lovers is replaced by liquor strong enough to keep one drunk. The Meissen figurines, the Dvořak manuscript, the Pampini violin, Jacobi's ring, all literally heirlooms – both inherited from the past and the inheritance of the past – are lost, destined to be broken, burned, stolen. Film itself becomes an instrument of propaganda, and Jan and Eva's nightmare simply someone else's movie.

For the first time, Bergman prises apart as distinct regions the private personal world of ordinary life and the public social world. Before *Shame,* the social had been only an aspect within the personal, something that impinged upon relationships and created certain problems but remained secondary. In *Shame,* the external social conditions come to dominate and ultimately revoke the personal. Before, it had always been the other way round. In *Prison,* it is suggested that if God were dead and Satan alone in charge, life would be no different than it is now, for daily existence already has all the features of Hell, and humans are better at the Devil's work than any demons. But it is also argued that this "hell" is an essentially internal and domestic condition comprised of failure and despair, loneliness, and the hatreds and recriminations of an imprisoning relationship. As a spiritual prison, life's bars are either those of despair and guilt, which shut others and life itself out, or those of "marriage," which chain people together. We may fail to free ourselves, but this is *our* failure, not due to the external bars of society or nature, which can, at the deepest level of things, always be set aside or overcome.[4] In *Shame* this is no longer true, and modern society has become an ultimate prison and a new kind of hell from which there may not be even internal escape.

1. Terrible Pictures

In *Shame*, Bergman finds in the public world not just a deadliness of spirit but a modern power to overwhelm completely the personal and individual. As a result, the old Bergman questions about life and its significance have to be reformulated and the old answers rethought.

The extent of this change in vision is seen most dramatically in the images that now characterize this world. The scene of Jan and Eva with their small wagon of possessions struggling early in the morning along the shore in hope of escape [see Fig. 3e] epitomizes its deteriorization as they recall the great silhouettes of the earlier films – the line of circus wagons moving on to their next performance in *The Clowns' Evening*, the majestic dance of death with Jof and Mia's wagon safe by the sea in *The Seventh Seal*, and Frid and Petra's dance through the wheat beside the great mill in *Smiles of a Summer Night*. Each of these events occurs at dawn, the dawn of a new day; in *Shame*, it is the dawn of what is in effect the last day and the ending of everything for everyone. The road that before always had another stop, and even brought one home again, now becomes a final path into the sea – their burial ground. Life's journey has become unspeakably shabby and unremitting in its pain and humiliation.

In *Shame*, the vehicles so central to this journey – the horse and circus wagon and the automobile – become first an old van that hardly starts and is finally destroyed and then an open handcart carrying a few bundles of clothes and food moving along a devastated beach. The mill and fields become a bombed-out church and rocky shore, and the dancers refugees trudging toward the landing.

The cyclicity and inherent renewability of life so central to these earlier films is also lost. Though the plague is virulent in *The Seventh Seal*, some do escape, and it is this escape that is the point of the film: the knight's "meaningful act." This kind of ending – sometimes exuberant, sometimes guarded and even skeptical – has been repeated again and again in Bergman's work. Albert and Anne continue on together. Evald and Marianne decide to stay with each other and to have their child. Fredrik Egerman gets his true mate and a Fredrik Jr. as well. Bergman's films have been structured in a way that holds out, however difficult it may be to achieve or to continue in place, the possibility of change and rebirth – a personal transformation that at the same time makes the world livable and casts it in a new light. In *Shame* this does not happen, and the old endings are pointedly rejected. Such "salvation" is only a dream of its own destruction, and Eva's beautiful landscape of white pillars, water, and roses consumes itself in fire. Mia holds the baby Mikael in her arms; Eva holds only someone else's dead child and an imaginary one of her own.

Finally, the humiliation suffered in *Shame* has become truly obscene. Jan and Eva must endure it without defense and with no way to escape or hide. *Shame* recalls *The Clowns' Evening* in this regard, but both Frost and Albert can leave the stage and retreat to their wagons with Alma and Anne. Their humiliations remain episodes in life, not its constant fabric. More important, the leering audiences are not themselves completely without shame, and each – at the seashore and at the circus – finally displays some unease and embarrassment at what they have abetted (though they still refuse to take responsibility for it). In *The Seventh Seal,* Jof is rescued from the taunts of Raval, who is punished by Jöns, and in *Smiles of a Summer Night,* Malcolm's wounds to Fredrik's pride provide just what Desirée needs to reinsert herself in his life. In *Shame,* humiliation has become the nature of the world itself, and its agents almost unidentifiable.

In all these aspects, *Shame* can be seen as providing a new version of these earlier films, a version that ultimately rejects them. And while Bergman's trilogy at the beginning of the 1960s anticipated some of this reversal, it continued to maintain the vision of the 1950s and reaffirmed a world in which the personal quest for rebirth had significance. *Through a Glass Darkly* is firmest in this regard (though, in retrospect, perhaps most desperate as well) and holds out at least the possibility of healing in David's attempt to speak to his son and Minus's joy with which the film ends, even if Karin's own desolated existence remains in the background. In *Winter Light,* Märta remains tenaciously ahold of Tomas, refusing to turn away from him even if he cannot accept her love or yet forgive God. Even *The Silence* – which comes nearest to *Shame* in its military setting and the squalor of its oppressive heat and stench – ends with Anna and her son, Johan, able to escape and a letter from Ester to the boy with words in this new language he must somehow learn (including those for face and hand).

The "resolutions" of the trilogy are perhaps more gestures than accomplishments, more symbolic than real. A place is kept open, but it becomes increasingly hard to imagine how these characters will move into or finally occupy it. In this regard, the trilogy represents a refusal on Bergman's part to give in to a foreboding and dread about the world he cannot dismiss or escape. *Persona* is at the brink of free-fall. Elisabet leaves the hospital and returns to her life without healing. We do not know what happens to Alma, the nurse who is revealed to have the same problem and is unable to help, and Elisabet's young son remains shut out, kept at a distance (his hand unable to touch her face). Life resumes where it left off, working again but still unsatisfactory and without any new promise. In *Hour of the Wolf,* though Johan disappears and has perhaps killed himself, his wife (another Alma), now pregnant, remains, reading his diary and awaiting his return.[5]

In these two last films, though they end in defeat and the failure of individuals to touch or be touched by others, this is a personal failure to find love and nourishment. In *Shame,* all this is put into a new context that overwhelms the personal and calls into question its capacity to achieve anything hopeful or of significance in life.

2. A Dream Play

It seems at the beginning (especially if the sounds during the credits slip by as ambient noise)[6] that the focus of *Shame* will be the marital discord between Jan and Eva. Jan's complaints – his nerves and emotional outbursts, his incessant need for pity and comfort – and his fecklessness have become more than Eva can manage. She wakes up already put out, angry at him for his constant demands on her attention and his ineptitude on the farm. She has tried to steel herself from being drawn further into his self-centered world. Her inspection of his tooth is cursory and betrays an indifference founded in the fear that his worries will utterly consume her.[7]

While *Shame* continues to examine this relationship, with its fluctuations between tenderness and violence and its growing deterioration, the film increasingly shows Jan and Eva as overtaken by external events and living in a world that is more dreamlike than dreams themselves – and far less merciful.

Bergman begins constructing this feeling of "dreamness" in the first words we hear. The alarm rings for a very long time before anyone stirs. No one wants to return to this world. Jan takes his heart medicine and tests out his sore tooth: "I had the weirdest dream. . . . We were back in the orchestra, sitting beside each other rehearsing the Fourth Brandenburg . . . everything that's happening now – it was all behind us. We remembered it like a terrible dream, and we were grateful to be back. I woke up crying. . . ."[8] Jan longs for what was and hopes that it will be again. For him, the present is less real than the past or a fancied future in its image.

Jan's dream is matched by Eva's at the film's end. As they lie side by side[9] in the drifting boat [Fig. 17c], Eva's voice-over is heard on the sound track.

I had a strange dream. I was walking along a very beautiful street. On one side were white houses with arches and pillars. On the other side was a lovely park. Under the trees by the street flowed a stream with dark-green water. I came to a high wall, that was overgrown with roses. Then an airplane came, roaring down and set fire to the roses. They burned with a clear flame. It wasn't awful because it was so beautiful. I stood looking down into the water watching the roses burn. I was holding a child in my arms. It was our daughter, she was only six months old, and she was clutching my necklace and pressing her face to mine. I could feel her wet open mouth touch my cheek. I knew the whole time that I ought to understand something important that someone had said, but I had forgotten what it was.[10]

Eva's dream reality comforts her with its peaceful detachment from the present and its fantasy of the child that could have been.

Through the course of the film, what was and might yet be becomes only what could have been – dreams of a better world displaced by the brutal reality of this one. But this present is also described as a "a terrible dream," and thus as something also unreal, almost even unimaginable. Jan and Eva have been taken to the community schoolhouse for "a decontamination" (p. 144). As they wait anxiously in a large room crowded with others, Eva whispers: "At times everything is like a dream. It's not my dream. It's someone else's that I'm part of. What happens when that person wakes and is ashamed?" (pp. 145–6).

It is a feature of dreams that they happen with their own logic and that within them we are more observers than actors in control. Several of the sequences in the film have this nightmarish quality – the shelling of the farmhouse, their abortive attempt to get away through a landscape of destruction and death (when Eva kneels beside the dead child [Fig. 17a]), their interrogation and filming by the "liberation" army and later interrogation (with its halted execution) by the "authorities," the ransacking of their house and execution of Mayor Jacobi, the burned-out forest through which they wander, their final drifting at sea. In all these scenes there are echoes of the plague-ridden land of *The Seventh Seal* and Isak Borg's own nightmares in *Wild Strawberries*. (As they lie in their boat, for instance, the hands of the dead soldiers almost reach out to grab them.) *Shame* is a journey like these earlier films but through a landscape where

Figure 17. *Shame:* Pietà / Madonna and Child. **a.** Eva with a dead child. **b.** Jan and Eva with the young soldier. **c.** Jan and Eva adrift at sea.

what then were only dreams or a medieval mystery play are now real yet even more dreamlike.

As Eva says, it is as though their lives are the creations of another dreamer to provide him entertainment and pleasure, a pleasure in violence and the suffering of the helpless. This dreamer is writing (or directing) a fiction just for himself: a story with its own characters and rules in which he can do what he likes to satisfy any desire. Nothing is owed to these creations, nothing about them matters, there is nothing to or for which this author must be responsible. They are playthings, puppets to be used as he chooses, like lead soldiers in a mock battlefield or actors in a porno-graphic fantasy or video game. If these imagined events were real with real people, they would be shameful; but for this writer-dreamer immersed in his dream such shame has no place.

Jan and Eva's world is now like that. Their own dreams have become even more implausible in a world that is no longer their own. They are indeed characters in others' shameless imaginings, but because this world is not a dream, no one will wake up. Now, unlike any earlier film, this is a shame that cannot transform itself to something better, a shame discon-nected from guilt. It can draw one to the better only in hopeless dreams of what was or could have been.

Eva, who is most aware of such shamefulness, is also least responsible for it, and in any event can do little about it. It is what happens with the paratroopers and at the schoolhouse, the burning farms and slaughtered people and the dead children, and Eva has no agency there. Indeed, she fails to protect those few things in her charge – her rabbits, her home, the frightened boy soldier, her husband. Could she have? Maybe if she had tried harder, kept on Jan's heels as he pushed the boy from the greenhouse and thrown herself over his body. Perhaps, and that might have reduced her own guilt; but it would not alter the other things or the situation itself.

The shamefulness of Jan and Eva's behavior to each other is not what matters to Bergman now, nor even Jan's failure to save Jacobi's life and his murder of the boy. Something like this would have happened soon enough anyway. What matters is that life itself has become shameful. They and all the people like them, all the ordinary people of their society, are not actors or agents in these events any more but simply the people to whom they happen, the people who must suffer and endure them while someone else is in charge.

Unlike Eva, the immediate agents in these events have no sense of shame themselves. Perhaps they once did, and perhaps at home with their families it reappears, but in the public sphere it is lost without a trace.

Jacobi is selfish and pragmatic, afraid to go to the front, and desperately lonely. He doesn't apologize to Jan and Eva for their interrogation; instead he only explains that it was "necessary." The paratroopers are callous and brutal and the home forces the same. Filip changes sides as it suits him. Beyond them there are disembodied voices on the radio: people somewhere in charge, setting policy, giving orders – remote and unreachable.

However, if those who can still be ashamed are not guilty, and if those who are guilty (if they can be located at all) feel no shame and cannot be touched or moved by what they allow to happen, then this guilt will be unrecognized and then unrecognizable. This is a social disaster and makes true politics impossible. Perhaps this has always been the tendency of political systems,[11] but none has been as totalizing or inescapable as those of modernity.

With this disappearance of shame, responsibility disappears, too. Life is transformed into an increasingly permanent condition of pervasive humiliation and people into some sort of human-thing. Public life becomes regulated by ideology, and guilt is replaced by error (and, of course, "mistakes," since "accidents will happen"). All this is the import of Eva's "vision" as she and Jan wait huddled together in the schoolhouse.

3. "But I Had Forgotten What It Was"

What possibilities remain for life in this kind of world? Can the old Bergman answers of turning toward and living together still be given? Can they mean at all the same thing or hold out the same horizon of hope and aspiration?

For Bergman, this seems less and less likely. The world has changed and darkened, and we have to accept it with very little chance of finding some backwater or enclave of escape. It is not simply that Jan and Eva are physically blocked from leaving the island; it's that in trying to stay alive, they have so easily taken on the behavior scripted for them. In self-defense, they become like their tormentors: shameless and unfeeling. Eva accepts Jacobi's gifts and privileges, obsequiously "crawling to him" (p. 159), while Jan becomes even more self-enclosed and inured to others but now calculating and efficient. He callously pretends not to know where the money is, later saying they would have shot Jacobi anyway. The man who could not kill a chicken finally steels himself, staggers forward, and shoots – and shoots again. Jacobi's body is put in a wheelbarrow, along with the animals slaughtered by the soldiers. The house is torched, and the partisans disperse. Eva stares at Jan with a look of incomprehension and hate when

Figure 18. *Shame:* On the way to market.

he shows her the money. They fight again, their roles reversed: Now Jan is the agent, forceful and efficient, and Eva is sobbing, overcome by her feelings. As the film progresses, Jan and Eva disappear bit by bit as persons who can see and touch each other, so that in Jan's case, finally, not even the pain can get through.

This change in Bergman's vision is suggested when Jan and Eva go to town to sell their berries (perhaps allusions to the wild strawberries of the

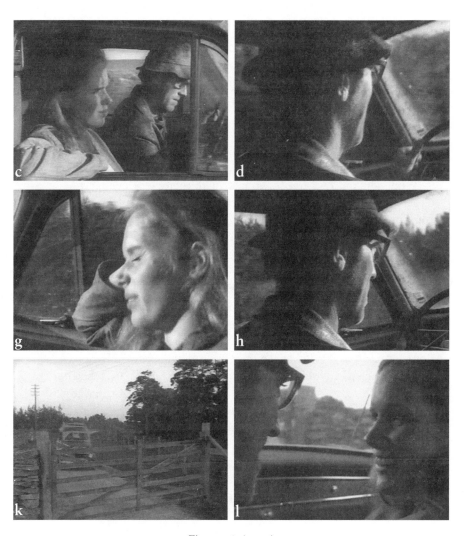

Figure 18 *(cont.)*

earlier films). The scene of them together in their station wagon [Fig. 18] recalls Marianne and Isak on their way to Lund. But now, although the issue of turning away or toward is still the same, they are shot differently and in a way that displaces, if not destroys, the shared space that turning requires. After an initial picture with the camera to the side and front, where it can easily show both Jan and Eva, the camera moves to the back seat like a passenger between them. It is now difficult to include both in the frame at once or to show the complete space they occupy. Bergman's primal image of overlapped faces can no longer be constructed. As the camera cuts back and forth, faces now alternate and are oriented in different, incompatible directions [e.g., frames e,f]. This effect persists even when we know they must be looking in the same direction. In this scene, it is as though Jan and Eva form one Janus-like head, its faces ever turned away from each other – coupled back to back, each talking and looking to where the other is not. The axis of turning is no longer apparent, and our most fundamental relationship with each other has been altered.

While Jan and Eva are shown later with their faces side by side in the classic Bergman manner, it is under conditions of extreme duress and terror. The separation between them grows and it is never repaired. The old narrative forms of renewal have failed, and there is nothing to take their place.

In her final dream, Eva feels there is something she should remember, something someone said that she has forgotten – something that will justify or make sense of the burning roses, what she and Jan have suffered, this shameless world. But what could this utterance be that will put what has happened in some perspective that can be accepted? "God's will be done, on earth as it is in heaven"? "This, too, will pass"? "Forgive us, for we have sinned"? None of these nor any other words are relevant, and there is nothing to say except that the world ought not to be this way. Eva's "forgotten memory" is only a desperate, hollow hope when all other words fail and there is nothing but silence.

Shame ends with Jan and Eva huddled down in the boat beside each other. They have just consumed their last food and water, a frightful version of Bergman's earlier festive meals and shared bowls of wild strawberries, themselves allusions to Christian communion. When they returned from town, they had had a picnic of fish and wine and then made love under the table, but this image, too, is replaced when on Sunday morning they sit in a drunken stupor at their table with Jacobi and individually sell themselves. Now, near the end, Jan stares blankly, perhaps asleep; Eva talks quietly. There seems little comfort here, only finality.

Eva's face is beside Jan's, behind him, her arms perhaps around him. There is here one last reference to the iconography of the holy family, with its promise of growth and flourishing, now replaced by that of the pietà, an image that assumes for Bergman a governing place in the geography of the soul.[12] This last bit of human warmth is all that is left between us and the terror of a night without dawn, or smiles.

4. The Life of the Marionettes

Accompanying this undoing of the old narrative structure and its images of renewal is an emerging sense of a new kind of dread, a sense of having fallen into some abyss where everything is out of control. It is different from the oppression grounded in the personal and domestic defeats of unfulfilling relationships, one's own failures, or the fear and anger at death. Now there is a sense of being up against something different, forces that one cannot escape, placate, or even identify.

This new oppressiveness is given its first major expression in *Shame* and *Hour of the Wolf*. In *Shame*, as well as in *The Rite* and *The Serpent's Egg* (and in the portrayal of the "art industry" in *Hour of the Wolf*), these forces are genuinely external to the domestic arena. But in *Hour of the Wolf* they are largely internal, a kind of power lodged within that, though it may originate in the domestic, transcends it and becomes demonic, possessing the soul as nightmares that cannot be exorcised. Like those agencies in *Shame* or *The Serpent's Egg*, these ghosts from the past (and most of all abusive parents) cannot be reached, touched, or engaged face to face. They are either recalcitrant, like Charlotte in *Autumn Sonata* (1978), or worse, dead, like Jenny's parents in *Face to Face* (1976).

The soul, for Bergman, is now under siege both from without and from deep within. The figures of this oppressive feeling are no longer cars and wagons and rooms, but planes and bombs, recurring nightmares, cries and moans and sobbing gasps for breath, as though one were drowning.

What these new forms of oppression produce is a sense not of being dead (like Isak Borg begins to discover in his first dream)[13] but of being a nonperson – something that is there, conscious and suffering, but passive and manipulated. It is the sense of belonging to someone else, whether outside in the sociopolitical world or lodged deep within one's own psyche. One is essentially an observer of one's body and actions, a kind of sleepwalker. This feeling finds its first full expression in the character of Elisabet in *Persona*. She is not cured and returns only to resume the motions dictated by her script, her director, her life: her persona. She is a marionette, a "wooden person" [Fig. 19].[14]

This figure of the marionette becomes a central reference for Bergman's later films, culminating in *From the Life of the Marionettes*. But as early as *Prison*, someone worries that if God is absent and the earth left in charge of the Devil, people will be made into puppets. The professions of actor and performer, often featured in these early films, also encourage a sense of not being in charge, of following someone else's script. Most of all, however, this figure is a transformation of a notion of beneficent fate that is given its fullest expression in the comedies. This is the rule of life itself with its cycles and seasons and patterns of harmony invoked at the end of *Smiles of a Summer Night*. One can resist it (as Fredrik does initially) or embrace it and then find oneself in its own special music.

This sense of a life-giving world order is expressed in the image of the eighteenth-century music box with its dancing figurines at the beginning and end of *A Lesson in Love* (1954) (along with a cupid winking to the audience). Both *The Clowns' Evening* and *Smiles of a Summer Night* use similar motifs, and the Meissen music box in *Shame* echoes them.[15] These ceramic figures are not puppets pulled from above but dancers at one with and animated by the music. In *Hour of the Wolf*, however, this harmony is grotesquely transformed when the Tamino figure in the baron's puppet theater of *The Magic Flute* is revealed to be a human being. And in *Shame*, it is only a moment of nostalgia in a shop of antiques – things soon to be destroyed along with everything else.

In this vision of human marionettes, there is also some residue of the underlying determinism and predestination of Lutheranism. We can feel the otherness of an omnipotent God of creation as malicious cruelty and an unfathomable difference in kind, like ants trying to understand the child who pokes them with a stick. Something of this sensibility is given expression in both *The Rite* and *The Passion of Anna*, and the feeling of being some kind of experimental victim is at the core of *The Serpent's Egg*.

God, however, is something with which Bergman has by now settled, for the most part, though his films never lose their indebtedness to Christianity's most essential themes. This new sense of oppression reflects a growing dread that the conditions of modern life itself cannot nourish and in fact produce poison that seeps into ordinary relationships, making them even more difficult and unpromising.[16] The most easily identifiable part of this modernity are its internal demons, from childhood and elsewhere. Bergman is less clear about the external forces of politics itself. The already noted instrumental and sectarian, ideological character of modern social life is certainly one aspect. Diffuse bureaucracies without accountability,[17] as well as political demagoguery, are others. The failure of art to matter and be an effective part of culture is another.

Little more is given in detail about any of these. They remain the general features of a failure of civilization and seem often to be represented in Bergman's films by a certain sort of person – the Dr. Vergérus of *The Magician* (1958) and his later incarnations, Hans Vergérus with his

Figure 19. Wooden people. a. *Persona:* Alma leaving the island. b,c. *Shame:* Jan and Eva near the end.

human experiments in *The Serpent's Egg* (and even in a way the bishop Vergérus who becomes Fanny and Alexander's stepfather). The first Vergérus is a medical doctor, a kind of scientist who performs autopsies to find the sources of behavior in the structures of the brain, not unlike the second Vergérus, who conducts and films experiments to determine the capacities of the human nervous system. None of the Vergéruses believe in the soul or a spiritual capacity in persons that is beyond analysis and control. They represent the growth of a scientific outlook and a social science that is analytic, reductive, and materialist. When anatomized, persons disappear, becoming simply entities that can be manipulated and treated.

It is from this modern view – we are only a physical mechanism – that the psychiatrists and doctors of the 1970s[18] come as successors to Isak Borg's good country doctor. They are typified by the brazen weariness of Jenny's colleague in *Face to Face,* who advises her to turn her young patient over to him for behavioral modification now rather than to have to do it a couple of months later, or the outright cynicism of Peter Egermann's psychiatrist in *From the Life of the Marionettes,* who advises him: "If you like, I'll arrange for you to be admitted to my clinic. There we'll give you every known injection so that at last you won't give a damn whether you're Peter Egermann or the emperor of China. Don't worry, we're phenomenal at obliterating people's identities. No self, no fear. Fantastic, isn't it?"[19] All this is little different than the caning the bishop gives to Alexander: Each is a similar denial of the soul, replacing it with the goal of obedient and mechanical behavior.

5. Children

Children are of great symbolic importance throughout Bergman's films. They are literally the future and represent both what life can become and that it can become something else than it presently is. Bergman thus often connects personal and domestic renewal with the new life of the child, and *The Seventh Seal, Wild Strawberries,* and *Smiles of a Summer Night* each end with a vision of a family ready to confront their future. In the 1960s, this vision darkens. Children are murdered in *The Virgin Spring,* whereas Alma has had an abortion and Elisabet's son seems abandoned in *Persona.* Indeed, after *Brink of Life* (1958), no child is born until *Fanny and Alexander* (1982). But in addition, the matter of children takes on a political character (recalling again some of the social realism of the 1940s) and may, in the final analysis, be the most important political issue of all.

Childhood's legacy is seen by Bergman as more and more problematic (as contrasted with the "healthfulness" and vitality of Sara and her friends in *Wild Strawberries*). Being a child seems now almost unavoidably to result in damage not easily repaired. This in part lies in the failure of parents but also significantly in the compounding effects of a dehumanizing sociopolitical order. For Bergman, the latter in particular is an inheritance of overwhelming humiliation. If this continues unabated, what will be its effect except hatred, both of oneself and those who cause it. What future can a society have in which hate is the deepest motive (and pain, because it at least gets through when little else does, the most satisfying emotion)?

This question is the meaning of the drained and hopeless faces wearily moving in slow motion at the beginning of *The Serpent's Egg* [Fig. 20b]. This scene is, on the one hand, a transformation of the enthralled (and prosperous) audience of *The Magic Flute* (especially the young girl whose smile echoes that work's joy) and, on the other, is itself transformed at the film's end into a crowd of mostly younger, harder, even belligerent, glaring faces [Fig. 20c]. Hans Vergérus explains the difference just before he kills himself:

> Look at all those people. They're incapable of a revolution – they're far too humiliated, too afraid, too downtrodden. But in ten years, the ten-year-olds will be twenty, the fifteen-year-olds will be twenty-five. To the hatred inherited from their parents they will add their own idealism and their own impatience. Someone will step forward . . . and *then* there will be a revolution and *our* world will go down in blood and fire.[20]

Perhaps Bergman's fear of another era of fascism is overwrought and *our* future's membrane much harder to see through, as likely to be some other animal as it is a serpent, or perhaps just something stillborn. Even so, the hatred and contempt of which Bergman speaks remain widespread and increasingly define public attitudes. Unless addressed, they will only fester and feed upon themselves and will be expressed as envy, resentment, scape-goating – and other forms of political violence. If Vergérus's second picture – the one leading to revolt toward a new society because man is "a misconstruction . . . a perversity of nature" who must therefore be remade (p. 118) – does not hold up, his first picture of a society simply weary and defeated remains. Even if Bergman suggests no answers, his question cannot be dismissed. If the legacy of society to its children is more and more structures of humiliation and hatred, what future can these children have, and how can they not hate their society, their parents, their lives? Moreover, how can this not be a political problem?[21]

6. Politics and Art

Cowie reports that "*Shame* was greeted with an unexpected amalgam of scorn and admiration when it opened in Stockholm on September 29, 1968. Bergman's film undermined the complacency of the ordinary Swede; it enraged the politically committed observer, however, by its refusal to take sides."[22] It is not true, of course, that *Shame* refuses to take sides or that it grants anyone, especially "contemporary Western intelligentsia," "total freedom from responsibility for Vietnam by turning this war into a metaphysical issue" (as one critic complained).[23] *Shame* takes the side of the ordinary person, the civilian whose life is being ruined; it suggests an analysis in which ideologies (including "neutrality") and politics itself are the problem; and it makes clear that the issue is a moral one – a deepening incapacity at all levels of social and personal life to recognize and respond to the shameful conditions of our existence. All this continues to be important since *Shame* is as much about Bosnia and Palestine as an imagined Baltic war.[24]

Such a stance will not appear as political to partisans or those who run for office, nor does it enjoin a direct cause of action or recommend a party platform. The charge that we are enmeshed in a *way of thinking* that turns people into kinds of animate things (human wood, as it were) and deforms our sensibilities, and that these two elements reinforce each other in a downward spiral seems beyond political address because it calls for an essential change in moral outlook.[25] To many this will seem inappropriate as a public goal; in any event, no one has any idea of how to go about it.

Moreover, it has its own limitations. In *The Serpent's Egg*, brownshirts beat Jews on the street and other "degenerates" and "undesirables." Such evil cannot be allowed, even if resistance requires using the same humiliating means of the enemy. Abel Rosenberg's flight and disappearance at the end of the film may buy him time, but it leaves the course of things unchanged, and, as his name suggests (recalling the first victim in Genesis), he will not escape.[26]

Bergman perhaps recognizes this view. Jacobi scorns the artist who thinks "the colossal sensitivity of your soul" gives some special privilege or immunity from taking sides and running the risks. "Are you afraid, Jan Rosenberg? Are you an artist or a sack? . . . The holy freedom of art, the holy gutlessness of art" (pp. 163–4). One should be clear, however, that the effectiveness of art in the face of this "twilight of the world" is a quite different question from the need for social systems that recognize the essential humanity of their subjects by refusing to humiliate them.

128

Figure 20. Modern people: Inside the serpent's egg. a. *Shame:* Jan and Eva taken for interrogation. b. *The Serpent's Egg:* the old. c. *The Serpent's Egg:* their children.

By this time, even as he continues to make such films, Bergman seems seriously to doubt whether all the work and effort are worthwhile. Images now seem to lie more easily than they tell the truth, critics distort and misunderstand, the public loses interest; and they are finally only films – things made up for diversion and entertainment. In his earlier works, film is celebrated as something that restores and nourishes (in *Port of Call*, Berit allows herself to be happy and hope again as she laughs at the movie to which Gösta has taken her; in *Prison*, Birgitta feels free when she and Thomas watch an old slapstick reel in the attic and then make love). But in *The Magician* the magic lantern is dark and ominous, and in *Persona* everything about film is put into question, so that by its end, both film itself and Bergman's own particular attempt have lost the power to transform or find something better. Elisabet remains as she was, and there is no vision of any other way that things could be. In all subsequent works (until *Fanny and Alexander*), when film itself appears it is used for purposes that deny its art – propaganda, family favoritism, human experimentation, and manipulation.

His own self-doubt aside, Bergman has greatly underestimated what he has achieved. As a political film, what *Shame* does is call on each person, wherever they may be placed, to refuse to join in these humiliations of our public existence. Perhaps this is just idealism and in no way practical politics, yet it has a place – an essential place, in fact – in our political life and thought. The political act of *Shame* is to bear witness to that about which we must always feel guilty and aspire to avoid. Perhaps Bergman himself sees little hope that any of this will matter or that such thoughts could ever make a difference, but the *film* itself refuses to back down. It shows that our political identity is most fundamentally a moral identity and insists that we recognize this fact, if not in a different course of behavior or new institutions, then in our own continuing shame.[27]

Here the political act and the artistic act merge. Bergman's cinematic art is above all concerned with providing us with portraits in which we recognize ourselves, no longer "through a glass darkly . . . but now face to face." It is very hard to be unmoved, to feel clean and at ease and unsullied after seeing *Shame* or to leave unimplicated and without our own guilt. And it is a film that, once seen, will not go away or be easily forgotten. In *Shame*, we recognize a civic and not just domestic shame and begin to become ashamed of ourselves as public beings and of our public life. Art can do no more than keep such a picture before us and provide us with images to accompany our actions always, images that always judge them – and us. In this regard, *Shame* is one of the great political films about and for "bourgeois" society.

7. Another Vision

There is a final aspect of *Shame* as marking a turning point in Bergman's vision. It is the fact that the script proposes a last motion of the spirit that the film itself cannot achieve and that must have seemed to Bergman no longer possible. This refusal of what was surely desperately desired is a measure both of the film's courage and of its greatness. There are two *Shame*s. One that was made and one that was not. The films of the 1970s represent a grand struggle between these two visions and Bergman's losing attempts to achieve this other ending in a way that is not hollow.

It is several days after Eva's dream with its anxiety over someone's important words that she forgot.

> In the night . . . the sky is lit up by a strong glare . . . bombs have been dropped by both sides. . . . They sleep a lot, waking from time to time and talking to each other. . . . Some . . . are already dead. Large, strange-shaped clouds drift over the sky.
>
> JAN: I was wondering what it said in those letters we wrote to each other during the summer tour. Whether it said "My hand in yours" or "Your hand in mine."
>
> EVA: It said "My hand in yours."
>
> On the seventh day a storm blows up, and there is a heavy rain. The survivors slake their thirst with the poisoned water. [The film ends.] (pp. 190–1)

This is a scene of aching beauty, one of the great lyrical moments in all of Bergman's work. It measures everything by its absence from the film. It is a moment in which Jan looks back and grasps, for both of them, what they did have in life and with each other: a time shared with some love between them that, though now past and over, is neither gone, nor obliterated, nor nothing; a time when the world was summer, and smiled. And because of which they need not regret being born.

Under the dire conditions of *Shame*, this is a form of redemption and goes far beyond the mundane comfort of two bodies holding each other as they die. Earlier, on the shore before boarding the boat, Eva confronted Jan: "How can we go on if we cannot talk to each other anymore." He walked away, saying nothing. But now he speaks, and these are perhaps the lost words that she cannot remember in her dream – the words that said "I love you."[28]

To make such a gesture would clearly be a return to the narrative forms of the 1950s. This is not done, and this moment remains a beauty and affirmation of life *Shame* itself refuses, even as a dream – wanted, perhaps, but not allowed. As a consequence, Eva's dream remains an elegy for what might have been, for a life that has been taken away before it could flourish, and so also a moment of regret.

This regret must stand, and Bergman can now find no way to undo it. In *Wild Strawberries,* the retrieval of such a time in Isak's final return to his youth canceled the regret about his life and its failures that had for so long left him for dead; it also turned him toward a future with hope. It provided both meaning and mercy, as well as a second chance. In the unmade *Shame,* there will be no second chance, but Jan's retrieval of that summer past would restore an old order and make it possible for them to die thankful for what they did have. In *Shame,* however, there is no retrieval and so nothing that, returned, can at the end reorder what has happened and cancel the regret and mourning that have taken hold.

One can still maintain that the old films are right and that the retrieval from the past of those times that were good is still a motion of the spirit that is achievable, even under the most difficult of circumstances. Bergman's own loss of faith does not invalidate this knowledge or require us to cast these films aside or reject their more comprehensive geography. We can still seek those possibilities and their "mercy and meaning." Yet it is a faith Bergman himself indeed seems to have lost and a step he can no longer take.

What can replace it? The regret that rises with such melancholy in *Shame* and the attempt to touch and retrieve in life something that will cancel it and return us to an old story are the preoccupations of Bergman's two greatest achievements of the 1970s – *Cries and Whispers* and *Scenes from a Marriage* (both 1973). In the end, the regret will remain.

With *Shame* a great sadness settles over Bergman's work. The waving hand of Isak's mother, both welcoming him and inviting him to join them, can, from the perspective of that lone boat floating on the sea, only bid farewell and mark the loss of a world that can never be regained. The laughter, smiles, and tears of joy of summer give way to a final autumn; the dawn with which the story began yields to only a closing twilight.

In the end, everything is reduced to two people alone together in an open boat on a vast sea, a boat that is but a speck in the distance. "One thinks of Frost's dream in *The Clowns' Evening,*" Cowie observes, "'I became smaller and smaller until I was only a seed – and then I was gone'" (p. 254). For Frost, this oblivion is a release from the humiliation and misery of his daily existence and it comes as he falls asleep in Alma's arms. But Jan and Eva's boat recalls other scenes as well: the carriage, disappearing down a long row of trees, in which Henrik and Anne Egerman steal away to their new life in *Smiles of a Summer Night;* Märta and Paul watching young Henrik and Maj row across the lake on their "elopement" and summer in Italy in *Waiting Women;* and especially Harry and Monika speeding away in their motor launch for that idyllic summer in *Summer with Monika* (1953), just like the "lawless lovers" in the movies. These earlier images mark the time of the first smile for young lovers, who hand in hand promise and know they will always be true to each other. And though we know what will happen and how these loves will become difficult, these summers remain a golden time. Their escape into the distance is not into oblivion but to joy and rapture and pleasure in each other's arms – safe for the moment. *Shame*'s picture of Jan and Eva adrift far off in a poisoned sea recalls this time (which Jan in the "other" film tries to retrieve) and is both the replacement and cancellation of these earlier images as well as a final elegy for what the new world has lost.

In terms of the lives of the people within *Shame,* there is only devastation and loss, and a slow, fitful sinking into a numb oblivion from which they cannot return. As a film about his other films and an earlier narrative form, there is regret and a deep sadness. As a political film directed to audiences that can yet feel and act, there is still embarrassment and rage.

6

The Illiterates: *Cries and Whispers* and *Scenes from a Marriage*

CRIES AND WHISPERS

The story line of *Cries and Whispers* is straightforward. Agnes is dying, and her sisters, Karin and Maria, have returned to the family manor to care for her, aided by Anna, their longtime servant and now nurse. Agnes dies in great pain, arrangements are made for the funeral, and the sisters depart. It is this pain and suffering and its attendant helplessness that is the source of the cries and whispers of the title.

The narration of the story, however, is neither simple nor direct, for the heart of *Cries and Whispers* lies in the memories and reflections these events bring about, and its structure is like that of *Wild Strawberries* and especially *Waiting Women,* with their interpolated stories, dreams, and reveries [see Table 2]. Here Bergman returns to the central narrative form of the 1950s and attempts to give the drama of rebirth, along with the religious immanentism of that period, new life. While questions of God's existence seem no longer important, the fundamental concepts and images of Christianity, particularly those of Christ's Passion and the communion meal, structure the film and provide its chief metaphors and allusions.

In the wake of *Shame,* however, the result cannot be the same, and *Cries and Whispers* ends more a cry in the wilderness and the reminder of a vision now faded, a looking back rather than moving forward. One sign of this is that such stories are no longer set (as they were even in the 1960s) in the contemporary present. They are real only in, and perhaps only for, the past. Thus, *Cries and Whispers* (like its companion, *Magic Flute,* as well as the subsequent *Fanny and Alexander*) takes place before (or near) the turn of the century and the onset of that modernity the other films of the 1970s cannot escape. It is a film trying to recall something said long ago that now may be lost.

1. Memories and Dreams

While Agnes's suffering is both real and her own, she is also a figure of Christ. Her very name – one who is pure or unblemished – recalls Christ's incarnation ("born without sin") and His subsequent role as sacrificial lamb (*agnus dei*). The family minister puts her in this position as well, imploring her to plead (in heaven) with God to recognize her suffering by pardoning those left behind. Yet clearly for Bergman, the only one who can die for one's sins is oneself. Thus, while Agnes's illness is physical, it is meant also to represent the spiritual sickness that Maria and Karin, in particular, must confront in themselves, and her life is not a sacrifice for them but the example from which they should learn.[1]

How to deal with betrayal and failed communion, and the despair and (sometimes bloody) passion that results, is what *Cries and Whispers* is really about. Each of the characters has undergone this abandonment in some way, and the film recounts their experiences in the form of reverie, memory, dream, or vision. Indeed, nearly half of *Cries and Whispers* occurs in such a mode of "qualified consciousness." These episodes (or "insets") are distinctively marked and carefully placed [see Table 2]. The first and last consist of Agnes's voice accompanied by scenes from the past: her childhood with her mother and a recent walk about the lawn with her sisters and Anna. Each of these is introduced by a fade to a person in white – from a white rose to her mother and from a candle flame to Agnes herself – and each ends with a red frame [RF in Table 2]. The latter, in particular, represents Agnes's vision and what she has to offer, especially for her sisters.

The other three insets are associated with Maria, Karin, and Anna. They are introduced and closed by a pair of red frames [DRF in Table 2] between which appears a face in half shadow. When the two parts are put together, a whole face is formed. This is the person (the soul) who "experiences" the scene shown and whose "portrait" it is [Fig. 21a,c, and d,f]. These moments are like Isak Borg's "apocalyptic" dreams of self-confrontation and represent decisive times in the lives of these women, times they here remember or, in Anna's case, dream or imagine. In them, the course of their life and its truth seems to be set forth. Each episode centers on a story of humiliation and abandonment (or broken communion), and of moral disgust, failure, and shame; and each ends with a particularly vivid image of turning away or turning toward.

Taken together, these five insets represent the ways these women have responded to the suffering, humiliation, and abandonment in their lives.

135

Table 2. *Cries and Whispers* and *Waiting Women:* Formal and Dramatic Stru

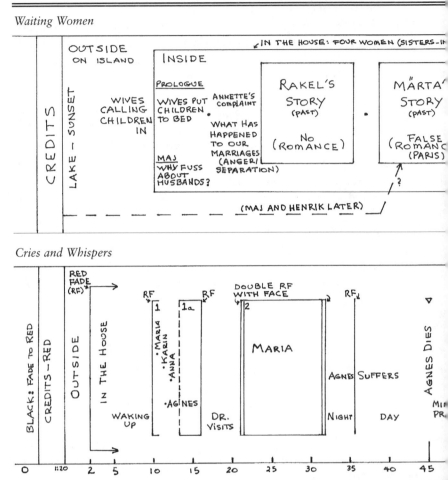

Waiting Women

Cries and Whispers

Note: Schematics are not to scale. *Run times:* WW, 107 min.; *C&W*, 91 min.

In the case of Agnes, it is to understand those responsible and to continue to see them and her life with a loving eye; for Anna, it is to offer comfort as a mother for her lost child; and for Maria and Karin, it is to turn away into themselves. But these two sisters, through the witnessing of Agnes's agony and death and the mirror of their own memories, are given a second chance, as in the films of the 1950s, and an opportunity to heal and repair the damage.

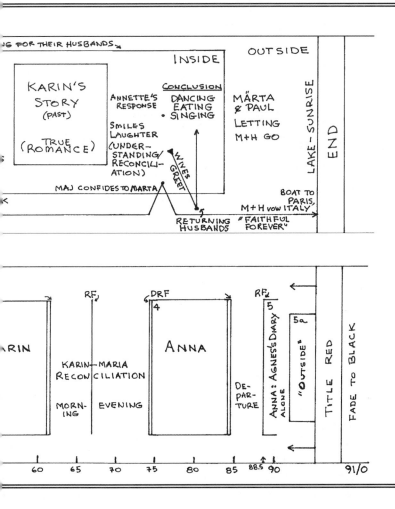

Their episodes are versions of essentially the same story of failure and abandonment. While Maria is unfaithful to her husband, Joakim, all her intimate relations, including with her lover, David, are hollow and loveless, just as much lies as is Fredrik's life with Karin. David's description of Maria fits Fredrik as well: a face that has become hard, filled with discontent, impatience, ennui, and most of all indifference, a face set into an almost permanent sneer; they are alike in their "selfishness, coldness, unconcern." Both are also associated with physical desire, but sexuality for them is something that has little to do with love. For Maria, it is a validation of identity, a kind of approval and recognition of her worth, as well as a means of freedom and escape; for Fredrik, perhaps only a sensual pleasure and need. They are each wrapped up in themselves, and their partners are lost to them as persons.

Joakim and Karin realize that the continuance of such relationships would be false, and this leads them to parallel acts of acknowledgment and negation – Joakim attempts suicide, and Karin mutilates herself. Each of their marriages is broken, like Karin's shattered wineglass, whose pieces can now only cut and disfigure, and these desperate actions make outwardly visible this inward truth. Karin uses a shard of glass to thrust into her vagina to show her husband what his lovemaking, and their marriage, is truly like; Joakim attempts to kill himself with a letter opener. Both acts indicate the kind of humiliation suffered and at the same time attempt to escape from the future demands of intimacy by making sexuality odious or impossible (an echo of Frans's attack on Albert in *The Clowns' Evening*, now internalized).

The blood that results is both real and symbolic. It completes the mystery of holy communion by transforming, as it were, its symbolic wine into the actual blood of human pain and despair. Communion proper, as the Christian sacrament, both commemorates Christ's own Passion and gives thanks for its redemptive power.[2] The meal of wild strawberries in *The Seventh Seal* and the outdoor lunch by the lake in *Wild Strawberries* are instances of this ritual transformed into a real event in which God's grace is human fellowship itself. But this "communion" can also easily be broken (as it is in *Shame*), and this is what has happened in *Cries and Whispers*. Thus, Karin and Fredrik are served fish and red wine for dinner before her self-mutilation; likewise, Maria and David are shown together at a supper where they share red wine and then later their bodies, a repeat of the betrayal of Joakim.

Here, the sharing of wine (and food) as a symbol of spiritual union has the same irony as in the biblical original, where it is followed by the betrayal by Judas and the denials by Peter and the other disciples. This figure of communion represents failure and possibilities lost. Now the divine transformation is reversed, and the wine becomes blood, their own. But, while this blood is the literal passion of those betrayed (like Frost and Alma's struggle up the hill), it is also a chance to restore what has been broken. Instead, Maria and Fredrik turn away in disgust, abandoning their partners for a second time.

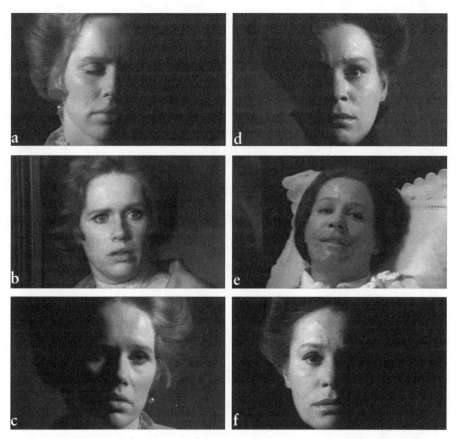

Figure 21. *Cries and Whispers:* The past in the present. **a–c.** Maria's "memory inset." **d–f.** Karin's "memory inset."

Maria's impulse is to go to Joakim, but when she sees him with blood smeared on his hands and face, she turns and flees (as she later does from Agnes in Anna's "dream"). She cannot bear to touch him. There is only disgust and perhaps embarrassment, no shame that he has been reduced to this because of her, no sense of his own suffering and need. In Fredrik's face there is a flicker of horror as he begins to comprehend what Karin has done and then disgust, contempt, and an even more complete withdrawal. There is no feeling of compassion or recognition of the truth of her accusation "that it is nothing but a tissue of lies"; only revulsion and a silent condemnation that she has violated the bounds of decency.

Maria and Fredrik finally see only themselves and respond to their own needs by escaping and remaining uninvolved, leaving Karin and Joakim abandoned and alone. In the third inset, Anna envisions the dead Agnes imploring each sister to hold her hands, take her in their arms, and keep her warm until the horror is over. They cannot – or will not. What Agnes asks is disgusting and repulsive, for she is already starting to decay, with foul spots on her hands (like Märta in *Winter Light*); there are also other obligations – children and husbands, as well as their own lives. Their response is the same as Fredrik's and Maria's was before to what is essentially the same need: They flee and stay turned away. Anna, moved by Agnes's pain and loneliness, takes her in her arms and holds her so that she can finally go to sleep, providing the compassion and love that was lacking for Joakim and Karin [see Fig. 23a].

This embrace and moment of comfort seems to complete the drama that unites these three insets, offering at least some version of a resurrection, as Christ's story promises, for it is indeed a turning toward and thus an undoing of the abandonment with which the preceding episodes end. (This completion is underscored by the fact that Anna's scene also ends with the same cello music that accompanies Karin and Maria's "reconciliation" just before.) But Bergman's resolution here is at best only limited or partial: It helps neither Maria or Karin nor their husbands, and it seems only to ease Agnes's death rather than truly bring her back to life. In the end, its real meaning will depend on the film's final events and qualifications.

It should also be noted that as a replica of Mary's gathering of Christ into her arms at the foot of the cross, Anna's cradling of Agnes is something temporary that is meant to be replaced by the true Resurrection of Easter morn (Christ's rising from the tomb). For all its reverence and tenderness, Mary's pietà is an act of mourning and a preparation for burial, not an anticipation of renewal (represented by Mary's caring for the Infant Jesus). As for Anna, all this is her own "dream," and it expresses both her devotion to Agnes and the feeling that only she truly loves her, as well as her doubt that Karin and Maria will ever really change. (It occurs just after, or even as a continuation of, their shared touches and embrace.) Still, it is a moment when love is present and the burdens and terrors of human life for the moment are given rest.

2. Karin and Maria

The physical in *Cries and Whispers* is both a sign of the spiritual and a dimension of life in its own right. Our existence is always corporeal and therefore sometimes also physically ugly and repulsive – we bleed, cough up waste, become covered with sores, and smell; and we scream in pain and fear as we die. Our lovers must embrace us in this form and sully their flesh with ours, cover themselves with our blood and waste. Bergman conveys this in a way few filmmakers have, and Agnes's suffering and death are both real and very hard to endure (or forget). Still, all this is easier than spiritual embrace, which requires putting aside our own pain, forgiving someone, and then making ourselves vulnerable to them again.

The inset "portraits" of Maria and Karin bracket Agnes's own death agony, itself shot as if it were a kind of crucifixion. Executed with Christ were two thieves – one on each side. The first mocks Him and is condemned; the other is promised paradise when, recognizing his own guilt, he asks to be remembered when Christ comes into His kingdom.[3] Perhaps this is just a matter of pacing and balance, but not only are Maria and Karin not innocent and even kinds of thieves living false lives, Karin is also importantly different from Maria (and Anna as well) in her awareness of guilt and the fact that she is ashamed and pleads for forgiveness.[4]

When David asks if there is absolution for people like them, people who are indifferent, bored, wrapped up in themselves, and selfish, Maria replies that she has no need of being pardoned. There is never a sign that she has asked Joakim to forgive her, and her willingness to resume the affair shows that even now she hardly cares how he thinks or might feel. Maria has no desire to be different than she is and sees nothing about herself that needs changing; she is thus shameless in her egotism, moved in her actions only by her immediate feelings and desires.

Anna, too, is unwilling to understand or be moved by the suffering of anyone other than Agnes. Maria does not see forgiveness as a need; Anna cannot forgive. When Karin, already desperate with guilt and dread, slaps Anna for continuing to look at her (for enjoying, as she thinks, her exposure and spiritual nakedness and anticipating her humiliation in her husband's bed) and then asks for her forgiveness, Anna shakes her head and says No – twice. She will not do it. She refuses even to make a gesture or an attempt to recognize what Karin feels or see how wounded she is. Perhaps it is the way she has been treated as a servant and the hatred and anger this breeds; perhaps it is jealousy and resentment that Agnes could be so fond of sisters who do not really love her. Whatever its source, Anna does not face or overcome it. Like Maria, she is spontaneous and emotional, and a bit childish.

Karin, however, does understand the need for forgiveness and the cost of these broken relationships. Her "reconciliation" with her sister begins with Maria's response to Agnes's death as Karin is doing accounts. Maria turns to her and asks if they can't be friends. "We could laugh and cry together, we could talk together for days and nights on end, we could put our arms around each other." Karin feels Agnes's loss and the need for comfort, too, but she is still fearful of betrayal: "Don't touch me. . . . I don't want you to be kind to me. . . . Leave me alone . . . don't touch me." Karin is in tears, sobbing and gasping for breath almost like Agnes. Impulse and desire cannot alone reverse a long-broken relationship.

Later in the day, as they are having lunch (another "communion" meal), Karin apologizes for losing control of herself and turns to the business of settling the estate. Then she pauses: "True, I think about suicide." Karin cannot keep her composure as her sister sits embarrassed and unable to escape. "Do you realize how I hate you? And how absurd I find your insipid smiles and idiotic flirtatiousness . . . [your] empty caresses and your false laughter. . . . Can you conceive of how anybody can live with so much hate as has been my burden? There is no relief, no charity, no help, nothing."[5] Maria's reaction is now no different than with Joakim: Embarrassed, cornered, uncomfortable with this real emotion, she flees.

Throughout this scene the two sisters have been pictured in a long sequence of alternating close-ups, each alone in her own space (even more separated than Jan and Eva in *Shame*), apart from the other, never together. As Maria goes toward her room, Karin's voice is heard: "Maria, forgive me. It may be you mean well. Maybe you just want to know me better. . . . Maria, look at me." Now we see them together against the deep red of the walls, their faces touching, their arms about each other, talking, stroking each other on the cheek, in tears. But instead of words, there is music, the rich voice of a cello. And then the screen fades to red.

How are we to understand this scene? It makes the right gestures of touch and embrace as the sisters begin to turn toward each other. It is brought about by Karin's guilt over their mangled relationship and her shame at her own failure to be better, as well as the hope of escaping the torture and humiliation she has had to endure. And there is a feeling of hope that things can change, as in the earlier films. But at the same time, everything seems exaggerated and even abstract. Moreover, in the old narrative this "reconciliation" is where the film would end (with Anne and Albert going off together, or Isak in bed at peace, for example), but to do so now would be to leave the story unfinished and badly formed. What was an ending before cannot be an ending here. Though the scene is not technically an inset of "qualified consciousness," it blends into one to become a kind of dream. The film can end only by coming back to reality.

The next morning, after the funeral, Karin speaks to Maria about how they came close to each other the day before: "Could we hold to all our resolutions?" "My dearest Karin, why shouldn't we?" As Maria turns away, anxious to leave, Karin grabs her by the shoulder and turns her back: "You touched me. Don't you remember that?" "I can't remember every silly thing." Throughout this scene there are the same alternating close-ups as before, each person again in their own space, again alone. "Dearest Karin. Give the children my love and keep well. 'Til Twelfth Night as usual, we'll meet then." As Maria moves to kiss her sister on the cheek, Karin flinches and turns away. "What a pity," Maria mutters, and turns away herself.

What has gone wrong? Maria and Karin's moment of surrender and embrace is followed (as though it were a continuation) by Anna's "dream" (or vision?) in which the sisters are tested by Agnes's demand that they embrace her, too. They cannot, and it is for the same reasons that their own reconciliation now falls apart.

For Maria, it is most of all her inability, or refusal, to see beyond herself or feel something in depth. Her facade of emotion is an armor that protects her from being touched far more effectively than the many layers of corseting in which Karin hides, for it transmutes what is real into something false and shallow while making the lie unrecognizable. At the very moment she is about to be truly touched by Agnes, Maria pulls away in horror; when touched by Karin, she later simply "forgets." She must ensure that her "feelings" do not make her vulnerable or take her beyond herself to a genuine contact with another. She now hardly remembers the night before and cannot imagine that she should feel or act differently because of it. Maria has no more recognized the truth of their relationship and Karin's needs than she did David's earlier portrait of herself. In both cases, she allowed nothing to get through.

For Karin, the fear of betrayal is so deep that the very touch of another is abhorrent. She must repress her feelings and desires like she clothes her body, with an iron will and layers of resistance so rigid that another's touch cannot penetrate. Still, they are there, and at the slightest alarm she must protect herself, make the body and all human contact odious so that she can turn away and not be touched or hurt again. She must lock herself inside, for touch can always turn to humiliation and betrayal. It is this constant possibility that Karin cannot forget or surmount, and her guilt and desire for something different is limited by this greater fear. How can she allow herself to be touched again, if no one can be trusted, or let herself hope any more?

3. Agnes's Vision

There is a great sadness in what happens to Karin. She does not deserve it. She has made the effort to move out of herself and turn toward her sister, responding to what she knew was better, and all she gets for it is a callous, even cruel, dismissal. In *Cries and Whispers,* Bergman seems to have replaced the old drama of abandonment and return with a new one of abandonment, return, and abandonment again. Karin remains one of those for whom Agnes is beseeched to pray, someone "left behind in darkness, left behind on this miserable earth with a sky above us grim and empty." "Plead with Him to pardon us [and] free us of our anxiety, and of our weariness, of our doubts and fear . . . that He may make sense and meaning of our lives."

Though her and Karin's origins and relations to their mother and Maria seem similar, Agnes has been spared from such a fate, but how? And what lessons can be learned from her life, and for whom? In her first reverie, we see something of her childhood: that her mother favored Maria and was withdrawn, often rebuffing or scolding her; that she was frightened and felt left out, the "only one who couldn't join the merriment" on Twelfth Night; that she was jealous. Why has she not given in to the hatred and withdrawal, or the loneliness and despair, that must tempt her?

Two special qualities set Agnes apart: compassion and gratitude. When she looks at others, she is able to go beyond her own desires and feelings and see the pain they suffer and why they might feel and act as they do. In the film's first inset, Agnes imagines her mother on the lawn "cold" and "playfully cruel," "Yet I could not help feeling sorry for her and now I understand her much better. I wish I could see her again to tell her what I understand of her boredom, her impatience, her longing and her loneliness." This is a love that supersedes forgiveness and shame. Seeing others as broken and damaged by life, hurting and needful of help, she is moved by their suffering to touch and comfort them. They are now only frightened and lonely people in need of someone to hold on to. At the very end of the scene, when Agnes expects her mother to scold her for spying, "instead she gave me a look so full of sorrow, I nearly burst into tears. I raised my hand and put it against her cheek, and for that moment we were very close."[6]

Accompanying this compassion is a special sense of grace that is felt as a deep gratitude for her life. Agnes sees it as a gift, or perhaps better, she is able to find in her life the gifts that it offers. Perhaps her long closeness to death has helped her recognize what she will lose and so led her to appreciate what she has. In her diary she writes (in a section seen by Karin and Maria), "I've received the most wonderful gift anyone can receive in this life, a gift that is called many things – togetherness, companionship, relatedness, affection. I think this is what is called grace." And at the end of the film, she (in her diary) recalls walking with her sisters on the lawn outside:

> It is wonderful to be together again like in the old days. . . . All my aches and pains were gone. The people I'm most fond of were with me. . . . I could feel the presence of their bodies, the warmth of their hands. I wanted to cling to the moment and thought, Come what may, this is happiness, I cannot wish for anything better.

The screen is filled with Agnes's face, radiant and smiling: "Now, for a few minutes I can experience perfection and I feel profoundly grateful to my life which gives me so much."

Agnes represents a vision of the world that recalls the thirteenth chapter of First Corinthians (one of the central texts throughout Bergman's work), which extols that love without which "I am nothing," a love that is patient and kind, without jealousy or pride, a love that "bears up under anything," "exercises faith in everything," "keeps up hope in everything," "gives us power to endure in anything," a love that never fails.[7] This kind of love is as much an achievement, a way of looking at the world and responding to it, as it is a gift. And if God is love, it is the presence of God.

This vision is not false. It is the ground of Agnes's triumph over pain and her refusal to give in to the temptations of hatred and despair. It is also the reason she can stand in for Christ and His promise of resurrection in Bergman's own drama or represent the answer to her minister's prayer and His only possible "pardon." Furthermore, Agnes has not been given something that has been withheld from others. She has simply seen and appreciated what is there for everyone. Has Bergman, in the figure of Agnes and her vision, at last restored the old drama of rebirth and its guarded hope?

Cries and Whispers even retains the open ending of the earlier films. Though Karin and Maria part separated, they are to meet again at Twelfth Night, the eve of Epiphany, the twelfth day after Christmas, when the wise men arrive and reveal to the world Christ's true identity with their gifts and homage. Is this a further chance for the sisters to see who they are and what they need, to undo what has happened, and again turn toward each other? What is to really become of them is, indeed, still open. Their own lives can be said to remain before them as questions they must still ask and decide. "Will I go? How will I behave? What will I say? What will it be like with Agnes gone?" Can Karin herself reach again toward her sister, for she more than anyone knows what is at stake? Will she retreat deeper into herself or find the strength to again move beyond her hatred and fear? Either is possible, and she must choose.

What, however, could lead something positive to come about between the surviving sisters? What further is there in their lives that could lead Karin or Maria to change any more than before? While Twelfth Night is "epiphany," and hence the "promise" of insight and recognition, it has already been encoded in Agnes's reverie as a time of false joyfulness and community, the time when their mother favored Maria. It is the time when something was revealed to *Agnes,* but why to anyone else? Maria is her mother's daughter, and what reason is there to think she will ever behave differently?[8] And Karin already knows what she needs to know.

It is also the time of family celebration and "communion." But what really do Karin and Maria have to talk about? It seems most of all an occasion for the children, not for them. Earlier, Bergman has to use music because there is simply nothing they have to *say* or share with each other (that will not bruise and hurt). Their touch and embrace can now be seen as only symbolic.

Finally, in *Cries and Whispers,* as always before in Bergman, the seed of change is found in coming to see one's life and relationships in a perspective that goes beyond oneself in a vision of something better. It is in virtue of this new sight that the desire to change will arise and grow more and more compelling. *Cries and Whispers* provides this vision in the form of Agnes's diary. And while Karin and Maria have had the experience of seeing themselves in their remembrances of the past, these, as we have seen, are not enough. The diary is Agnes's testimony to them of the reality of compassion and grace and is of crucial importance if their lives are to change – yet they do not have it.

Though the sisters know about Agnes's diary, and have seen at least a small passage, they do not take it with them. It is kept and hidden by Anna. As a consequence, they do not have the special mirror the diary provides that would allow them to see themselves as Agnes saw them – not as they actually were but as they could be. That Agnes did not recognize their self-centeredness and lack of real feeling for her, or in fact ignored and looked beyond it, should fill them with shame. Leaving this testimony behind is Agnes's act of faith that the love she has experienced can touch the lives of her sisters ("How could she say these things?" "What could she mean?"). Without it, all they have are vague impressions and memories of her life as it appeared from the outside; and these are not enough. (What we have, as viewers, is more – the whole picture.)

In the old narratives, there was always some chance for change and re-birth for the characters *within* the drama. *Cries and Whispers* is under the shadow of *Shame,* and these possibilities now seem remote. The earlier truths remain and have been articulated here again with passion and force but now seem primarily for the audience – things *we* can see and that can perhaps affect our lives. While Agnes may seem more saintly than real, her vision itself remains powerful, though now in a minor key in which the earlier animal exuberance of life is replaced by a more detached and aesthetic appreciation.

Within the film, the essential image of communion – the hand stroking the cheek or cradling another – remains undone. Maria forgets, and Karin takes it back. As such, it is less than the Madonna and Child or the holy family of Jof, Mia, and Mikael ("Life" itself) celebrated in the earlier films. This Mary is replaced by the Mater Dolorosa and the grief of the Stabat Mater. In *Cries and Whispers,* the pietà is a gesture of solace before the end, not an opening to the future, just as it is in *Shame.* But outside the film, it can perhaps stand for more: as a sign of the tenderness and com-fort we each need and can give and as the beginning of a genuine turning toward.

4. The Soul Inside

If the old drama of discovery and rebirth is now qualified and its central images muted, there is nonetheless something new in *Cries and Whispers* – something still as startling today as it was in 1973 – color. In 1969 with *The Passion of Anna,* Bergman, with Sven Nykvist as director of photog-raphy, turned permanently to using Eastmancolor for his remaining films until his "retirement" in 1984.[9] They had earlier tried it for the comedy *All These Women* in 1964 (actually, with some success), but its use in *An-na* and *The Touch* in 1971 is basically functional (though perhaps, be-cause of Nykvist's consummate artistry, always a bit more than ordinary). In *Cries and Whispers,* however, color is a distinctive element operating almost on its own.[10]

Visually, the film is more than beautiful – it is ravishing, even rhapsodic – and one of the great achievements of world cinema. Its deeply saturated colors interplay in a system of regularities (if not a code). The sisters and Anna (as well as the other characters) are ordinarily dressed in white or blue or black (Maria's dress is always a bit lighter, frillier, more "sexy"), while Agnes (and often Maria) is in white or red. Outside, there is yellow and green and a hazy blue of sky and water (the grounds in late summer and the sisters' walk in the autumn) and inside there is red everywhere (the walls, drapes, and rug; Agnes's robe and Maria's gown; wine and blood). In all this there is a rhythm and harmony that is felt but not understood, itself a drama and final balancing that effaces individuals and hints at deeper, more animal forces and the flow of life and death itself, of which we are only parts.

As sheer spectacle, *Cries and Whispers* is an almost abstract visual poem that is musical in its structure and effect (intensified by the accompanying Bach and Chopin at key passages). Bergman has several times spoken of his films, especially the later ones, as being musical in form and as expressing most of all a rhythm of imagery and emotion that is to be *felt* intuitively rather than *understood* intellectually.[11] From this perspective, *Cries and Whispers* is a kind of visual string quartet (or perhaps sonata for piano and string trio), and what matters most is the struggle between the different voices and their ultimate resolution and harmony.[12]

Visually, the film is a stunning creation that is both deeply moving and deeply satisfying. The elation and joy that one finally feels stands in contradiction to the suffering and terror of death the film portrays and to the desolation of Maria and Karin's parting. Against these losses Bergman has set the gift of beauty and the celebration of existence that is the film itself as an aesthetic achievement. This vitality of color and formal composition resists the spiritual despair of the lives within the film and presents in its own register a world that is much more positive and filled with hope. Indeed, Bergman's (and Nykvist's) camera exemplifies Agnes's own vision of compassion and gratitude. It never fails in its honesty to view its subjects also with sympathy and respect; and it is in love with the world and lovingly gives it back to the audience as a place of aching beauty. Cinematically, this represents the difference between Agnes and her minister: She can see things in a way he cannot, and this power of a loving sight is emphasized in the final scene, when the film's vision and Agnes's become one and the same.

If there are two films, the internal one of Agnes and her sisters and an external one built from its "surfaces," their "messages" are not easily combined or reconciled. They play off of each other, and the viewer is bounced back and forth between them – between developed characters left with little hope in a concrete world and something more abstract. But this "second film" goes deeper than aesthetics. If the colors of *Cries and Whis-*

pers are coded, red is their key. The manor house and its outside grounds are various shades of yellow and green, while within it is red, as though this were the blood-filled interior of some person's body. Bergman says that ever since childhood, "I have pictured the inside of the soul as a moist membrane in shades of red."[13] When we enter the manor at the film's beginning, we thus enter the human soul with all its mysteries.

The body as a house for the soul, and as that to which the soul gives animus, is an old image, and one can think of *Cries and Whispers* as presenting a picture of such incarnation (and what it means for us to have to have a body). In this sense, the film is a kind of essential portrait of the embodied spirit as it faces life and the agonies of dying, where the different voices represented by Karin, Maria, Anna, and Agnes merge as the feelings, faculties, thoughts, and experiences of one being.

Our incorporation in matter and space is an entry also into time, and the many clocks and chimes of the house at the beginning of the film mark this passage. Agnes awakens and opens her eyes (*and* the blinds shading the windows of her room), bringing the house to life as the others also awaken and begin the day's activity (the soul thus born into the world).[14] These four women, each dressed in white when they first gather in the morning, loosely represent aspects of human being: Karin's self-awareness and guilt (as well as her rational control), Maria's sensuality and self-deception (as well as emotion), Anna's physical ministering (as well as secretiveness), Agnes's reflection and appreciation (as well as faith). Taken together, they can be seen as an image of the psyche as a whole, with both its needs and resources, as well as its hidden, hardly conscious, fears, desires, dreams, and memories (whispers) and its sufferings of loneliness, terror, and pain, with its pleas for someone to help (cries).

Understood this way, the "focused" nature of the characters, such as Agnes's saintliness and lack of sexuality, should now not matter. Though "she" has not had lovers or children, or even apparently any sexual experience, the "others" have, and it is thus clear that this is both a fundamental aspect of embodiment and a central source of torment and turmoil in our lives. Moreover, the physicality and even "simpleness" of Anna, along with her devotion to being a mother (of both Agnes and her dead daughter), can also be seen as essential elements of life – the need (and capacity) for nurturing from both food and physical affection. The same approach holds for Maria's superficiality and Karin's repression.

The major events within this house, now itself a version of the "metaphysical reduction" that has occupied Bergman throughout his career, are those of abandonment and passion, self-confrontation and second chance, and facing death, but also children, appreciation, memory and the past's hold on the future, music, and perhaps most of all *trying to understand* – *saying* what it means and writing it down, so that even a little can be passed on to others. These events are placed by the film within the cycle of nature and particularly its twilight. The house is first seen in late summer, and the film ends with Agnes's memory of her sisters' autumn visit, as they leave to avoid the threat of a heavy snowfall that will close the roads.[15]

Seen in this way, *Cries and Whispers* is closest to *The Seventh Seal* – a modern allegory or morality play, with the true "soul of man," as before, not just Agnes but all the characters interacting together. This time, however, death is not escaped, and the film's "Gloria" – Agnes's vision – is followed by a final chime of the clock. Perhaps the two versions ultimately come to the same thing, particularly given the great beauty of what we see. But its tone now is nonetheless more somber and tinged with a final note of sadness.

This is the new story of Everyman: There is an empty screen, and the film begins with frames of a deep blood red, with its title and credits and the soft sound of clocks. Then there are some few moments of life and finally death, as each of the soul's "parts" leaves and its last thoughts trail into silence. There is a last chime and an abrupt cut to a red frame with the words, "And so the cries and whispers die away." Then empty screen again.[16] As the story and fate of everyone, *Cries and Whispers,* and its fundamental image of an ensouled house, is an encapsulation both of the central fact of human existence – that there was nothing, then someone is, and then there is nothing again – and of its phenomenology: In our consciousness *of* ourselves, we find both ourselves and the world already there and under way, beautiful and terrifying, yet also never fully revealed, subject to mysterious forces and haunted by impenetrable secrets and burdens of the past.

As noted, such an abstract and formalistic reading is in tension with the more realistic "internal" drama of distinct and individual persons. Taken this way, *Cries and Whispers* uses elements from many earlier films but perhaps is closest to *The Silence* from ten years before, and thus to the trilogy as a whole. There, Karin and Agnes are combined in the figure of Ester, while Maria is Ester's sister, Anna. Ester suffers the same torment and repression as Karin, and her illness appears similar to Agnes's (her convulsions are even shot in the same manner). At the film's end, however, she is left to die alone, abandoned by her sister and nephew (Johan), and crying for her mother.[17]

In *The Silence,* the metaphor for the house of the soul is a foreign country with a strange, unknown language. *Cries and Whispers*'s eighteenth-century manor, with all its tradition and cultural heritage,[18] is replaced by a squalid modern city in which the new visitors are now illiterate. Only what is most basic can be communicated without need of translation: sexual desire, hunger, fear, sickness, and music. (Indeed, "music/musicke" and "Sebastian Bach" seem the only words in common with the new language.) If a person remains illiterate yet must live in this place, he or she will be condemned to loneliness and surely die. Ester is a professional translator (as is Agnes a kind of amateur one, with her painting and writing), and she has promised to set down for her young Johan the few words she has managed to decipher, words that will make life possible for him in this new world. These she puts in a letter that he takes with him as he and his mother leave the city to continue their journey. *The Silence* ends with a shot of Johan's face as he intently studies the list Ester has provided.[19] We never see it nor know, aside from a couple words ("face" and "hand"), what it says. Karin and Maria are worse off, for the words they need – Agnes's diary – have been forgotten and lost.

SCENES FROM A MARRIAGE

5. The Illiterates

Is there any other way to learn? One can take this as the final question of the 1970s, in which the "faith and hope" of *Cries and Whispers* is examined from a much more psychological perspective, ending in the particularly dark and nihilistic *From the Life of the Marionettes.* But it is in fact the immediately following contemporary and completely realistic *Scenes from a Marriage* (1973) that provides the best answer Bergman can give in the attempt to translate *Cries and Whispers* into nonreligious and nonmetaphorical terms and thereby restore a little of all that has been lost in *Shame.*

Scenes from a Marriage recounts six stages in the marriage of Marianne and Johann as their relationship moves from the appearance of enviable "perfection"[20] to crisis to reconciliation. It was produced for Swedish television and shown in six weekly installments (in England and the United States as well).[21] It may be Bergman's finest script and would work equally well as a series of staged dramas.[22]

Bergman's "miniseries" shares the same concerns as *Cries and Whispers* and can be seen as a reworking of its story in which all its characters have been conflated back into the two protagonists. The film begins almost immediately to question the core of Agnes's vision about love (and what has been a continuing text throughout Bergman's work). Marianne is asked as part of an interview of modern couples for a "woman's magazine" to "say something about love," and replies:

> No one has told me what love is. And I'm not even sure it's necessary to know. But if you want a detailed description, you can look in the Bible – Paul told us what love is. The trouble is, his definition squashes us flat. If love is what Paul says it is, then it's so rare hardly anyone has known it. But as a set piece to be read out at weddings and other solemn occasions, those verses are rather impressive. I think it's enough if you're kind to the person you're living with. Affection is also a good thing. Comradeship and tolerance and a sense of humor. Moderate ambitions for one another. If you can supply those ingredients, then . . . then love's not so important. (p. 13)

Marianne is a divorce lawyer, so in a sense, love is her business, and she has found that it has created intolerable burdens: "In my profession I'm dealing the whole time with people who have collapsed under impossible demands for emotional expression. It's barbarous. I wish that . . . that we were not forced to play a lot of parts we don't want to play. That we could be simpler and gentler with each other" (p. 13).

These are the two central themes of *Scenes from a Marriage* – the understanding of love as something demystified and within ordinary reach and the need to accept both one's partner and oneself without the demand (or desire) that they be someone else. Love as a kind of friendship and unconditioned acceptance becomes the final meaning of the gestures of hand and face, comfort (the pietà), and mutual embrace that inscribe themselves throughout Bergman's films. And in the end, there is revealed a surprising capacity for the healing of the wounds we give each other.

Even though she is a successful lawyer and mother of two, Marianne has the feeling that she has never been allowed to discover herself and has been only what others have wanted her to be.[23] The love of her parents expressed itself as plans for her future and the "ordering" of her life: "My father's a lawyer. It was decided from the outset that I was to be a lawyer, too. I'm the youngest of seven children. Mother ran a big household" (p. 5). Her marriage and relationship to Johan seems in a similar way something with which she has gone along, fitting herself to its demands and to the conventions of being a wife and parent. This growing sense of having to be someone else (and a new awareness of her own sexuality),

152

more than Johan's infidelities, becomes her chief motivation for not resuming their marriage but rather going through with a divorce.

This conflict between the approval of others and of oneself seems particularly to affect women in the films of the 1970s (and thus reflects concerns of the times) [Fig. 22]. Its most acute expression is given in *Face to Face* (1976) through Jenny Isaksson, herself a successful doctor and the acting head of a psychiatric clinic. She has suffered a "nervous breakdown" and, in one of the most harrowing scenes in any film, fractures herself into the voice of her grandmother, her present voice, and the voice of herself as a young girl, and in these three personae scolds herself for not behaving as she ought, curses her grandmother, and begs for forgiveness.[24]

Jenny's sense that she has always been assuming an identity to please someone else is expressed in an image of herself as half-hidden in a doorway or behind a curtain. It is as though she now has the need to step forward into the open and find what is real. There is a similarity here to the framed half-faces in *Cries and Whispers* and, especially, to Agnes standing veiled behind the curtains watching her mother at her desk. And indeed, Agnes's childhood sounds like it could have been Jenny's, for she expects to be scolded again as she had been so often before.

Somehow Agnes escapes the destructive force of her childhood and is able to develop her own sense of herself (perhaps because she is largely left alone by her family?). But for Marianne and Jenny (as well as Eva in *Autumn Sonata* and Maria in *Cries and Whispers* – all played by Liv Ullmann), there was no such independence and no vital sense of self as they grew up. Stepping from behind the veil and through the doorway now is for them a confrontation with something they must defeat and exorcise. It is unclear what success they can have. Only Marianne seems to move forward a little, whereas Jenny suspects they have all been damaged for life, a "vast army of emotionally crippled wretches."[25]

What is important here is not particularly independence but being accepted for oneself. Being a whole person and being loved unconditionally are intertwined. Marianne's parents and lovers want her to fit the image they have constructed, and she wants very much to please them and have their love. So she acts to cover the gap and tries to be another person. In the process, she never shares their love, for it will always seem to be conditional and thus really directed to someone else.

In the previous section, we questioned whether Agnes overlooked her sisters' failings or even imagined they were not there. What we should now say is that these faults do not change her love for Karin or Maria, which is prior to and more basic than anything they might do or be. Yet, while it may never fail Agnes, finding even a modicum of this accepting love is for Johan and Marianne a difficult and treacherous journey, requiring greater and greater amounts of violence to overcome and undo the resentments that ferment beneath the controlled surfaces and dishonesty of their lives.

While couples have bitterly hated each other throughout Bergman's films, actual violence is relatively rare. It is thus shocking in *Wild Strawberries* when Alman's wife strikes him and draws blood, even though we can understand her desperation. In *Shame*, Jan and Eva become more and more physical in their relationship, hitting and slapping and pushing each other about, whereas in *Cries and Whispers* people turn this violence on themselves. But there is nothing in Bergman that matches the brutality of Scene 5 of *Scenes from a Marriage* where, as they are about to sign the divorce papers, Johann is goaded to slap Marianne and bloody her nose and then kick her as she lies on the floor.[26] It is a separation from and negation of the other that seems so complete that we cannot imagine how they could ever have anything to do with each other again. The depth of hatred it measures seems bottomless and the rupture between them absolute, without the possibility of reconciliation or rebirth. Here, they are truly illiterates, unable to find any way to speak to each other or even be civilized, much less more generous or understanding.

Nevertheless these wounds *are* healed, and in some way this explosion of hatred is a catharsis that clears the ground for the growth of a real love between them. There is a kind of miracle here, for Marianne and Johan's final relationship of acceptance and affection in Scene 6 seems both impossible and yet natural and understandable. Six years after their divorce and new marriages, they begin seeing each other, and they have an affair that has lasted for over a year.[27] They go away for a weekend to a friend's cabin, where for the first time they honestly talk about themselves and their lives. They now seem very close, and it is clear that they do indeed love each other. How has this happened?

The violent expression of anger and hatred that ends Scene 5 is the first moment of true and open emotion between them (as Marianne's confessions later reveal). They are now not who they believe they should be, doing what they think they should be doing. What emerges is who they really are and what they are really feeling, and it is given such complete expression ("I could kill you," Johan shouts, and very nearly does) that no remainder is left to fester or continue as something that needs to be hidden. In breaking their marriage so radically, they become free of their

Figure 22. Mothers and daughters. *Cries and Whispers:* **a.** Maria and daughter.
b. Maria with her mother. **c.** Anna and daughter. **d.** Agnes with her mother.
Face to Face: **e.** Jenny and daughter. **f.** Jenny with her (dead) mother. *Autumn
Sonata:* **g.** Eva and daughter. **h.** Eva with her mother.

mutual bondage and complicitous deception and begin to see each other without unpaid emotional debts, no longer the other's victim. In Scene 6 Johan is struck by this result, "that you and I have begun telling each other the truth." "Didn't we before? No we didn't. Why didn't we? That's odd. Why are we telling the truth now? I know. It's because we make no demands" (p. 196).

In their divorce they have come to see themselves more clearly and gain a better grasp of their own lives. For Marianne, this includes becoming more independent and living a life more of her own direction; for Johan, it is to see that his previous "independence" has been mostly appearance and that he has long followed the desires of others, acting out a life for their sake or because it was easier not to resist. "It was my father who had the great expectations, not I. But I wanted so desperately to please Daddy, so I tried all the time to live up to *his* expectations. Not mine. When I was little I had very modest and pleasant ideas as to what I would do when I grew up" (p. 195). His dream was to own a "books and toys and stationery" store like his aunt and uncle.

Sex, too, is demystified and separated from love. This is partly the result of direct experience and partly the perspective of age and the growing awareness that the core of love is something else. Marianne asks:

Do you remember what we had drummed into us as children? All that rubbish about physical love being the most sacred and beautiful thing there was? . . . To make love to someone was almost a sacrament. [No wonder] we got the jitters when we tried to put it in practice. At the other extreme was pornography, with lurid descriptions of the sex act and colossal feats of incessant orgasm. That was also pretty depressing. (p. 205)

Here sex stands also for all the promises of life and our high expectations in general. Everything is less than we had thought or hoped, and it is better now (and would have been better then) to accept this as part of our coming to terms, and peace, with the world. "Someone said I'd grown slack and gave in too easily. That I diminished myself," Johan reports. "It's not true. If anything, I think I've found my right proportions. And that I've accepted my limitations with a certain humility. That makes me kind and a bit mournful" (p. 195).

Finally, there is the moment of seeing behind the other's facade. The script begins Scene 6 with an encounter (not included in the film) between Marianne and her mother that is a more realistic version of that between Agnes and her mother in *Cries and Whispers*. In talking about her father, who has recently died, Marianne discovers that her mother's life was as restricted and directed by others as her own, that her parent's sex life was for his benefit and "at times . . . rather horrible" (p. 179), and that the two lived together a whole life "without touching each other" (p. 180). She also learns that her mother was "a little scared" of her and always felt anxious and insecure, though to Marianne she seemed perfect (p. 181). Inside, she and Marianne have been the same all this time – uncertain and lonely children in a world not quite made for them. At that moment, they share a great tenderness toward each other.

Johan and Marianne have also dropped their facades to discover they, too, share much the same fears and worries, each lonely, afraid, needing a friend to talk to and someone to hold them. Johan has revealed how desperately he wanted to please his father, how he is still a child with women, and how he still wants meaning in life. And though Marianne at first appears more vital and upbeat, in fact she is no different, no less powerless and lost than Johan. In the middle of the night she wakes up in terror. She has dreamed she has no hands and only stumps cut off at the elbow for arms. No one can grasp or hold onto her and keep her from sinking into the soft sand. "Put your arms around me, I'm shivering so terribly." "There, there. You'll soon feel better" (pp. 208–9). Finally, everything that got between them or distorted their lives has gone away.

"Sometimes it grieves me," Marianne worries, "that I have never loved anyone. I don't think I've ever been loved either. It really distresses me." Johan replies: "I think I love you in my imperfect and rather selfish way. And at times I think you love me in your pestering, fussbudget way. In fact I think that you and I love one another. In an earthly and imperfect way" (p. 211). Love, like sex, must be demystified and not too much expected of it. It is not really a matter of special feelings and emotions, and if we "harp on it too much, love will give out" (p. 212). Nor is it a matter of great romantic seriousness. Johan laughs at Marianne's impulsive suggestion that they sit up all night holding each other. "One leg has gone to sleep and . . . I'm very sleepy." "Well then, let's snuggle." "Yes, let's." "Good night." . . . "Good night" (p. 212).

Both Marianne and Johan say they don't know what love really is, but here we have a glimpse. It is all that *Scenes from a Marriage* has shown us, brought back to earth from Agnes's more saintly vision. And while compassion and forgiveness and sexual desire may still be parts of it, the love that matters most seems to be acceptance and companionship along with a deep affection and caring for each other that has ceased to be possessive. All of this is part of the film's last image of Johan and Marianne holding each other alone together "in the middle of the night in a dark house, somewhere in the world" [Fig. 23c]. Though they may have learned to "read and write" late, they are no longer entirely illiterate, or as lost.

6. The Last Smile

Scenes from a Marriage stands between the despair and regret of *Shame* and the abstraction of *Cries and Whispers*. Unlike the saintly Agnes, whose gestures of compassion seem to flow only outwardly, Johan and Marianne need and touch each other. Shown entwined together, they are in fact Jan and Eva in their lifeboat, except now the world is just muddling on, not come to an end. Bergman achieves in *Scenes* the ending he could not reach in *Shame,* in which something in life and being alive is affirmed, as limited as this may be. Here, they discover that they have been (and are) loved, the words someone once said that Eva could no longer remember, the something that makes it possible to accept their existences without "grief" or "distress." These words also continue Ester's struggle to extend the primitive vocabulary of *The Silence* to include more than sexual desire, hunger, fear, and sickness, and they provide a step in what is needed if we are to be more than illiterates along the "dangerous road" of this new, modern world.[28]

The old narrative is still not restored, however. Instead, *Scenes from a Marriage* has taken the themes of the 1950s and reworked them in a new key, shifting their weight to something less spirited and less hopeful (from summer to autumn). Marianne and Johan are not like Albert and Anne moving on into a new day but like Frost and Alma retiring to their wagon. Their reconciliation creates not a new family with great expectations, as it does for Fredrik and Desirée, but only the acceptance of loving "imperfectly" and "in their own way," like Charlotte and Carl-Magnus. The last smile of the summer night is for them as well – "the sad and the sleepless, the confused, the deceived, the frightened, the lonely." In *Scenes,* this smile is neither of celebration nor anticipation of the future, but only relief and melancholy pleasure in a brief moment of peace and mutual comfort.

They must soon return from their retreat in the woods to a world they do not accept and in which they do not feel at home. For Johan, himself

---

Figure 23 *(facing)*. Bergman's pietà. **a.** *Cries and Whispers:* Anna comforting Agnes. **b.** *Fanny and Alexander:* Emilie comforting Alexander. **c.** *Scenes:* Johan comforting Marianne. **d.** *Fanny and Alexander:* Helena comforting Alexander.

a doctor of psychology and Associate Professor at the Psychotechnical Institute, it is a world of scientific clarity in which virtually everything about us can be explained, but it is still empty.

> I refuse to accept the complete meaninglessness behind the complete awareness. . . . Over and over again I try to cheer myself up by saying that life has the value that you yourself ascribe to it. But that sort of talk is no help to me. I want something to long for. I want something to believe in. (p. 206)

Like Antonius Block in *The Seventh Seal* or Tomas Ericsson in *Winter Light,* Johan still has a longing for the transcendental and its seeming security and direction.

For Marianne, less philosophical, it is a world without shape or bearings. "Do you think we're living in utter confusion?" "You and I?" "No, the whole lot of us. . . . Fear, uncertainty, folly. I mean confusion. That we realize secretly that we're slipping downhill. And that we don't know what to do" (p. 209).

Marianne's nightmare of having to travel a dangerous road and slipping into the sand because she lacks hands and arms to grasp others or to be held by them is an expression of the doubts and needs of both her and Johan. It occurs in the early morning, at the hour of the wolf. Our fears of abandonment and desires for a meaning beyond ourselves or a sense of larger order and security never disappear. Their discoveries that night provide only a partial answer, for the "something important we have missed" – that we do and can love each other, though "in an earthly and imperfect way" – "really is too late" (p. 210).

Rather than falling into the oblivion of nonexistence that Frost seeks with Alma in their wagon, Johan and Marianne have become even more aware of themselves and their situation. In terms of the old narrative, the exchanges of confidences and past secrets and fears throughout Scene 6 are a more somber version of the earlier comedies of embarrassment, such as Fredrik and Karin's encounter in the elevator in *Waiting Women* or Desirée and Fredrik's first reunion in *Smiles of a Summer Night.* Bergman's targets then were a pretentious seriousness about life; but now there is a crucial difference. Before, the point was (for the men in particular) not to take oneself as the center of the world and thus to become able to see other things (and relationships) as genuinely important and as included in the true, larger picture of things. In *Scenes from a Marriage,* only the deflation remains, and the wider point of view is now to take nothing as finally very important.

In their cabin in the middle of the night in a dark house somewhere in the world, Johan and Marianne attain a philosophical and emotional perspective on that world that leaves them no longer fearful, nor alone, nor overcome with regret at all their mistakes and sufferings. But their new acceptance of life is bought at the paradoxical price of a greater distance and detachment from it that, though it may restore some good feeling and make life more manageable, in its stoicism constitutes everything as not mattering that much after all. It is somewhat like looking through the wrong end of the telescope – everything and everybody becomes smaller and not so significant. It is seeing things *sub specie anticlimacticus.*

It is not just that love is imperfect and earthly; love has always been that way in Bergman's films, and, of course, that is probably the only way it can ever be. It is that there is now no ideal, no vision of something better (of wild strawberries, a "holy family," or the aspirations of St. Paul's epistle on love). Johan and Marianne will separate what they have learned this night from the world to which they return. What they have discovered will change little about them; they will go on living the same empty lives of pretense and sexual musical chairs. And now there is not even shame or guilt. Both will continue to deceive their spouses and go on to have other lovers.[29] They will probably remain wrapped up in themselves and do little to care for their children or help them grow up. The amoral (or anesthetized) world of *Shame* continues to underlie everything, a world worn out and near to exhaustion. While this world is less frightening for Johan and Marianne, and they have genuinely touched and turned toward each other, they – and most everyone else – will remain "emotional cripples" "damaged for life," and the moments of satisfaction and appreciation they can have will be only as spectators off to the side of the world, not as participants within it.

The division between the "internal" story of *Cries and Whispers* and its external aesthetics is thus replicated in *Scenes from a Marriage,* but here it is the world and their lives that have become a spectacle and Marianne and Johan who have become its audience. The split is now within life itself. The older dynamic of coming to see oneself as seen by others in order to change is replaced by a stance of self-centeredness as actor and distanced acceptance as observer. Johan and Marianne are more and more alone, friends mostly at a distance, no longer a couple. Their turning toward has become, if not abstract, only a kind of holiday. They know they are living half-truths with their spouses and, along with them, prefer that and not to become deeply involved with anyone else beyond themselves. In the acceptance of this, there is little that remains of Agnes's sense of gratitude or the earlier films' exuberance and feeling that life and the world are a gift (and a place of dance and song). Rather than trying to live between death and the devil, both now seem for the most part acceptable enough, and the mercy is to be found in no longer seeking the meaning.

PART THREE

A FINAL LOOK

7

The Little World: *Fanny and Alexander*

Bergman announced that *Fanny and Alexander* (1982) would be his last
film and, with the exception of the immediately following *After the Rehearsal* (1984 – itself a kind of coda), this had been basically the case until
the 1990s, when he began directing again for Swedish television. The film
exists in three forms: a film script published in 1979, a five-hour television
production premiered in Sweden on Christmas Day 1982, and a shorter
"theatrical" film (3 hr., 15 min.) edited for international release shortly
thereafter. Although there are significant differences between the two film
versions, as well as between those and the script,[1] the fundamental story
and its themes do not change.[2]

The film's release was a major event, and it was advertised as both a
summing up of Bergman's filmic career and a farewell to his audience –
with some justice. With forty years of films now past, *Fanny and Alexander* can be seen as an attempt to restore the filmic vision of the 1950s and
finally to overcome the discouragement, and even despair, of the 1960s
and 1970s.[3] It is, in the literary sense, an apology for this earlier vision
and, in particular, for the theater, which has played such an essential role
in it. It is thus also a justification of Bergman's own life's work as a filmmaker and a refusal to end his career with a film like *From the Life of the
Marionettes*.

1. The Little World

Fanny and Alexander begins the day before Christmas and concludes in
late spring a year later. Its center is the Ekdahl family – Helena, her oldest
son, Oscar, and his younger wife, Emilie (who together manage the family
theater), and their two children, Fanny and Alexander. They are joined

that evening by Oscar's two brothers – Gustav, with Alma and their three children (and their maid Maj), and Carl, with Lydia (his berated wife), as well as the Jew, Isak Jacobi, Helena's old friend and lover. This is the home that is soon brought into disarray by Oscar's death and Emilie's abandonment of the theater to marry Bishop Vergérus and live with her children in his church apartments, and it is the home that must be restored by rescuing Fanny and Alexander from their new prison and returning Emilie to her senses.

The life that Emilie rejects, and that is now on the verge of collapse, is that of "the little world" (in contrast to the "outside," "real" world that threatens always to intrude upon and overcome it). This "little world" of family and friends is the site of a joyful appreciation of being alive and participation in life's ordinary pleasures. This, as Gustav says in his christening speech at the film's end, is "the little world [of] good food, gentle smiles, fruit-trees in bloom, waltzes" and most of all each other's company and friendship. Because of it we should "be happy while we are happy . . . kind, generous, affectionate, and good."[4]

Yet as necessary and nice as it is, the little world can never be enough to close out all dangers or satisfy all needs; and it cannot be a guarantee against trial or doubt. The emptinesses and despairs of life cannot be avoided. The crisis of the film is precipitated fully as much by Emilie's dissatisfaction with her life in this household and the theater itself as it is by the intrusion of Oscar's death. Thus, being overcome by life is – along with being taken away from home – the other great peril in *Fanny and Alexander*, and it threatens both Emilie and Helena. Though mostly a danger for adults (even Gustav worries that the world is getting worse day by day and that no one will escape its ills), Alexander, too, is terrified by death and rages at God for His injustice and cruelty. The boy has no perspective, and the adults about him are losing theirs. The understanding and wisdom needed are not just the self-knowledge so emphasized by Bergman before; now this awareness must be coupled with the stories and imagination at the heart of the theater.

Oscar, in his speech backstage after the Christmas pageant, describes the theater as a small place of "orderliness, routine, conscientiousness, and love," and includes it as part of the little world. "Outside is the big world, and sometimes the little world succeeds for a moment in reflecting the big world, so we understand it better. Or is it perhaps that we give the people who come here the chance of forgetting for a while . . . the harsh world outside" (p. 26).

Together, Gustav's companionship and simple pleasures and Oscar's more reflective theater constitute the heart of the little world. Both are forms of the appreciation of life, one immediate, one more detached and thoughtful. Bergman here rejoins what became separated in *Cries and Whispers* and *Scenes from a Marriage* – the actual lives of the internal drama and an external aesthetic form available only to the removed film audience, in the first film, and ordinary ongoing life and its detached observation where it is understandable only in an escapist retreat, in the second. In the little world, one is both actor and appreciative audience united in a single life, though a life now lived as much as possible in separation from the larger commercial and political "big" world "outside" and so still not a life fully whole: The breech brought about by the 1960s is not completely healed. In *Fanny and Alexander* both parts of this little world are threatened by Emilie's departure with the children to the bishop's house.

The bishop and his household represent what is most opposed to the little world, and *Fanny and Alexander* pictures their conflict in terms of these two essential places – the Ekdahl home with its theater and the bishop's austere church quarters. Vergérus's desire is to replace the first with the second and its entirely different kind of life. He has seduced Emilie with promises that he offers something more and purer than her life with the Ekdahls, and with her permission takes the children to submit them to this new discipline of piety and self-denial in which there is duty but never joy or pleasure. What he offers in place of the little world, and the imagination and theater on which it is founded, is a more literal and supposedly better truth that does not depend on or express itself in fictions (which are always falsehoods) – a truth knowable apart from any story about it.

In this struggle, Vergérus is most in conflict with Alexander, whom he tries to confine to literal speech alone (punishing him for his lies) and thus to his own speech as his (new) father, taking the boy's creative power over words and meanings away from him. Alexander resists, even to the point of murder. In the end, it is the strength of the little world that finally prevails, for the bishop's defeat is ultimately accomplished through those elements he so adamantly rejects (in the form of Isak and his nephews, Aron and Ismael, and the third essential location of the film: their mysterious house and workshop).

It is clear, for Bergman, that the theater has a special role beyond being its own form of celebration or a respite from life's care and worry and that it indeed exists "not for pleasure only."[5] It, and all its kindred imaginative forms, are most of all to defend the life of the little world, and in turn this life owes its continuance within the world's darkness to its – and imagination's – protection and support. In the end, it is the theater and the power of its stories that is at the heart of *Fanny and Alexander* and is its true hero.

2. Emilie and the Bishop

Edvard Vergérus seems to Emilie Ekdahl everything that she herself is not – clear about his duties and who he is, disciplined and confident, a whole person. As a minister, he is unselfish and dedicated to the service of God and morality. Most of all, he seems not to be an actor. He believes what he says and has no doubt about what he does. There is a purity to his being and to the simplified life he lives that has the ring of truth. In contrast, Emilie's own life seems just the opposite. Everywhere she seems to be acting, and offstage feels no different than on. Everything feels false and theatrical in the worst sense: a series of actions belonging to someone else, a flitting between roles she continues to play that never truly represent herself. Her life seems only an impersonation with few real emotions or sincere thoughts, now made all the more hollow by Oscar's passing. Everything is merely a performance – only a pretense at being someone and thus artificial and empty. (Helena expresses similar feelings later on.)

Emilie thinks that if she is to find her life again, she must stop acting. This is what attracts her to the bishop.[6] By sharing his way of life, she can become like him – whole, pure, one person. And the more she desires what Vergérus seems to represent, the more she desires Vergérus himself. The two goals become one, and Emily is swept up in an eroticism that was absent in her relationship with Oscar (which Alexander soon notes). Her seduction is both spiritual and physical and is complete.

A seduction it is indeed. None of these promises of a reality that shows itself "as it is," without roles and with just one face, can be satisfied. Our being is always multisided. Any face (or role or even motivation) is also a mask that hides or puts aside other desires and needs. We can never be only what we appear to be. It takes a long time for Emilie to discover this about the bishop and see that the escape from acting he promises is an illusion; but Alexander knows it almost immediately, and this knowledge is the ground of the deep enmity between them.

Alexander knows that the bishop, if not a liar, is a lie. His words about love and concern or right and wrong are no different than Alexander's own tales and make-believe, not "literally" what the bishop believes and practices. This is not only because he has substituted rules and rigid principles for love and wisdom: His own body betrays him. When Vergérus reaches to console Alexander, it is as though a vise had begun to grip him by the neck, and pats on the head or strokes of the cheek verge on blows. The whipping Alexander receives is simply the true and unrestrained desire hiding in these gestures. The bishop's concern is not love for Alexander but an instinctive hatred at being caught out and the fear that he will somehow be undone. Alexander must be silenced and controlled.

What has made Vergérus this way we do not know. Of all Bergman's creations, he is the closest to being a caricature, and it is often hard to have sympathy for him.[7] Yet there are clues and we can guess. Fifteen years before, his wife and daughters drowned in the icy river below. At that moment love disappeared from his world. Life became dark and austere, a trial to be survived only through the severest self-discipline. As for Bergman's other minister, Tomas in *Winter Light,* this was Edvard's first real experience of God, now revealed as a supreme authority who did not care that His creatures suffered. Still, instead of giving in to doubt and despair as Tomas did, Vergérus reasserted his faith with a single-mindedness and conviction that left no room for doubt and became as much like this God as he could: a man of principle and obedience for whom love is following the rules without hesitation or excuses – or feeling and mercy. His own desires and stirrings of the heart have no place within this God's law; there is to be only guilt and punishment and continued sacrifice.

Not only does Alexander challenge the bishop's submission to such a God[8] – bringing out the latter's suppressed hatred of the tyrant who has taken his wife and children (and so exposing his Christian moralizing) – but he also sees how much this man is sexually attracted to Emilie and how much his faith is the desire for a wife's love and vitality. For Alexander, there is no God in any of this: Vergérus lusts after his mother and wants to replace a lost woman with a new one. This is not religion, it's sex, and it makes him all the bigger hypocrite. But for the bishop, the two goals are not so distinct: While on one level he seeks his salvation in obedience to the law, on another he knows that the void in his life will be filled only by a love like the one he has lost. Emilie, too, is his salvation and a path to God.

That is, she might be, if he could allow himself to love her and respond to her as a person with her own cares and needs, as perhaps he loved his first wife. But he cannot; he can only try to possess her and make her as much like himself as possible. (This becomes painfully clear in his refusal to cede custody of the children and in his accompanying threats.) Vergérus can offer Emilie not the freedom from acting she craves but only a new role in another script – that of his own struggle with God and search for salvation. In closing out doubt, he has closed out feeling as well; he has nothing with which to respond and no way to be touched by another.⁹

The bishop in his destitution is finally a terrifying figure with his one mask "branded into his face" (p. 188). Taken away, there is a raw and bloody mass, crying out in pain in its loneliness and separation. Here is that original wound of abandonment that he can hide but cannot heal alone. Is this reality, the truth face to face, the unscripted world that Emilie has most hoped to find? In a way it is, for here she discovers something that is not pretense: her desperate fear for her children's safety, her own strength, the terror of a world without feeling and touch, and the truth of what she had left behind in the "little world" – that little of it was simply and only pretense and so false and unreal. She has made a terrible mistake, and her only way of escape is to turn away coldly, brutally, from this man and his world.

Bergman's portrait of religion in *Fanny and Alexander* is more scathing than in any other film, though it is a particular interpretation of Christianity that emphasizes suffering, guilt, and fear of punishment founded on the soil of disappointment and its concomitant hatred of life.¹⁰ Still, the Ekdahl children say their bedtime prayers, and the Christmas story is read and celebrated both at home and in the theater, where it is their holiday gift to the community. All this echoes Bergman's earlier religious immanentism, and here, as before, he reverses the Christian imagery, placing the Crucifixion first, to be followed by the Madonna and Child. Thus, Emilie holds the terrified and bleeding Alexander in her arms after he has been whipped in her absence (this pietà replacing and canceling the crucified Christ in the attic background) [see Fig. 23b], and the film's final image is of Alexander resting in Helena's lap as she gently strokes his head and reads aloud [see Fig. 23d].¹¹

3. Saving the Children

As awareness of the true nature of life in the bishop's palace grows, it becomes clear that the children must be rescued at any cost. But here there is an unsettling mystery at the heart of *Fanny and Alexander* – how do they in fact escape? What is shown seems impossible: The bishop, suspicious some trick is being played by Isak, rushes upstairs and, in the presence of both his sister and Emilie, sees the two children lying asleep on their bedroom floor. Yet just a moment before Isak brought them downstairs and hid them under a cloth in the chest he was buying, which remains in our sight throughout. They could not have gotten out and run upstairs, nor could they have then gotten back and into the chest before Isak's helpers took it away. Nor can they be in two places at the same time, as the evidence of our viewer's eyes seems to require. We next see them safe in Isak's apartment. They have been rescued, but how?

Throughout the film there is a basic realism: It is a story set in the ordinary physical world. True, Alexander sees the ghosts of his father and stepfather, as well as a statue moving; but this we understand as his imagination. What happens in the rescue cannot happen because it is physically impossible, nor is it the internal subjective state (or imagination) of a character in the drama. Their escape occurs in the shared public world and is agreed to by everyone; as such, it requires specific agents and adequate causes, and thus a proper explanation. It cannot be that the children are carried out the front door while they are also asleep on their bedroom floor.

How, then, can these events be explained? Most ingenious is the suggestion that the Fanny and Alexander seen on the floor are a pair of Aron's puppets smuggled up to Emilie from outside while Isak is talking with the bishop (since she forbids him to touch them or otherwise make sure they are really what they appear to be), or perhaps some other form of illusion and sleight of hand (Aron's profession). Though we see none of its preparations, the rescue has obviously been well planned.

Another suggestion is that the *entire film* is Alexander's retelling of his childhood in which what happened is colored by how he felt and thought at the time. His boyish imagination has transformed a more straightforward (and consistent) rescue into an exciting and fabulous adventure (that may have appeared to him as miraculous at the time) in which the bishop is utterly defeated – the same sensibility that led him to tell his schoolmates he was being sold to the circus. All of this, including the accidental fire, may have taken much longer than his "memory" suggests (or even be an embellishment). Perhaps Emilie even prevailed on the bishop behind the scenes for a peaceful separation.

Alternatively, one could try a different sort of psychoanalytic/symbolic reading. Adulthood for Alexander requires freeing himself from his stepfather's power; he must become independent, assert himself against and even "kill" this new father who wants to exercise authority over him.[12] This event is figured as a dramatic, even magical, rescue accompanied by a psychic murder and the ultimate repossession of his mother. How this achievement of independence was in fact accomplished or the actual time it took is again left open. For Alexander (or Bergman) to mature as an artist and take up his own life, it had to happen. This is the symbolic importance of this section of the story.

Though attractive in one way or another, each of these interpretations has its difficulties. (They cannot explain, for instance, the white flash after Isak's howl.) What Bergman has done is deliberate, and the question must be, Why? Fanny and Alexander could have been rescued without the story committing itself to a contradiction or losing in excitement. All this would take is a little more time: The bishop and his sister can fumble longer at the lock to the bedroom door, Emilie can bar their exit, and Aron can hurry in sooner with his assistants and carry the chest off before Vergérus can return and stop them.

As viewers, we are faced with something we cannot take as real, even in the extended senses just suggested. What we see can be understood only as something else – as pure fiction, where even the illusion that reality is being represented is undercut. The more we focus on its explanation, the less possible it is to suspend disbelief and the more the "storiness" itself of the film is thrust upon us. The only other place Bergman has done this is in *Persona*, where the celluloid that carries the story seems to burn and break, and the entire screen becomes blank with light.[13] A similar "whiteout" is inserted between Isak's cry of rage (and uplifted hands calling for . . . ?) as Vergérus goes upstairs and the bishop's discovery of the children in their room. Neither sudden whiteness has any place *in* its story, and that is the point: Each is a metaevent outside the film's own constructed reality calling attention to its status as a fiction and hence to its truth, not as a reproduction of reality, but as a *story* about it.

Recognition of the film's explicit fictionality requires us to abandon psychological and practical realism as basic interpretational frameworks and accept *Fanny and Alexander* as instead a modern fairy tale, with a special fairy-tale (moral) logic. This in turn changes the nature of the activity that accomplishes the children's rescue.

To say that *Fanny and Alexander* is a kind of fairy tale is to say that its events are ordered not by ordinary physical or psychological causation but by moral need. Fanny and Alexander escape because that outcome reflects the moral necessity of their well-being and the way the world *should be*. As a fairy tale (or comedy), rather than a tragedy or horror film (such as *Marionettes*), their story must have an essentially happy ending that reaffirms faith in life and the possibility of the world's goodness. The world can be good only if they can be rescued, returned to their true home, and the "little world" brought to life again. Therefore, they *must* be rescued.

That things can turn out well, that we can survive the assaults of the real world, and that our own children can be saved from its brutalities and enabled to have their share of its joys and pleasures has to be affirmed, for how else can we continue to live in a similar world? What matters for the story is not *how* this is done but *that* it is done. This is the moral imperative that overrides all practical considerations, even the regularities of causality or the laws of logic, which Bergman here brings into focus.

This imperative has operated before in Bergman, and especially in the films of the 1950s, but now something is added: In revealing *Fanny and Alexander* as explicitly a *story*, the audience's responsibility for its success is also exposed. When Bergman breaks the illusion of realism, he does so to show (if for the briefest moment) the machinery of stories, and it is this machinery alone that produces the children's rescue. It includes not just the activity of the maker(s) of the film but that of its viewers as well. Put most bluntly, what ultimately keeps the story going is the viewer's belief in it and his or her willingness to continue, not Bergman's.[14]

Here, viewers are complicitous performers through what might be called their "activation of belief" (an expression more accurate than the traditional "suspension of disbelief"). They take the story up in their imaginations and allow themselves to be taken in by it. They believe *in* the story though they do not (literally) believe *it*. Bergman can succeed in continuing his story in spite of the impossibility of the events he has shown because his viewers accept this almost without hesitation. Here the machinery of storiness explicitly supersedes, and stands as more important than, the machinery of realism.

Fanny and Alexander are saved by the story. This event and everything that follows from it is sustained and held together only in our imaginations, and Bergman's choice to disrupt the film's realism parallels our own choice to ignore that disruption and carry on with the story. "How it's done doesn't matter," we say, whereas we could insist (as some viewers have) that the rescue does not make sense and could not have happened. For them, the story falls apart and is ruined (and they are left with a world in which Bishop Vergérus is master).

To save *Fanny and Alexander* and allow it to succeed requires, for the moment at least, accepting its governing moral order. We must allow ourselves to believe in this world and, as a result, momentarily share its values and recognize the truth they represent. Bergman has upped the stakes from our normal encounter with art. We cannot just be observers, and it cannot be just his view that is at issue. If the film is to succeed, we must be necessary participants. If we stumble and balk and insist on realism at this point, we shall not only cause the story to fall apart but will become like the bishop in our literalism, losing contact with what is most important. The film – and Bergman – asks us to, and makes us, take sides.[15]

4. The Empress of China's Chair

Much of *Fanny and Alexander* is a meditation on how our lives are essentially defined by the stories we tell and the kind of truth and falsity they can have. These stories, extending from deep in our pasts to far into our futures, arouse desire and direct action, ordering our lives and making them coherent. In the longer television version, Oscar makes up a tale that seems to epitomize both stories' power and danger.

Late on Christmas Eve, after the children have been playing with Alexander's new magic lantern when they should be asleep, Oscar stays to tell them about the special chair he holds in his hands. Though it looks like one of the ordinary wooden chairs in the nursery, it is "the most valuable chair in the world," made by the emperor of China out of the rarest metal from the center of the earth for his empress three thousand years ago (p. 41). "Now it belongs to you! . . . Take care of it. It is very fragile and breaks easily. . . . Touch it gently, sit carefully, talk to it, and breathe on it at least twice a day" (p. 43). The children are enthralled. But then Oscar pretends the chair is trying to bite him and starts to fight back. Almost immediately, Fanny cries out, "Don't do that to the chair!" (p. 44). She has been completely taken in. (This is a version of our own actions later when, confronted with the rescue's "impossibility," we say "Ignore that! Go on with the story!")

What Fanny imagines is not just a chair that now shines with a special glow and whose appearance hides its real nature, but also the pile of dust it will soon become and the disaster that will be if her father is not stopped. Oscar's story, with its vision of a possible future, pushes everything else aside, marshals her energies, and moves her to action.

We, of course, recognize Oscar's tale as something completely made up and smile at Fanny's gullibility. But adults also tell stories to themselves and are as easily taken in by them. Thus, at this same time, Gustav tries to seduce Maj with the promise of a coffee shop and an apartment where he will come to her visit every Wednesday and Saturday at three o'clock (p. 53). Maj doesn't believe a word of it, but not because she thinks Gustav is lying about his intentions (he has already signed the "document"). Rather, it is a story she doesn't believe *in* and one that will not be good for either of them. Gustav can see none of this and remains immersed in his fantasy of a carefree pleasure garden. His brother Carl is no different, for he humiliates both himself and Lydia with his continued tale of cowardice and failure. He cannot see that this is only self-pity and that Lydia is too afraid of being left alone to insist on another, better story.[16]

In all this, the issue is not that sometimes there are stories and sometimes not. There are always stories, but some are better than others, and though they are all in one sense made-up, only some are delusions or mere fantasy. How to tell the difference is the ultimate question Bergman raises in *Fanny and Alexander*.

How, for instance, should we take Alexander's two tales for which he is punished? Are they false as the bishop insists and thus to be recanted and no longer told? We cannot believe that what they say is true as a statement of fact: Emilie has not sold Alexander to the circus, and the longer version of the film makes clear that Vergérus did not drive his first wife and daughters to their deaths. Yet each story gives a truer picture of Emilie and the bishop than their own rival claims that these are lies and perhaps even malicious slander; for Alexander's sense that his mother is about to abandon him to a precarious world where he will be on his own is correct, and Vergérus is indeed a man capable of driving his wife and children to their own deaths, as the events of the summer go on to prove.

At one level, these two stories are simply products of a vivid imagination, but at another they are truer than the literal "facts." Alexander is better off believing (and believing in) them, for the vision they give of the bishop and his own situation will keep his guard up and reinforce his resolve to resist. These stories are an integral part of his wariness and begin to define him to himself as an outsider. Certainly, Emilie would have done well to take both more seriously and search for the truth at their core.

Vergérus forces Alexander to admit that what he has said is "false," that is, fictions he has made up. The bishop only dimly senses that this in no way prevents them from telling truths about Emilie or himself (even if taken simply as metaphors and figures of speech). How are we to understand this literalism? At its heart is the fact that the bishop's own character and motives are under attack in these stories and that what he says and thinks about himself can be true only if what Alexander says is simply made up and thus entirely false.[17]

The underpinnings of this rigorism and the absence of any attempt to understand Alexander's feelings, however, lies in stories of his own, stories he does not recognize as such: for instance, that God has an order and His bishop is its minister. The perceived literal truth of this story is all that prevents apostasy and despair. Vergérus cannot otherwise face the fact that the meaning of his wife and children's death rests only on himself. (He is thus like Antonius Block in *The Seventh Seal,* who even at the end and after the wild strawberries waits to hear from God directly.) But for Alexander, Vergérus's "facts" are nothing but blind faith (only a story the bishop believes *in* – like Fanny's belief in the emperor's chair, yet even more fantastic and stupid).

This faith is dominated by two fundamental images. The first is explicit in the film: It is the crucified Christ, bleeding and in pain, waiting to be returned to God and restored in Heaven. His story is to be ours: This earthly life is unworthy, to be replaced, if we pass its test of punishment and suffering, by an otherworldly future. At its best, this story rejects the joys of "the little world" to "live in an atmosphere of purity and austerity" and religious discipline (p. 96); at its worst, it requires one to get on the cross oneself, humbled and humiliated in God's "loving punishment" (p. 156). "I must teach you and your children to live in reality. It is not my fault reality is hell. In this world, Emilie, in this reality Jesus Christ was tortured and put to death" (p. 157).

The other image is Abraham about to sacrifice his son. In the script, a picture hangs in the bishop's office: "The naked Isaac is already lying on the altar blindfolded. Abraham is holding the knife against his son's taut, backward-bent neck. An angel with a furious expression is approaching out of the clouds" (p. 95). It is not in the film, and that is a loss, for it dramatically focuses much of what we feel about Vergérus. Nothing in this world matters as much as what he takes to be the commands of God or his Christian duty. Emilie finally abandons him because he will not relent in his demand that the children come back, even if it means that things between them will become hopeless: "I don't care about what is hopeless or not. I care only for what is right" (p. 186). Like Abraham, he believes that God can command the sacrifice not just of what is precious in life but of another human being, and that this can be understood as fatherly love. And like Abraham, he believes God will somehow keep His promises and make everything right.

For Vergérus it is most of all the visions of what is to come in these stories that sustain him. Like Abraham, he will find an angel who will intervene and vindicate his harshness and apparent cruelty; and like Jesus, he will be taken down from the cross and given his own place in heaven at the right hand of God. The faithful servant will be justified and have his reward. Vergérus, as much as anyone else, relies on stories for his life.

For Bergman, it is clear that the stories matter most and that they are the only difference between the little world and the bishop's "hell." The same events occur in both: the death of a lover or child, the eating of daily bread. Their meanings and possibilities, however, are entirely different according to the stories that define them and that hold their lives together. The bishop's "real" world is hell because it excludes as sinful the sentiments and activities of the Ekdahls' "little world" and for no other reason. It needn't be so – and in this sense, *Fanny and Alexander* is one of Bergman's strongest affirmations of human existence.[18]

5. Another Hamlet?

Though willing to try Vergérus's first story, Emilie cannot accept the second and allow herself to be Sarah or Alexander to be Isaac – and not just because Alexander is too precious or because permitting his mistreatment cannot be love. She, too, sees that Vergérus's motives (unlike Abraham's perhaps) are impure, and that he is jealous of Alexander, fearing and even hating him.[19] Though Edvard says he loves her and promises to be different, Emilie refuses to stay. As he stumbles about drugged, he calls for her: "Are you there? I can't see you. I can't see. . . . Help me." "I don't dare to help you," she replies, and leaves to return to the "little world" and her family (pp. 196–7). Two days later and now in mourning, Emilie visits the theater with Fanny and Alexander. Everyone is deeply moved, and Hanna says what they all hope: "You'll stay with us now, won't you?" (p. 205).[20]

For his part, Alexander accepts the image of the suffering Christ the bishop forces on him but as an act of rebellion, not submission. Martyrdom is heroic, and punishment will steel his resistance. For him, both God and Abraham are bearded tyrants of the Old Testament who confuse power with goodness, and the bishop is their living image (a "piss-God" and a "piss-bishop"). He must oppose their stories, which sanction his own acquiescence and even destruction, with one of his own that gives him control of his existence and ensures Vergérus's defeat. He will be Hamlet and his mother the Gertrude who has abandoned him and betrayed his father to marry her wicked "uncle."

And why not? The Ghost Hamlet was the role Oscar was rehearsing when he collapsed, and since Alexander must find some way, some story, by which to make sense of what has happened since then, why not this familiar one that comes recommended by his own father and seems to fit and capture his stepfather's true villainy (and now pits the theater against the religion that would deny it)? Although Emilie tells him when they first arrive that he is no Hamlet, she no Gertrude, and the bishop's house no Elsinore Castle (p. 111), she is not convincing. The place looks the part, and his father has died suddenly and mysteriously, just as Hamlet senior, while his mother has just as suddenly become involved with a man he had hardly noticed before, precipitously marrying him and changing all their lives. Like Claudius, this man has robbed him of his inheritance, as well as of his mother, and now stands against him as a mortal enemy. Perhaps Emilie, too, protests too much. "O, horrible! O, horrible! most horrible!/ If thou hast nature in thee, bear it not,/ Let not the royal bed of Denmark be/ A couch for luxury and damned incest" (pp. 67–8).[21] These are the last words Alexander hears his father speak before he is "struck down," words that now might seem prophetic and appropriate to him as well. Indeed, the time is out of joint, and must not Alexander set it right . . . even if this should mean the murder of a bishop?[22]

When this last thought indeed comes true, the bishop's stories are even further canceled by being shown to have been all along the real lies, since in Vergérus's own words to Alexander, "life punishes liars ruthlessly and indiscriminately" (p. 137).[23] It is hard not to side with Alexander in all this. In accepting and even approving of and finding satisfaction in the bishop's death, for all its pitifulness and gruesome horror, we also find it part of the better story.

Alexander's story is different from the bishop's in two important respects. First, it knits together events only in this world and is thus dependent only on worldly possibilities and agencies. This means that, at certain points, anyway, stories can be tested. Fanny's chair will not crumble to dust, and seeing this will usually break that story's hold. We as audience share the pleasures and sorrows of the Ekdahl family and easily recognize how good a life this would be. But the stories on which the bishop relies cannot be tested: They look in another direction, away from the here of this life and often in direct opposition to it. Emilie tries but can find nothing she finally recognizes as love in their life together, whereas it was palpable, even if not sexual, in her relationship with Oscar.[24] She, like Alexander, chooses the world of experience over that of faith.

At one level this is a stalemate, advocating one kind of story over the other. But at another, it is the question of which story you can believe in without self-deception, and what Bergman suggests is this: If a story so departs from the ordinary meaning of its words as to include what appears to be just the opposite (an "act of fatherly love" encompassing a brutal beating), it cannot be accepted as the story it claims to be. It is either a different story, or we must begin to *pretend* that it is not. If its words cannot be tied to their usual meanings – and so tested by our own lives and experience – we shall never quite know what to believe in and will be tempted to suppress our experience and feelings, replacing them with fiat in order to keep our story in place.

This is the path of the bishop (which, rather than freeing Emilie from masks and roles, demands she embrace them even more completely). Though Vergérus believes in what he says, he does so with his eyes shut. Bergman demands our eyes be open, and this is a second feature of those stories that are better: They have a perspective that includes the other stories as well and even an awareness of their own storiness and of story-telling itself (like *Fanny and Alexander*). In the case of Vergérus, it is this sort of self-knowledge, finally recognized in the face and look of another, that causes his own story to begin to lose conviction: "I always thought people liked me. I saw myself as wise, broad-minded, and fair. I had no idea that anyone was capable of hating me" (p. 188).

Awareness comes, most fully, from Emilie. When earlier in that last evening Edvard asks, "Won't you forgive me?" she replies, "I'm staying with you, am I not?" (p. 186). But by the night's end she has drugged him and is preparing to leave forever to go back "to my children, to the theater, to my house, and my family" (p. 196). Nothing of hers is left with him and nothing of his taken with her. His last words are these: "I am awake. I am horribly awake. . . . Help me" (p. 196). For a moment, Vergérus has seen himself as he is seen and all his stories are shattered, for they do not include this kind of self-knowledge.

Alexander, too, lacks perspective: He sees his dying father only as a grotesque and terrifying corpse reaching to grab him, the bishop as a ridiculous and hostile adult, and God as a shit who doesn't give a damn about us. He is, after all, only a ten-year-old boy from a rather sheltered environment who has not yet had the experience that will check the bravado and posturing in his tales. For now, and perhaps for a long time to come, he is their hero, and they are the stories of a hero's trials and triumphs.

It is in Isak's apartments that Alexander begins to see beyond these stories with their crude casting of heroes and villains. He has three encounters, together a kind of initiation in which he begins to learn what imagination is and to what it is ultimately answerable. It is here that he first recognizes himself as an author responsible for his stories (what the bishop could never accomplish with his punishments) and thus starts his life as an artist. He also takes the first steps toward that encompassing perspective he now so contemptuously dismisses.[25]

The first he must keep stored away until he can recognize it in his own life and art: It shows by what these will both be measured. As he wanders about at night looking for a place to relieve himself, Alexander meets his (dead) father, who, when his son rails against God and then against people themselves ("Idiots. . . . The whole lot of them"), tells him, "You must be gentle with people, Alexander. . . . By and by you will understand –" "What damned by and by? I see clearly. People are absurd and I dislike them" (p. 184). (Here, ironically, he is not unlike the bishop, nor even, sometimes, Bergman himself.) Although Ismael later deflates this self-certainty and arrogance, his father's words now seem only for someone else. He cannot yet understand Emilie's attraction to the bishop (the next shot is of Emilie with Edvard) or the exhaustion and blindness with which everyday life wears people away and makes them desperate (the substance of Isak's story). Nor does he see that he too will become like them, no longer a hero.

Alexander's other encounters are with Isak's nephews – first Aron and then Ismael. Aron allows him finally to free himself of God, who becomes simply a puppet and somebody's prank, replaced by the human counterparts of magic and art. Ismael confronts him for the first time with himself ("Perhaps we are the same person") – with his deepest feelings and desires and with who he may become as an artist ("'a wild man; his hand will be against every man,'" someone "considered dangerous," and with an "awkward talent" of exposing the truth [p. 198]). Through him, Alexander also sees what it really is to want another man dead and for the first time discovers something terrible and disturbing about himself and the sources from which his (and Bergman's) art will come. He shrinks back, but Ismael holds him fast and makes him look, makes him tell his story and see the "shapeless burning figure moving across the floor – shrieking" (p. 200). "Don't be afraid."[26] As the bishop dies, Alexander ceases to be a child.

6. Hideous Winter[27]

There remains only Helena to save. She says to Isak on Christmas Eve, "Last year I enjoyed Christmas; this year all I wanted to do was cry. I suppose I'm getting old. . . . Now, you see, I'm weeping. The happy, splendid life is over, and the horrible, dirty life is engulfing us. That's the way of it" (pp. 46, 50). It is this melancholy that is so striking about her from the very first, and so puzzling. We notice it immediately as she makes her rounds checking on Christmas preparations (looking at the world outside through a cold, frosted window) and find it strange and out of place.

Others share her sense that the world is deteriorating hopelessly: "Worse weather, worse people, worse machines, worse wars," laments

Isak too (p. 49).[28] But something more than this has gripped her. Her life seems now only parts and pieces, one role after the other but from different scripts: "I enjoyed being a mother," she tells the dead Oscar the following summer, "I enjoyed being an actress too, but I preferred being a mother. I liked being pregnant and didn't care tuppence for the theater then. . . . Suddenly I am playing the part of a widow. Or a grandmother." Nothing comes together anymore. "Everything is acting. Some parts are nice, others not so nice" (p. 129). As she said that Christmas Eve, "We play our parts. Some play them negligently; others play them with great care. I am one of the latter" (p. 50). And now: "But what became of it all, can you tell me that, Oscar?" (p. 129). Life has passed, come to this and nothing more, and left behind only memories and old photos.

As she talks with Oscar (a more animated photo and such a memory) and holds his hand, Helena tells him how she grieved at his death, how it "shattered reality." "Reality has been broken ever since, and oddly enough it feels better that way. So I don't bother to mend it. I just don't care if nothing makes sense" (p. 129). Like Emilie, Helena is distressed that life now seems nothing but fragments and parts left dangling, but unlike her, she knows these "scripts" cannot be escaped and that no life exists outside them. Her melancholy will continue until two things happen: She achieves some understanding of and reconciliation to life as simply a series of passing parts; and she discovers how to find herself in her current part, not just to give a workmanlike performance but to enter in and enjoy and be nourished by it.

This is what Helena is thinking as she sits sorting her husband's old pictures during that rainy summer. They represent one life but fit together only as an album, something without any intrinsic or necessary order. All this heterogeneity and compartmentalization – his roles as husband, father, philanderer; hers as actress, wife, mother, discreet spouse – is there and acknowledged. For Helena there is acceptance of all this but not yet approval (in this she is still like Johan and Marianne). She tells Gustav that the nice-smelling woman with the décolletage was not one of "Papa's lady friends," only a schoolmate who had twelve children and "grew the size of a house." Gustav in reply notes how he has "always admired the adroit way" she has handled "Papa's amours" (p. 148), suggesting that his mother is still disguising something that was over long ago.

Helena needs to become her own audience and laugh and be warmed by these performances as we are. This is what she did earlier when she remembered her youthful affair with Isak as a "farce by Feydeau" and a love "like strawberries." She is not yet, in Oscar's words to Alexander, gentle enough with people, herself included. For Bergman, this step goes beyond acknowledgment and reconciliation to the shape of life to an awareness of its inherent goodness. Helena is turned in this direction by an event out of the blue: Young Jenny and her little brother bring their grandmother a string of wild strawberries to cheer her up. The emerging smile of growing bewonderment caused by this entirely free and unexpected act brightens Helena's entire world and begins to show her that it is still (as it has always been) a good place to live, changing roles and all. Here she is confounded a second time, not by death and summer made winter, but by life and summer's return. Not all strawberries belong to yesterday.

Conceptually, this unexpected visit is both an instance and emblem of God's grace that is always present and available, and of the little world that has become so distant. It recalls Bergman's earlier visions of "charmed spaces" and his recurring figurations of Madonna and Child, and like them it represents the enduring possibility of something better. But to Helena herself, it shows, through her other grandchildren, just what joyfulness and vitality Fanny and Alexander have lost, and just what is at stake if nothing is done. It is this vision of what could and should be that at last moves her from her mood of melancholy hopelessness.

Thus, though it may at first seem only a nice bit of summer detail or even a sentimental indulgence, this scene – only twenty-five seconds long – is essential for the drama.[29] It occurs after Alexander's punishment and Emilie's visit home, where the desperateness and danger of the situation becomes clear: The law will not let her take the children if she leaves, and neither the bishop nor Alexander will back down. The children enter at the end of Helena's reminiscence over her photographs, which itself begins immediately following Emilie's discovery of Alexander in the attic. In the television version, the cut juxtaposes the three, cinematically identifying Helena as the person who must do something about Alexander's plight if disaster is to be escaped. This she does, though we do not see it happen, and soon thereafter Isak steals Fanny and Alexander back. He could not have acted on his own, and one way or another, Helena must have made sure he understood what was required.

Helena's return to the world is completed with Emilie's invitation to act again in the new theater. What was fractured re-forms itself into a new life, a new set of roles to be played with enthusiasm, as she also becomes a special mentor to Alexander. The final scene of grandmother and grandson together on the sofa recalls the beginning of the Prologue, when Helena calls Alexander to her and out from under the table. The little world is restored, and what was started then now resumes its course.

9. This Wide and Universal Theater[30]

In *Fanny and Alexander,* Bergman achieves something important: a kind of story that addresses the doubts and fears we feel as we face our lives and so often find our identity dispersed into different roles and fragments. It is like the stories of the 1950s, particularly *Wild Strawberries* and *Smiles of a Summer Night,* though its problems seem more modern and its world more embattled. This being Bergman's last "synoptic" film, all the earlier structural elements are present – abandonment, passion, turning, shame, judgment, and vision – now in a form that is explicitly reflective and self-conscious, about both life and its story of life. The two fundamental questions – Who are we? and How can this question be answered? – are confronted through this story-and-metastory-in-one.

It has three central elements. First, as noted earlier, *Fanny and Alexander* includes within itself many other stories, both by following the lives of different characters of many ages, types, and positions and by having many of them tell stories of their own as they try to order and comprehend what has happened to them. Presented within these tales are the main stages and events of life, as well as many of the roles in and out of which people go, each time interpreting them anew. This is a portrait of life as an essentially theatrical space, and its picture is fairly extensive in scope (more than just the "little world") though never complete – almost a catalog of the likelihoods and probabilities of this life.

Second, as also argued earlier, the film discloses something fundamental by which any of these stories can be tested, a bedrock in human experience itself that can be pointed to outside our stories. These experiences can be appreciated as the core of our lives and are, most essentially, human companionship and the pleasure and love that can be found in life itself. They – by their presence or absence – are the terms by which to judge the many answers to the questions of meaning that beset us.

Third, *Fanny and Alexander* shows how these two aspects go together, how in becoming an audience to life without retreating from it one can come to both accept and appreciate it for what it is. Here the theatrical and the real confirm each other, and the understanding that results is a perspective on both life and stories that, though conveyed and disclosed by stories, is not itself a story. This stance of appreciative participant is displayed within the film (from Gustav's gusto to Helena's return to the theater), it is the film's own view of itself, and it is the position its audience must assume as it enables the film to continue. Its emblem, as suggested, is Fanny herself.

Together these elements achieve a comprehensive view of our existence and a mundane wisdom to seek the best it offers. This is a perspective for all perspectives, a standpoint from which youth and old age, self-righteousness and despair, death and birth, ardor and weariness, love and abandonment, parent and child, Hamlet and Abraham and any other character and story, and all the commerce between them, can be observed and understood. Such a story form presents what I have called the geography of the soul, and *Fanny and Alexander* is Bergman's final attempt to provide an encompassing view of this terrain in which we all must live.

Here it is a geography of places rather than one of traveling, as in *The Clowns' Evening, The Seventh Seal,* or *Wild Strawberries.* Initially, these are distinguished – the Ekdahl apartments, their summer house, and the theater, the bishop's residence, Isak's shop and chambers – and represent different aspects and even faculties of life. By the end, however, they are brought more fully together than in any other Bergman film (recalling the "house of the soul" of *Cries and Whispers*). In the Epilogue, the Ekdahl residence includes the extended families of Helena and Emilie, the theater (Alexander's own dramatic productions with Fanny, as well as Emilie's new projects and the scripts of Strindberg), the realms of mystery and art associated with Isak, who has become an even more "official" member of the household (and father-figure to Alexander), and even religion and conscience in the form of Oscar's and the bishop's ghosts (Alexander's other "fathers"). The newer part of the house – Emilie's rooms – is filled with modern paintings and furniture, while the older part – Helena's – has moving statues and ghosts of the past.

So, indeed, *Fanny and Alexander* does stand as a confession of faith and as Bergman's attempt at the "close" of his career to again give both a "reduction, in the metaphysical sense" and a final credo that affirms life and art.[31] The film ends happily, with singing and celebration, parents and children reunited and safe, the villain killed, and plans being made for the future. But compelling as it is, this vision is not quite the same as before, at the end of the 1950s. It is older, a bit more wary, and its dark places are even darker and more disturbing.

In *Wild Strawberries* or *Smiles of a Summer Night,* for instance, people may be selfish and ungenerous, but no one has the sinister threat of the Vergéruses or the palpable maliciousness of Justina (not even in *A Clowns' Evening,* though it is closest). And it now seems that we could as much find ourselves to be like the bishop's dying aunt as like the bishop himself or Emilie or Helena or Alexander. She is "repulsive . . . rotting, a parasite, a monster. Her part will soon be played out . . . a loaf that hasn't risen in the world's batch and it is no use wasting pity on such an utter failure" (p. 187).

This description of the aunt, Elsa Bergius, occurs in the script shortly before Bergman kills her off and is genuinely shocking. Does he think there is no story about her that will reveal her interiority and humanity, that inside she is not a person too? It may be that there are always people left out (Carl and Lydia, perhaps), but they have remained people (the Almans, Evald or Charlotte and Carl-Magnus, or even Vergérus himself), but never hunks of fallen dough. Here, Bergman sounds like Alexander with his father. The world of the 1960s and 1970s have not disappeared in *Fanny and Alexander*, and the need for luck to escape both death and the devil is stronger than ever.

Light and dark go together, and this darkness becomes a necessary part of the story's perspective and the wisdom it provides. A story that shows both can promise nothing more than possibilities.[32] (Remember: Fanny and Alexander are rescued not because this has to happen but because it is the *best story* and the one in which we choose/need to believe.) Thus, for all its joy and genuine affirmation of life, there remains in *Fanny and Alexander* – metaphysically – the same deep neutrality as before. In Bergman's "last testament," failure is as possible as success, and life is the opportunity for either and for both (the hand can caress and strike, make love as well as punish). Still, things *have* turned out for the best.

Fanny and Alexander ends with the face of Alexander as he rests in Helena's lap listening to the words of Strindberg: "Anything can occur. Anything is possible." For the moment, as befits a fairy tale, the wisdom of the old and the creative power of the young join in alliance as Helena and Alexander prepare to enter together their new lives and a world of "new patterns" where, indeed, anything is possible.

10. Final Words

Still, none of this will last, either for the Ekdahls or for Bergman. Though it may be refound again and again, each little world is as mortal as any other form of life. As the film makes clear, the family that has been restored and brought together to celebrate the beginnings of new life will soon be pulled apart again, never to be the same. Gustav's own dreams in particular will be shattered, for he will lose his eldest daughter, his young "mistress," and above all, his granddaughter, the "little empress" he holds in his arms, Helena Viktoria. They are going, against his wishes, to Stockholm to open a milliner's shop and so face and struggle with life them-

185

selves. Will they fare any better than those young adults in that city in Bergman's very first films? There is no reason to think so.

What Gustav has been celebrating does not even last the day. It ends and disappears without any continuing effect, particularly for the children, exactly those for whom it is most especially intended. They want only to get on with their lives, which are going to be played somewhere else with other people. These will be their own and "new." All this is captured in the christening photograph taken at the end of the celebration: Everyone is arranged and posed – the whole family, including Isak and their friends from the theater; the picture freezes, then it fades into gray and white, colorless and already of the past, a picture of something from another time and place, something already over.[33]

Bergman, too, soon adds his own external epilogue to his "last film," putting beside the uplifting cheer and hopefulness of *Fanny and Alexander* a reminder of the 1970s and its moods of sadness and defeat. *After the Rehearsal* (1984) explores the thoughts of a stage director at the end of his career as he prepares a new production of Strindberg's *A Dream Play*, just the piece Helena begins to study for her new life. It is a moment of looking back. All is over, and there is little more that can occur, little that is possible. Even imagination is exhausted. In this final moment, everything – even the world-weary melancholy that afflicted Johan (or Helena) earlier – becomes purified into a desireless acceptance. Life is seen finally as nothing greater than a list of its contents, and understanding as simply the acknowledgment of an inventory: There was this and there was that – emotion, desire, need; love and hate; despair and joy; dreams and fears; coming together and coming apart.

In this vision, life is seen as not even anticlimactic but from a point of ultimate detachment and disinterested observation (like that of a visiting anthropologist). The rage and anger of the 1970s is gone, as is its despair and yearning for answers. Both questions and complaints have been superseded by a simple knowledge: This is what life is, what it will be for others, what it has been for us, and there is nothing more to say. At the end, we are left alone on the stage and the lights go out.

Which is the answer to Bergman's original question about mercy and meaning: Celebration of life, with its possibilities of rebirth and renewal of the future, or acceptance of a gray and sometimes vicious modern world where our greatest peace is as detached and stoic observers? The metaphysics of existence (in which human being is seen as forever constituted by the axis of turning) cannot provide the answer. In the end, Bergman gives us a choice, as he always has before.

Afterwords

Biographical Note

Erik Ingmar Bergman was born early Sunday morning, July 14, 1918, in Uppsala, Sweden, of parents Erik and Karin Bergman. He had an older brother, Dag (later a career diplomat), born in 1914; his sister, Margareta (who became a successful novelist), was born four years later in 1922. His mother (née Karin Åkerblom) had influenza, and Ingmar was apparently sickly and undernourished in these early months. Throughout his life, Bergman seems to have had a somewhat fragile constitution and a nervous disposition. He recalls being fed gruel at the age of one or two and vomiting over everything – "This is probably my very first memory."[1]

Bergman's parents were second cousins, though her family was economically better off and part of the upper-class bourgeoisie that came to replace the landed aristocracy. Both families included pastors and churchmen, and the influence of Lutheran religion went especially deep. Erik Bergman's own father died when he was very young, and Erik was raised by his mother, aunt, and grandmother (Ingmar's grandmother, grand aunt, and great grandmother). Karin's mother (Ingmar's maternal grandmother) deeply opposed the marriage, but in spite of this the two were wed in 1912 after Erik was ordained and given a chaplaincy in a small rural mining community. Before Ingmar was born, Erik accepted the position of curate, or assistant pastor, at the prestigious Hedvig Eleonora Church in Stockholm, and the family moved to the city. In 1924, Erik was appointed chaplain at the royal hospital nearby, Sophiahemmet (where Bergman recalls being locked in the mortuary when ten by the somewhat malicious caretaker),[2] and then parish priest at Hedvig Eleonora in 1934 (where he continued until retiring in 1957). He died April 26, 1970. Karin Bergman had died several years earlier, in March 1966.

Erik Bergman appears to have been a good pastor and a very effective preacher, genuinely loved and admired by his parishioners. Privately, matters were more complicated. He was a disciplinarian (not unusual, of course, for the strict, even oppressive, standards of the time) but also given to sudden changes of temperament and moments of rage. In *Sunday's Children,* the aged Erik, after finding in his deceased wife's secret diary her conclusion that her – their – life was a "fiasco," "a life-fiasco," says to his son: "I couldn't sort this out. What have I done wrong?" After a while Bergman replies: "We were frightened. . . . We were frightened of your fits of rage. . . . It always came so quickly, and sometimes we had no idea why you were shouting at us and hitting us."[3] In addition, there was an undercurrent of domestic (personal and sexual) tension that stressed the parents, leading even to a nervous breakdown for Erik in the mid-1920s. At various times divorce had been considered (at least by Karin), and for a period around 1925 she had an affair with a younger man, which she confessed to her husband. All this was as much as possible hidden from the children, and the affair itself unknown to them until revealed in Karin's diaries after her death.

Nevertheless, much, or even most, of Bergman's childhood and youth appears to have been pleasurable (sometimes even idyllic) and normal (as he remarks, it all *seemed* normal to him). His father was the only male authority in the family, and most of Ingmar's upbringing was by the many women surrounding him, including especially his maternal grandmother. Summers were usually spent in the countryside or at the shore, while in Stockholm he could walk to the theater, the opera, and the moviehouse – which he did often. In 1927, he was given a magic lantern for Christmas and the next year traded "100 lead soldiers" for the movie projector given to Dag "by mistake" by their rich aunt. In the summer of 1934, he spent six weeks on exchange with a minister's family in Germany (there was a second trip later). As a supporter of Hitler, the pastor took the children to a Nazi rally, and Bergman reports being deeply impressed by Hitler's charismatic person. (He later remarks that this was as far as it went. Although there were many Swedish supporters for Hitler throughout the war, little was known clearly about the true consequences of Nazi policies or the camps. Erik Bergman was responsible for helping a number of Jews escape to Sweden, which remained officially neutral.)

While Bergman hated the routine and atmosphere at Palmgren's gymnasium in Stockholm, he was an excellent student and completed his qualification exams in 1937. After a brief time of compulsory military service (excused for stomach distress), he entered Stockholm University, nominally as a student in the literature and art-history departments. He was more interested in the theater and directed his first play (*Outward Bound* by Sutton Vane) in May 1938. This lack of seriousness, and the fact he was regularly sleeping with a fellow student and actress, led to a fierce, physical quarrel with his father and to hitting his mother when she tried to intervene; he immediately left the house, and they did not meet or speak for four years (though some messages and money were sent through a friend). It is clear that these strained family and childhood relationships[4] are one of the sources and subtexts of Bergman's films, though interpretation of this connection is never simple or without many ambiguities and pitfalls.

In the next half-dozen years, Bergman continued to direct, wheedled a production assistant position at the Stockholm Opera, left the university completely in 1940, produced his own play (*The Death of Punch*), joined the script-development department of Svensk Filmindstri in January 1943, married Else Fisher, a dancer (a daughter, Lena, was born that December), and had his first screenplay filmed in the spring of 1944. Released October 2, *Torment* was a critical success, winning a Swedish Film Society "Charlie" for best screenplay (and later in 1946, after the war, a Grand Prix National at Cannes); it also occasioned considerable social debate for its criticism of the Swedish school system.

For Bergman, both careers – in theater and in film, and as writer and director in each – were now launched (as well as his series of marriages and affairs). In April 1944, he accepted appointment as director of the Helsingborg City Theater and the following year directed his first film. Inexperienced and insecure, he was excessively authoritative and peremptory in both spheres, beginning his reputation as the "demon director." Though he soon learned his craft and directed more judiciously, Bergman seems always to have needed a high degree of control over his productions (and even his personal relationships).[5] In the fall of 1946, he became the director of the Gothenburg City Theater. By this time he had also divorced his first wife and remarried, and had an additional daughter and son. This in general became the pattern of Bergman's professional and personal life. While some productions and films were more successful and better received than others (and his own stage plays seem to have been the weakest of his efforts), work of greater and greater consequence was achieved. Some marriages and relationships lasted longer than others, but terms of friendship seemed to remain (or eventually to develop) even after the breakups. Children were cared for by their mothers.[6]

In 1959, Bergman officially joined the Royal Dramatic Theater in Stockholm as one of its regular directors and became its head in 1963 (resigning under some pressure in 1966, though he still continues his association). In 1967 a small house on the island of Fårö in the Baltic Sea (about a hundred miles south of Stockholm) was built for himself and Liv Ullmann, and he has since spent much of his time there. That year, Persona Limited was incorporated in Switzerland to receive income from foreign sales and as a production company for films in Italy provisionally planned with Fellini. His own production company in Sweden, Cinematograph AB, was established the next year. In 1971 he married his fifth wife, Ingrid Karlebo, eleven years younger (just divorced from Count von Rosen); at this point "all other traffic ceased" and his life became more settled and emotionally mature (his "long adolescence had ended"). A close relationship – "something extraordinary" – developed, lasting until her death twenty-four years later in 1995, which Bergman described as the "cruelest thing to happen to him . . . making life itself a heavy burden."[7]

When nothing came of his foreign production plans, Bergman dissolved Persona Limited in 1975 to return the funds to Sweden. The tax authority, however, asserted that it had been a dummy corporation and a tax scam all along. On January 30, 1976, Bergman was taken from a rehearsal in Stockholm of Strindberg's *Dance of Death* for questioning. His apartment was searched and his passport confiscated. Three days later he entered a hospital mental ward (eventually going to Sophiahemmet itself). He stayed for two months, until he decided to stop running and fight back. In March, charges of fraud were dropped, but it was still claimed that he owed back taxes. On April 22, in a letter to Scandinavia's largest evening newspaper, Bergman explained his side of the issue and announced that he was leaving Sweden. He eventually settled in Munich, where he filmed *The Serpent's Egg* and later *From the Life of the Marionettes*. A new production company, Personafilm, was created for *Autumn Sonata*, filmed in Oslo. Bergman also became director at Munich's Residenztheater (fired in 1982 but shortly reinstated). In April 1981, he presented simultaneously (at three theaters) Ibsen's *A Doll's House*, Strindberg's *Miss Julie,* and his own *Scenes from a Marriage.*

The tax case was settled in November 1979, with a general vindication for Bergman (final taxes of only $35,000). Though he had been to Fårö (celebrating his sixtieth birthday with all his children, who before this time had not all been together at one occasion) and even to the mainland a number of times since leaving, Bergman officially ended his exile and returned to Sweden in 1981 for the filming of *Fanny and Alexander,* announced as his "last film." This was a retirement more in word than deed. Bergman has never had an adult life separate from his creative work. For the past twenty years he has devoted himself to the theater, memoirs, and the fictionalized reflection on his parents' lives, and more recently to some television and film work. (See the Filmography, especially note 1.)

Bergman and Existentialism: A Brief Comment

Bergman has often been classed with existentialist writers, especially in more academically inclined criticism. More significant, his films, and particularly the most well-known, such as *The Seventh Seal, Wild Strawberries,* and the trilogy, have been widely examined and discussed in terms of existentialist themes. A number of collections and essays have fruitfully explored this line of interpretation. What I want to do in this short section is raise two questions and offer some reflections on this relationship. First, can we say that Bergman himself is an existentialist? Second, what is the relation of his "world view" as given in the films (and my interpretation of them) to Sartre, Heidegger, and Camus, in particular?

I.

Very little information is available – either from biographers or from Bergman himself – about his intellectual background and antecedents, that is, what he read in his youth or even throughout his life. He "studied" at the university (with courses on drama) and seems widely read in theater and literature, particularly Scandinavian, "long Russian novels," Dickens (which he especially enjoyed), and Shakespeare. In his comments and memoirs, he cites two psychological texts – Eino [Eiono] Kaila's *Psychology of the Personality* (c. 1950) and Arthur Janov's *The Primal Scream* (1970) – as being influential.[8] There is little or no mention of any specifically philosophical texts (except for Nietzsche), and he remarks that he always read slowly and found discursive writing hard to stay with and understand. Plays (and novels) were just the opposite: They immediately connected through their imagery, characters, and action.[9]

The most fundamental influences on Bergman as a thinker/writer/filmmaker seem, first, his own life and especially childhood–adolescence; second, Lutheranism, both as practiced at home and preached weekly by his father at church services; and third, Strindberg (whose plays and other writings he came to know early on and for which he felt a particular affinity). In addition, there were various ideas "in the air" at the time of his more advanced schooling and throughout the 1940s (most certainly including the French existentialists). One classmate recalls Bergman ardently reading and espousing Nietzsche,[10] who, at least in a quite summary form, would be one of the liberal, intellectual currencies of the time. Little of Nietzsche seems present in Bergman's work, though he perhaps thought of himself as a kind of Overman (*Übermensch*) exempt from ordinary rules, particularly as an artist (his inbred Lutheran conscience would always spoil that), but at this level it is hard to distinguish this from ordinary egoism and self-centered insecurity. For instance, there seems no informative application of a distinction like the Dionysian–Apollonian to Bergman's work – so central, for example, to Thomas Mann, and one of the primary critical categories of the first part of this century. Bergman's films focus again and again on certain kinds of personal relationship and experience, never really on larger-scale entities, whether these be art, politics, or social structures, except as they are experienced by and impinge upon individuals.

Also a part of this intellectual atmosphere (especially prior to WWII) is the prominence of materialism and scientific reductionism, or, more exactly, a cultural conflict between the claims (and successes) of science and the claims of religion, in particular, and "spirituality" in general. Though certainly not new, this modern conflict, particularly in Europe, was propelled by the nineteenth-century successes of, especially, biology (evolution) and medicine (vaccination, sterilization), and ultimately physics. There was an optimism that science would lead to the control and hence improvement of life, and a more theoretical reductionism that the only true entities of understanding and analysis were physical ones. This seems to be a view of which Bergman himself has always been suspicious, and the conflict is posed throughout his films. It is in part the contrast between Jöns and Antonius Block in *The Seventh Seal,* and it is the subject of difference and dispute between Sara's two suitors (between whom she cannot choose) in *Wild Strawberries.* Bergman himself can choose, at least when the choice is between science and poetry (as, perhaps a replacement for religion and an antidote for science – at least, when represented by Isak Borg, himself a doctor now doing medical research). In later films, science becomes both darker and clearly not an answer. In the "psychiatric" films of the 1970s, it is where one turns when there are no real answers or solutions, something that can achieve behavior control as a last resort (good for the rest of us but not the patient, and so a failure).

One of the companion beliefs of this scientific materialism was atheism: Modern physics and biology allowed no place for a transcendent

God, creation, or providence. Here, scientific culture and Nietzsche coincided (without paying attention to Nietzsche's rather different reasons) in the belief that "God is dead." Bergman's own version of this, both in his films and as he recounts his own life, seems fundamentally psychological (in a nonmaterialist way) and personal. There is little analysis, or even citation, of causes (not even Dostoyevsky's accusations in "The Grand Inquisitor," though echoes of them and "the problem of evil" appear from time to time). Rather, God is something people cannot, or even just do not, believe in any more; this is modernity and in coping with it, they are thrown back on themselves and, like it or not, other people. Nietzsche's broader analysis is absent, and for Bergman recourse to the Overman (in its common popular interpretation as a "super-man" who achieves a true self through his "will to power")[11] does not occur as a solution.

Kaila's psychology, so positively cited by Bergman and summarized as "Each man does what he needs to do," may have these Nietzschean tones of someone who can rise above life and master it in his or her own way. But there has been almost no discussion of how this "psychology of needs" really applies in Bergman's films, if it does. If anything, it points to what turns out to be a kind of defeated egoism in the character of Evald in *Wild Strawberries,* who seems to quote Kaila in defense of his refusal to accept Marianne's pregnancy,[12] but in fact offers only the excuse of, as Marianne says, a coward afraid to live (itself a kind of Nietzschean charge without any of the Nietzschean background). While Bergman himself may feel an affinity for Evald and the force of his own "needs," there is always more, as the context of *Wild Strawberries* and Bergman's films in general makes clear. Egoism may remain a deep strand of human psychology (with a concomitant "will to power"), but it is not all that there is, either in the films or Bergman's own life.

In Bergman's own case, the struggle with religious faith, perhaps because fundamentally psychological, lasted a long time. In *Sunday's Children,* which takes place when he is about eight, Bergman describes himself as even then an atheist (think of Alexander), and this seems to be how he continued to *believe* but not what he was able to *feel* or *feel comfortable with* until much later. The sense of sin and guilt as transgression (and the accompanying requirement of a kind of perfection) attached itself to all aspects of his life, independently of his disbelief in their supporting background system (persisting as a kind of *residual* guilt). Only with the making of *Winter Light,* he says, was he able to free himself psychologically (emotionally) from this oppression, and then God – alive or dead – disappeared. Though he articulates this finally won freedom as the conclusion that "we are the makers of our own meaning," this was not a new truth just discovered but something known or even believed for a long time that was then at last really felt and accepted – accepted as a result of some process of struggle largely occurring unawares (grace?) but not as a form of "existential" choice.[13]

In Kierkegaard the problem of religious doubt (and so the *feeling* that God is at least absent, if not dead) is central (as it is for Christian faith generally). It is a darkness that any believer must endure and transcend. As both Scandinavia's major philosopher and internal critic of the Lutheran Church, and one who enjoyed a revival of attention after WWI, Kierkegaard might be expected to be an influence here, but this does not seem to be the case. There is no indication that Bergman read any Kierkegaard or that Kierkegaard was a topic of interest to Erik Bergman or in the household.[14] And when a specific reference might be in play in the films, notably with respect to Abraham's sacrifice of Isaac (or readiness thereto), a different, non-Kierkegaardian tack is taken: Abraham is ignored or replaced (negated) by moving to Sara/Sarah as the "caretaker" of Isak/Isaac in *Wild Strawberries* or to Emilie as both the caretaker of Alexander (and Fanny) and the Holy Mother, again in place of the bishop/Christ. Kierkegaard's story of Abraham is thus turned on its head: Abraham is not the focal point but a destructive wrong turn (and certainly not a hero of faith).

Some writers have interestingly related Kierkegaard's thought to Bergman's films, for example, Richard A. Blake's discussion in terms of the three stages of development in *Either/Or* (1843): the aesthetic, the ethical, and the religious.[15] If the aesthetic is more generally the evidence of sensual and personal experience, the ethical is an awareness of a context beyond this. However, the religious – as defined by any kind of "leap of faith" or move to the "transcendental" in some form – is rejected from the beginning by Bergman (as we saw with his account of Abraham), both in the films and personally. And the ethical – as both a realization and perhaps affirmation of one's dependence on others (whether only as object of humiliation or as source of something that helps and sustains, as in love and friendship, or even as just someone with whom to share life so as not to be alone) – seems always to fall back toward the aesthetic, the realm of feeling and experience rather than principle or moral duty or some more abstract realization, where, if anything, people are (rightly) substituted for God.

The place of the psychological is perhaps the crucial issue in how one classifies Bergman the person with respect to being an existentialist or not (as distinct from whether one can provide existentialist interpretations of his films). In his account of his mother's infidelity, one sees more clearly what may be the main question for Bergman himself: What hold does our constitution (something more than but including character) have on us (no matter how it came about)? How does it relate to and constrain our freedom? (In Lutheranism, this is the "conflict" between the doctrines of predestination and the possibility of sin insofar as the latter requires a measure of free choice). It is posed by Karin Bergman (as *written* by Ingmar sixty-five years later) as whether to tell her husband Erik of the affair she has had (and is still having) with a younger theology student. She says that she cannot, for she knows how Erik will react, that he won't be able to take it, that he is both too insecure and in need of control, and that things will be far worse if she does (see the Biographical Note about Erik's unpredictability and rages). Her favorite uncle, Jacob, also a minister, counsels – and indeed, as her confessor, requires – that she tell him. There are reasons for this that have to do with truth, the difficulty (and falseness) of living a lie, and what is owed to others, especially in a marriage; but relevant here is Jacob's assertion not to underestimate Erik and his power of choice, or his ability to rise to the occasion.[16] If one has already read, or seen, the first two parts of Bergman's "family tryptic," one shares Karin's fears and feels an ominous sense of disaster. How can Erik be – become – such a different person than he has been? He behaves differently at home than at church. How, why should this change? Can psychology be trumped by awareness of what is right or better, and by an act of will?

I think Bergman's own feeling on this is "in principle, maybe, but not likely" – people rarely change, or act out of character, though they may struggle as they stay the same. This is what happens time and again in the films (though in my account I have emphasized the *possibility* of acting otherwise, and indeed of changing), from Antonius Block in *The Seventh Seal* to Maria in *Cries and Whispers*. In the case of Bergman's father, it is what happened too, though not as soon or in as violent a way as Karin fears. Erik cannot forgive, but rather than raging, he cuts her off emotionally and withdraws into himself while asserting an even greater (both suffocating and threatening) control. ("In any divorce the children will go to me.") With his nervous breakdown, now binding himself to Karin as her dependent and an (always) ill, mentally precarious husband to whom she must tend (she is a trained nurse), Erik secures his domination over her – until death do them part – in a loveless marriage. This result, as bad as or worse than Karin predicted, is fully in character.

For Bergman, what "makes us tick" is, I think, beyond our understanding and rarely do we succeed (or even really want) to change it. Change

195

is possible but just saying that, or even realizing its need and "choosing," is not enough. Something below the surface must happen, too, and perhaps it will always be the case that other people will also play a necessary (loving, nurturing) role in any "conversion." I've continually put these points in as psychological a way as possible, as I think Bergman would do himself, but this may conflict both with other things he sometimes says and (perhaps often) with aspects of the films themselves. This would only show that being a person is much more complex than we can say, and that Bergman is an intuitive thinker not a systematic one: a thinker who, even with his psychologizing, seems always to return to the fundamental categories – even if secularized, transformed, or resisted – of Lutheran Christianity, not those of any other modern "ism."[17]

II.

Though I don't think Bergman can himself be said to be an existentialist, the pervasiveness of his Lutheran background, with its emphasis on both determination (facticity) and sin (choice and freedom), and his almost exhaustive attention to our inner lives and our struggles, with their sense and senselessness, certainly make him a "conversational partner" and ground a special affinity that goes beyond the fact that existentialism, as a coherent and important philosophical perspective, should be able to illuminate nearly any significant literary or filmic work. But while there may be this shared ground, Bergman's own account often goes in a different direction than what is found in classic existentialist texts.

Perhaps symptomatic of this, it is notable – given Bergman's own remarks about the relative accessibility of literary versus discursive writing, coupled with the prominence of stories, novels, and plays as forms of existentialist expression in the 1930s, 1940s, and 1950s (particularly in French) – that Bergman has directed no play by Sartre, Beckett, or Ionesco, and only farces by Anouilh; the exception is Camus's *Caligula* in 1946. He has thus avoided the dominant existential and absurdist drama of his time,[18] preferring Shakespeare, Molière, the American "psychologists" Albee and Williams and later O'Neill, as well as Strindberg, Ibsen, and other Scandinavians. This is not just a preference for a kind of realism, for many of his productions (as well as films) have a fantastic, nonrealist dimension to them. (He has produced Strindberg's *A Dream Play* five times.)

For instance, his very first play as a student director was the American playwright Sutton Vane's *Outward Bound* (1923). In it, passengers discover themselves on a boat set to sail but don't remember how they got there or know where they're going. In fact, they are dead, and this is the beginning of the "afterlife." Where they're going turns out to be a continued version of where they were – the same world, with some alteration. The good continue on essentially as they were; the bad have their lives reordered and are in effect placed in the charge of the good. They must either change or else endure an indefinite misery now knowingly living their failure. *No Exit* (1944) is a much better play with related themes: The "afterlife" is really this world, and hell is other people, themes especially congenial to Bergman. (The portrait of the Almans in *Wild Strawberries* is in effect a miniature *No Exit*.) But two things are missing from Sartre's play that are present in Vane's: There is no good or immanent "heaven," and self-knowledge – Sartre's existential awareness – does not offer a second chance, at least for the characters in the play (precisely because they are dead and so have no future).

This is in part a difference of tone, for the point of *No Exit* to its audience is precisely that *they* are not dead and hence are always able to change and always rechoosing (or rejecting) past choices. But what is absent in Sartre is the specific idea of a second chance, of a decisive moment of self-confrontation where one's life may be turned around and changed from living death to living life (as in, for instance, *Wild Strawberries*). Sartre's concern is taking responsibility for one's life, whatever it might be, not any specific change beyond this; Bergman's concern is, in its secular, "immanentized" form, salvation: a new, better life.

There are three aspects to this difference. First, certainly in *The Flies*, Sartre describes, and advocates, a conversion – to truth, to responsibility, to authenticity. But in existentialist texts it is never clear that this is more than a formal commitment to freedom as such, more than acting in the terrible awareness of the utter groundlessness (arbitrariness, absurdity) of one's situation and choice. This suggests that the content of the choice could be anything (or at least almost anything – for Genet, it is crime; for Orestes, justice/punishment), as long as it derives from a choice made self-knowingly, without regret or excuse, a choice that is truly free. For Bergman, there is good and evil in the world, in its (our) very nature. One's second chance is not just (or really) for an "authentic" life but for a better one, in which one becomes a better person.[19]

Second, "bad faith" (living, and even in some sense choosing to live, a lie) is not as central a notion for Bergman as it is for Sartre. There are parallels, and much of facing judgment for Bergman is seeing and confronting the falsehoods of one's life. But this is never enough; it only turns one around toward something (and someone) else. In *Cries and Whispers*,

Maria afterward retreats to her non-self-awareness (her lies); this is wrong not because it is falsity and bad faith (and so *nonresponsibility*), but because it leads to loneliness and so condemns both herself and her sister (and her husband and her daughter . . .). Karin does not retreat; she knows and is radically self-aware (and responsible); her mutilation of herself before her husband is an overt recognition of this and an authentic act. But she remains miserable, alone, and filled with hate and despair. The recognition, and even the act, does not free her, as it does Orestes. Life for Orestes will not be easy, and he may have future doubts (since he must act over and over again in an unaccepting world), but in his freedom there is a heady satisfaction – a peace. Karin can find no peace and cannot escape her loneliness even though she has tried, and it is now not her fault. (Contrast Agda in *The Clowns' Evening*, who is at rest but also dead in her isolation.)

Third, there are no "existential heroes" in Bergman, no champions of freedom or rebellion. Part of this is the priority of loneliness and the need for other people (and hence the centrality of love and touch) over falsity/bad faith/inauthenticity in Bergman. The fundamental structure of turning relates one to the other as needful of them (as well as giving or taking) and hence as incomplete without them. Orestes (like Mathieu in Sartre's *Roads to Freedom* series of 1945–9) does not need other people (not in the same way), though he does need (or certainly chooses) an audience and a cause (freedom, then justice). Orestes, Sartre, and Beauvoir have something to promulgate aggressively (and "convert" others to). They can also stand alone, in their truth, as warriors in this battle. Others may need them, but they don't *need* others to be authentic (though they do need them to make, or remake, the common world they must share). Camus's Caligula can also stand alone in his (negative) rebellion against life's absurdity – its inherent meaninglessness and sheer neutrality – and be a guide to others to rebel themselves. But for Bergman, such freedom is not and cannot be such a cause.[20]

We can now begin to see why, and to discern what may be the most fundamental difference between Bergman and Sartre (as well as Camus, and perhaps the early Heidegger). Much of the existentialist picture – captured by Heidegger's notion of "throwness" – is that one is interjected into the world as something different from it (a *pour soi* not an *en soi*), and thus is in it as a kind of alien, not the same as it. One has "fallen in" to something different than oneself (or abruptly woken up to see for the first time who and what and where one is and that one is different, merely as a human being). One recognizes oneself as a stranger. But Bergman's sense of things is different: One's fundamental experience is of being abandoned, and the ontology of the axis of turning is both the seeking for others and the awareness of silence where they have *withdrawn* (and hence were before). What is fundamental is not strangeness but in fact a kind of familiarity, that entailed in loss and absence. This is not the experience of nothingness as underlying or even being a constituent part of existence, nor of nonmeaning simply in the sense of *just* being there (without reason, like Sartre's chestnut roots in *Nausea*), but of silence as the absence of what one once heard (the "something important that someone had said" at the end of *Shame*).

The world, or our condition, is thus not something to rebel against or to transform aggressively by decisive action; it is something to listen to. This tension is apparent in *The Seventh Seal*. There is a decisive action – the knight distracts Death so "the spirit of man" can escape – but this does not save *him*, for he does not comprehend what has (always) been before him: the companionship of the wild strawberries. He does not *hear* what his own life has to say to him and so dies in a wretched silence of his own making. (This picture is perhaps closest now to Heidegger's later notion of *gelassenheit* – an openness and listening to being – but without any notion of the transcendental or beyond-human; one turns not toward being, or even the world, but toward particular persons.)

What seems central in Bergman is an openness (a willingness to see from a perspective outside of oneself, and so to see oneself along with others) that enables one to find and recognize the images that provide a guiding vision of what can and should be, and an accompanying persistence in remaining turned toward them and one's others (shown, for instance, in different ways by both Märta and Tomas in *Winter Light*: Märta by her refusal to abandon Tomas to his loneliness and self-pity, and Tomas by his continuance with the forms of the church, i.e., the rite of communion as a kind of prayer and hope).[21] In *Wild Strawberries* this is what Isak must do if his relationship to Evald (and Marianne) is to be really repaired; in *Scenes from a Marriage,* it is the carrying on by Marianne and Johan over many years and ruptures of a relationship that was/is genuine (both the obverse of Karin and Maria in *Cries and Whispers* and the response to silence that Block cannot find). In theological terms, this is the openness to grace that must precede it. Only in the later Heidegger is there some version of this openness and its accompanying notions of grace and gift, but they are radically non–person-centered.

This finally explains in a more theoretic way Bergman's lack of interest in the political and social, at least in his films, in contrast to Sartre, Camus, or Beauvoir. It is the difference between an ontology of freedom versus an ontology of abandonment. Freedom for the existentialist always has a material manifestation – my freedom, in my acts, seeks to (re)make the world; as such, it both impinges upon and involves, and so ultimately requires, yours to act with it. To be fully free I must have a free world, not just "internally" (that is, in each individual's recognition of their own inescapable responsibility) but socially and politically. Thus political freedom (and so politics) is the cause of causes (the proper ontic expression of this ontology). For Bergman, and the ontology of abandonment, the social and political world is secondary (and its most fundamental need, as indicated by *Shame*, is respect, not freedom). *Our* most fundamental need is to turn toward and to be turned toward; this state cuts across all political conditions and is not more realized in one rather than another.

A few further remarks about death and humiliation. One thing the encounter with death does is direct one back to his or her actual life. In Bergman, this is often followed by a renewed appreciation and sense of *being alive*. This isn't really the point for Heidegger or Sartre (or the only point for Bergman).[22] When Heidegger introduces the topic in *Being and Time* (see esp. §§52–53), he is addressing the question of what kind of completeness *Dasein* – human existing – can have, since, unlike things, its very being includes an open and indefinite future. Death[23] – as the always present "possibility of the impossibility of any possibilities at all" – delineates that wholeness as an existing constantly to be cared for (this is "being-toward-death"). This awareness *may* make the present more precious, but it most of all raises the question of self – Who am I? – and of responsibility – Who will I be? I am what I yet will be, what I yet will do. In Bergman, this is crystallized as the moment of judgment in which one is given oneself as *not yet dead* and so given a second chance. And it reinforces Bergman's sense of both the finality of our finiteness (the lack of anything beyond this life) and the immanence of any of life's measures.

For Sartre, death is not central, but questions of unity and wholeness are. One development of this line of reflection was "existential analysis" in which a person's life was to be understood as playing out what Sartre termed a "fundamental project" that at some decisive point they *have* chosen.[24] Jean Genet, on Sartre's analysis, does not as a youth *realize* that he is a thief but rather at that point *chooses* this as *who he will be/become*. My own way of putting Erik Bergman's response to his wife's confession (see end of §i, above) verges on being such an account. All it needs is reference to some underlying project in which Erik is engaged as his way of being-in-the-world, a project that is fundamentally deliberate and not just the result of "needs" or other psychological forces. For Erik, it would include the *intent* to control others by being weak and thereby forcing them to behave as he wants or needs. But Bergman never moves to this level of intentionality (or internal unity) in the explanation of our behavior (and similarly shrugs off the suggestion that he might be either Freudian or Jungian in his approach).[25] Rather, his true concern is not with this kind of unity but with the *moral* unity of what a life comes to: Has it turned toward or away from others, has it succeeded or failed at life itself, has it sought what it can see to be the better? In his mother's terms in her diary, this is whether ours has been a "life-fiasco" or not; in Alman's terms in *Wild Strawberries*, it is whether we have been incompetent or not.

For Sartre, the idea that death, in ending our existence, completes our being has special difficulties. As indicated in *No Exit*, death renders one not just "ended" but also an object now unalterably defined by the "look" of the other. Since the dead can no longer act to control or even resist such interpretation, who they are has become subject to (whatever) interpretation others now choose to give. This is the final outcome of what is for Sartre a constant battle between consciousnesses. It is the nature of consciousness to turn others into objects by interpreting them and investing them with particular descriptions and significances, while at the same time trying to resist and counteract similar attempts by others. This is a game of dominance and control, even though false at its heart, since no (living) person is or can be an object. As a *pour soi* ("for itself") it has a future and can always act/change: Its "existence precedes its essence." Yet this struggle remains for Sartre a game we cannot escape, and consequently it is hard for him to account for something shared between persons – love, friendship, companionship, and especially the need to turn toward and be turned toward. For Sartre, we seem always turned away, even when we might cooperate on a political level, and as a result are almost necessarily and unremediably alone. For Bergman, we neither are nor have to be.

There is a complication, however. Since it is a common world, for my interpretation ("look") to prevail (or even last) it needs, if not confirmation, at least nonresistance or noncontradiction from others (hence the power of rebellion, for instance). In this regard, for Sartre the weak have an ultimate power over the strong – to look back at them, expressing their own subjectivity and thus showing the dominators' inability to control where it most matters. One cannot make the other an "object" without that person's cooperation (and even then it's very dicey). At the extremes, the torturer needs the assent of the tortured and is defeated by his or her refusal. The more ordinary form of this struggle is humiliation; but here,

I think, Bergman makes clear the way that Sartre's account (and perhaps the more general dialectic of master and slave derived from Hegel, at least when moved from classes to individuals) is wrong (or at least significantly limited). For Bergman, the humiliator does not need the complicitous look of his victim: The latter can be beaten to a pulp, with no look at all, or still glare ferociously or defiantly back. What the humiliator needs is the look of an audience – other soldiers, other actresses, admiring women. Against a gang, victims may indeed be powerless and completely vulnerable, as shown by the shore and circus scenes of A Clowns' Evening.

Finally, there is the matter of shame itself, connected in Sartre to the look of the other catching us when we wish to remain hidden (spying through the keyhole, for instance). This is also a way of thinking about God and about the sources of guilt (whether the looking other is transcendent or simply a parent). But for Bergman, the issue here is really two things. First, the look of the other, insofar as it also humiliates (or even perhaps just judges), produces not guilt so much as anger and hate (and it is rather love, or being loved, that produces guilt). Second, shame, in its most morally proper sense, is a recognition (a vision) of the better and the failure of the present with respect to it – not embarrassment at being caught and seen doing what "one ought not to." This kind of shame is absent from the dialectic of control so central to Sartre and at the heart of his account of interpersonal relations.

Thus finally, with respect to the existentialists, Bergman seems furthest from Sartre, where one might initially expect a closer agreement. He shares some features with particularly the later Heidegger but only to a limited extent. He may in the end be closest to Camus, particularly with respect to tone and in his political championship of the "ordinary person" in the face of social and state violence. This closeness is perhaps greatest in The Plague, which one might envision as an earlier version of Shame.[26]

A Note on Woody Allen

Vincent Canby, perhaps unfortunately, described Woody Allen as "America's Ingmar Bergman" (New York Times, April 24, 1977). Allen's own admiration for Bergman is well known, as is his use of various Bergman motifs and images, sometimes seriously, sometimes as comedic reference (most notably in Love and Death [1975]). Another Woman (1988) is an almost scene-by-scene version of Wild Strawberries, and Interiors (1978) and September (1987) are attempts at a serious Bergman-style drama. How close are their world views? Although the idea of a second chance and the transforming possibilities of self-knowledge persistently occur throughout Allen's work, I think he is much less optimistic about their effect and not really committed to the value or need for such change (or its realistic possibility). In Bergman – surprisingly, in fact – there is a dogged commitment to relationships and marriage; in Allen, these come and go, continually reconfiguring themselves. (Almost no Allen character has not been divorced – often more than once.) There is a kind of seriality and hence underlying solitariness that permeates his stories, its depth masked by the comedy. In *September*, I think, all this is out in the open. Here, everyone is mismatched and all loves are unrequited, unreciprocated (Howard loves Lane who loves Peter who loves Stephanie who is married . . .). Here, our personal world is another version of the universe itself: Neither "matter one way or the other. It's all random. Originating aimlessly out of nothing, and eventually vanishing forever. . . . Just a temporary convulsion. . . . Haphazard, morally neutral, and unimaginably violent" (Lloyd to Peter). In the face of this, all notions of morality seem to collapse and lose their hold; all that remains is desire (cultured and civilized desire, perhaps, but only desire nonetheless). "The heart wants what it wants,"[27] and there is finally no other measure of things. In *Crimes and Misdemeanors* (1989), perhaps Allen's central film, the notion of sin (and right and wrong) is replaced by expediency and what individuals can afford in their own economy of desires. Judah escapes all punishment for the murder of his (now inconvenient) mistress – internal, external, or divine. Does Allen approve of this? Does the film? Maybe not, but the point seems to be that that's the way things are and we need to accept this; or perhaps sublimate it. Curiously, rather than making his account more optimistic, Allen's recourse to comedy makes it even darker and more despairing: at bottom and in its heart darker and more despairing than Bergman ever is. (Hope becomes a useful illusion like the enchanted wood in *A Midsummer Night's Sex Comedy* [1982], the cinema in *The Purple Rose of Cairo* [1985], or an alternate world like the circus in *Shadows and Fog* [1992].) At the very core of Allen's world view, laughter is a diversion, and this diversion – rather than love or companionship – is the best we can hope for.[28]

Notes

Preface

1. These and other details are from Peter Cowie, *Ingmar Bergman: A Critical Biography* (New York: Charles Scribner's Sons, 1982) [hereafter Cowie], pp. 26–31. Also see Frank Gado, *The Passion of Ingmar Bergman* (Durham, N.C.: Duke University Press, 1986) [hereafter Gado]; Birgitta Steene, *Ingmar Bergman: A Guide to References and Resources* (Boston: G. K. Hall, 1987) [hereafter Steene]; and Hubert I. Cohen, *Ingmar Bergman: The Art of Confession* (New York: Twayne, 1993), for additional (and more extensive) biographical information.

2. Beginning with *Through a Glass Darkly* in 1961, Bergman wrote all the films of the 1960s and 1970s except *All These Women* (done with Erland Josephson) and *The Magic Flute* (which significantly alters the Mozart–Schikaneder original).

3. This theme is present from the beginning in Bergman's work. See his first plays, especially *Jack among the Actors* (written in 1942/3) in which God is a bored puppeteer (and theater director).

4. See Steene, p. 30.

5. Gade reports that Bergman was moved in this direction after a director friend complained about his "depressing stories" (p. 495).

6. Quote by Ullmann, *Poughkeepsie Journal*, Aug. 12, 1999. *Faithless* has been followed by *Sarabande* (2003), said now to be his (really) last film.

7. While it is clearly Bergman's vision and account of our existence that is given form and voice in his films, one should never underestimate the artistry and contribution of his collaborators (and his ability to involve them as co-makers of his art). These include the actors Gunnar Björnstrand, Eva Dahlbeck, Harriet Andersson, Max von Sydow, Bibi Andersson, Ingrid Thulin, Anders Ek, Gunnel Lindblom, Liv Ullmann, and Erland Josephson, as well as the cinematographers Gunnar Fischer (twelve films) and Sven Nykvist (twenty films, including all those in color). Even for someone as singular and demanding as Bergman, filmmaking remained a cooperative art.

1. Introduction: The Geography of the Soul

1. *Through a Glass Darkly* (1961), *Winter Light* (1963), and *The Silence* (1963). See *Three Films by Ingmar Bergman*, trans. Paul Britten Austin (New York: Grove Press, 1970) [hereafter *Three Films*], p. 7. See D. Z. Phillips, *Through a Darkening Glass: Philosophy, Literature and Cultural Change* (Notre Dame, Ind.: University of Notre Dame Press, 1982), chap. 9, for another account of the trilogy and the idea of a reduction. For an early version of this introduction, see Jesse Kalin, "Ingmar Bergman's Contribution to Moral Philosophy," *International Philosophical Quarterly* 17:1 (March 1977), pp. 170–81.

2. Or more specifically: "*Through a Glass Darkly* – certainty achieved. *Winter Light* – certainty unmasked. *The Silence* – God's silence – the negative impression." *Three Films*, p. 7. These are retrospective characterizations since Bergman did not originally plan the three films "as a suite. They just followed one another." See Hubert I. Cohen, *Ingmar Bergman: The Art of Confession* (New York: Twayne, 1993), p. 171.

3. A figure of God in the form of the Holy Spirit, presiding over the events below. See Revelation 8:1.

4. First Corinthians 13:12.

5. In *The Seventh Seal* and *Cries and Whispers* death is final, though the knight postpones it long enough to do the significant deed for which he longs. In each film, however, there are central protagonists that live – Jof and Mia with little Mikael, and the sisters Elizabeth and Maria with Anna the housekeeper. Death is also final in *Shame*, which is discussed at length in Chapter 5.

6. It is unclear whether Bergman thinks God is dead or simply absent (or even absence itself). Perhaps they come to the same thing. In either event, God is now silent, and it is this silence that is so devastating in *The Seventh Seal, The Virgin Spring*, the trilogy, *Cries and Whispers,* and even *Fanny and Alexander*, the films where God is a central theme.

7. *Three Films*, pp. 84–7.

8. Frost's drunkenness in *Naked Night* is such distractedness, a way of silencing the silence.

9. And to Emilie as well in *Fanny and Alexander.* She leaves the theater, too, and, in an effort to find her true face, marries the bishop.

10. If one is not a coward, as Marianne suggests to Evald in *Wild Strawberries* (*Four Screenplays of Ingmar Bergman* [*Smiles of a Summer Night, The Seventh Seal, Wild Strawberries, The Magician*], trans. Lars Malström and David Kushner [New York: Simon & Schuster, 1960] [hereafter *Four Screenplays*], p. 272).

11. The line from Auden is from "September 1, 1939"; *Three Films*, p. 86.

12. See *Three Films*, pp. 45, 47; 85, 82; 136.

13. It is to emphasize this interdependence that Bergman usually binds people together by ties of family (parent–child), of marriage (spouse, lover), and even of profession (doctor–patient, minister–parishioner).

14. *The Best Intentions* begins with the young Henrik Bergman (the fictional representation of Bergman's own father) summoned to a hotel room by his

paternal grandfather. When Henrik's father died, his well-off grandparents refused to provide needed aid to the young mother and her child. His grandfather asks Henrik to go to the hospital where his grandmother is dying, ridden by guilt, and reconcile with her. Henrik resists: "Tell that woman she chose her life and her death. She will never have my forgiveness. Tell her that I despise her on behalf of my mother, just as I loathe you and people like you. I will never become like you." Yet, of course, in this refusal he has. (Trans. Joan Tate [New York: Arcade Publishing, 1993], p. 7.) Bergman's behavior toward his own long-estranged father was different. After his mother's death in 1966, he began weekly visits to the then eighty-three-year-old man. There was no reconciliation and a reluctance on Bergman's part to enter conversations that brought up the past, while at the same time his father seemed unable to understand what had happened or to escape his profound loneliness. Bergman remarked that "When he died, we were friends" (see John Lahr, "Profile: The Demon-Lover – After Six Decades in Film and Theatre, Ingmar Bergman Talks about His Family Secrets and the Invention of Psychological Drama," *New Yorker* 75:13 [May 31, 1999], p. 66 ff., at p. 69), but this is perhaps not accurate. At the time of his father's death in 1970, Bergman describes himself as having no feeling: "I look at him and think I ought to forget, but I don't forget. I ought to forgive, but I forgive nothing. I could have felt a little affection, but I can't bring myself to feel any affection. He's *a stranger*" (*Sunday's Children*, trans. Joan Tate [New York: Arcade Publishing, 1993], p. 150). Yet twenty or thirty years later, as he works through these relationships and his family history, something changes, a connection is made with some measure of understanding and affection, and the old feelings pass: "I hold out my hand and ask him for forgiveness, *now*, at this moment" (*Sunday's Children*, pp. 151–2; see also pp. 85–91, 123–9, and 148–51).

15. In Märta's case (*Winter Light*), this has caused her to hound Tomas (like God after a sinner) because the good, or how life can be, requires him to be different. This is her discovery of love (and his possibility of grace).

16. An ending Bergman himself later regrets. See G. William Jones, ed., *Talking with Ingmar Bergman* (Dallas: SMU Press, 1983), p. 67.

17. Karin in *Cries and Whispers* overcomes her fears, promising with her sister that now things will be different, only to be betrayed the next morning by Maria who hardly remembers what has happened.

18. From Karin in *Through a Glass Darkly* and Ester in *The Silence* to Agnes in *Cries and Whispers*. *Three Films*, pp. 52–4 and 117–18: "She [Ester] whimpers and swears by turns: it's so humiliating all this, I'm just not going to put up with such humiliation . . . oh God, help me, let me die at home at least."

19. Such references in Bergman first appear in the trilogy with Jonas's fear of the Chinese's nuclear capability and in the setting of *The Silence*, some foreign city under curfew with tanks in the streets. Death begins to shift from a figure that confronts us personally as individuals (as in *The Seventh Seal*, even though it is the time of plague) to an impersonal, global force. In *The Seventh Seal* humiliation is felt at the hands of others – the mob in the tavern – not from nature itself or the plague.

20. Followed closely by *The Rite* and *From the Life of the Marionettes*.

21. Cowie, p. 343. This applies, he says, "just as the journey matters more than the arrival." But for Bergman the pleasure and joy *of* the journey *is* the arrival – life does not exist somewhere else.

22. "They burned with a clear flame and there was nothing particularly terrible about it, because it was so beautiful" (*"Persona" and "Shame": The Screenplays of Ingmar Bergman,* trans. Keith Bradfield [New York: Grossman Publishers, 1972], pp. 188–9). Beautiful perhaps, but terrible, too, for Eva's last name is Rosenberg, and the rose itself is a symbol of the Madonna, the Holy Mother; Eva's dream in *Shame* replaces Jof's vision in *The Seventh Seal,* and now the viewer of Bergman's work must consider them together.

23. This is in fact the position of Thomas and Birgitta as they show the film in the attic of his aunt's house, and while it brings them closer together and perhaps saves him, it is not enough to finally keep her from taking her life.

2. The Primal Seen: *The Clowns' Evening*

1. The most egregious example of this practice is *Prison* (1949), which is still shown on videotape as *The Devil's Wanton.* Even now the video cover for *Naked Night* exploits Harriet Andersson's near undress, as did the preceding *Summer with Monika,* with its brief scenes of nudity. (Some distributors added clips of nudist bathing to enhance this appeal of "soft pornography" – see Steene, p. 70.) Remember that at this time it was something of a scandal when *The Moon Is Blue* (Otto Preminger, 1953), a perfectly innocuous Hollywood comedy, openly used the word "pregnant."

2. Especially in comparison to Britain's *Sawdust and Tinsel,* though that picks up on the film's juxtaposition of circus and theater. Regarding the English-language release titles, Gado writes: "Aware of the fact that neither of these comes close to the original, several critics have referred to the film as *The Night of the Clowns* – an exact translation of its French title, though a shade away from the Swedish" (p. 513). His translation is *Evening of the Jesters,* but I think *The Clowns' Evening* is better. It retains the meaning of *afton* as evening rather than night, and renders *gycklarnas* as clowns, which is precisely what they are – circus clowns.

3. This is a more primal version of Sara's first kiss from Sigfrid in *Wild Strawberries,* a kiss she both resists and acquiesces in. The scenes should be read together.

4. The stories of Albert's and Anne's visits in town are intercut, and the transitions between them function to identify Anne and Agda. When Albert replies that her life of "fulfillment" would be "emptiness" to him, she pauses in her sewing, eyes shut. Agda's head fades into that of Anne as she enters the theater. At the end of this section, as Anne begins her sexual ordeal in Frans's room, the shot fades back from her to Agda finishing her sewing. It is as if Agda were in these moments recalling everything about the circus and the life with Albert she hated; her feelings then and Anne's now are the same. When Agda says no, there is a final fade from her to the image of Anne in the mirror afterward, a corroboration of her decision. Agda is Anne escaped.

5. Frans's room is literally a locked prison, while Agda's is a kind of museum

208

where human relations are no more vital than those between the pictures on the wall. Isak's study and his mother's drawing room in *Wild Strawberries* have a similar effect on the viewer.

6. John Simon, *Ingmar Bergman Directs* (New York: Harcourt Brace Jovanovich, 1972), p. 89 ff. Simon's book and Robin Wood's *Ingmar Bergman* (New York: Praeger, 1969) provide the two best discussions of Bergman's "first period" films, and I am deeply indebted to both.

7. Thus, when he promises Anne he will return, his appearance reveals that he really wants something else.

8. Agda, too, has this chevron on her dress. Does she represent the bear who has escaped the circus and found her freedom, or is it the sign that she has exchanged one cage for another, more subtle, one?

9. As he says to Anne, "You're from the circus – how do you make the bears dance? Do you use red-hot irons?"

10. The bull on which Simon puts such emphasis occurs only in the theater and is only the *image* of an animal, not the real thing. With its papier-mâché reality, it is more an emblem of Frans, whose sexuality is far removed from the primal drive or raw sexuality real bulls suggest. In the end he must buy what he gets, which is only a body for a few moments.

11. Even though Paul, in describing the world as "without mercy or meaning" at the beginning of *Prison*, recommends suicide as one way out, and in that film Birgitta does kill herself, it is not Bergman's answer, and so he usually doesn't let it happen. The meaning of life isn't our failure or humiliation but what we do with them afterward.

12. When Albert confirms that the circus will continue, a horse whinnies, itself ready to go – acknowledging, as it were, this new identity between them. There is a fade to a wagon wheel, it begins to move, and horses and wagons pass by. The circus is under way again.

13. The very last image of the film, painted on the side of the calliope, is of these three – Albert, Anne, her horse – together in the circus ring. (Anne's earlier boast to Frans – "I can ride geldings bareback" – is now also a reference to Albert and further identifies him as a kind of horse.)

14. There is only the fox fur around Jens's neck, a reminder of the fate of all "beasts."

15. Ever repeating the same tune, as Simon notes, p. 93. As Frost remarks of the circus, "Horned music for horned people [those cuckolded], brass music for the herd [the masses, like cattle; it is a play on words in the original]" – it is the same music for both.

16. R. G. Collingwood, *The Principles of Art* (Oxford: Oxford University Press, 1938), p. 122.

17. Such clowns no longer exist, at least in American society where they would be too crude and "obscene" for television or children. (Circuses are for children, after all – for birthday parties and hamburger commercials.) Their place has been taken by "professional wrestling."

18. Anne's reaction to Albert's initial success with the whip is not that different.

19. Sartre emphasizes a reciprocity of desire in which, because of one's embodiment and thus essential objectness ("being-for-others"), one needs the look

of the other to confirm one's status, even as victor or tyrant. Here, Sartre has missed something in the modern that is deeply antihuman (bestial), deeply hateful (negating, annihilating), and that expresses itself in the totalizing practices of state terrorism and torture, though by no means confined to these realms. (For Bergman, confirmation is provided by the exchanged gazes of the crowd, not the victim.)

20. Later Raval uses a flaming torch, which recalls Frans's remark about using red-hot irons to make the circus bears dance.

21. The more closely one examines Agda's life, the more disturbing one finds it. Everything about her shop and home is controlled, ordered, kept in place. It begins to suggest the bishop's house in *Fanny and Alexander*.

22. When Alma confronts the crowd and pleads for help, "we got mad and told her she had herself to blame." Seven years later, Jens's final word is still, "That's women for you."

23. As Albert lies on the floor and the crowd begins to shuffle in uneasy silence, Frost enters the ring, announces the evening is over, and starts the band. Everything is once again the circus and one more evening's entertainment.

24. This sequence is also an homage to the silent film itself and to Bergman's own filmic origins. It was filmed by Hilding Bladh; the circus-tent scene at the end (with sound) was handled by Sven Nykvist. See Steene, p. 73.

25. Frans keeps his coat on. Here he is not the one who will be exposed or tested. In his dressing room with Anne, he wears a robe and what we (and Anne) see is his true self.

26. In *Wild Strawberries*, Isak's wife offers much the same complaint as justification for her own infidelities.

27. One can find in this structure of abandonment, passion, and return both Bergman's interpretation of the Christian Gospel and the doctrines of original sin, repentance, and divine grace.

28. This irony of nonrecognition is a persistent theme in Bergman. In *Waiting Women* (itself a version of *Smiles of a Summer Night*), the young Maj pays little attention to the stories the other women tell, yet each represents a stage in her own future, a turning point she will have to survive. It is this fact that makes her elopement at the end with Henrik and their promise to love each other forever so bittersweet. They experience spring without realizing it is a season. For Bergman, we have always been warned, already been offered help. Part of the joy of his version of *The Magic Flute* is its prologue in which the camera ranges over the audience, finally settling upon a young girl. Everything that is going to happen in the opera is for her and she is ready. All art should be so fortunate.

3. The Journey: *The Seventh Seal* and *Wild Strawberries*

1. Marianne also travels back to her home, with the result that her own marriage is reestablished, at least for the time being. One can see this journey as also the basic structure of *The Clowns' Evening*. Albert begins to retrieve what has been lost by replacing one person or relationship with another – Agda with Anne.

2. "Borg" is, of course, the surname of Evald, Marianne, and Isak's mother, and will be the name of Marianne's child – a terrifying inheritance. Is it a coincidence that both "Evald" and "Eberhard" (Isak's true first name) have the ancient meanings of being bound to law and legalistic, which defines exactly what their relation as father and son has become? (Gado takes "Evald" as "ej vald" – not chosen, since he was "an unwelcome child in a hellish marriage" [p. 218]).

3. This is the part Jof is to play, because he's "such a fool," at the saint's feast in Elsinore.

4. Jof emphasizes this point because he has just seen what Jöns does to thieves.

5. According to Jöns, it is Raval who "poisoned the knight" with "holy venom," convincing him of "the necessity to join a better-class crusade to the Holy Land." Is it that he envied the wealth and good fortune of the knight with his beautiful young wife and precious faith? Was it resentment that they had more than he and appeared to be blessed and graced by God, that "our life was too good and we were too satisfied with ourselves," that nourished such hate?

6. See Revelation 8 ff.

7. "And the city has no need of sun or moon to shine upon it, for the glory of God is its light, and its lamp is the Lamb" (Rev. 21:22).

8. And in that sense "shall hunger no more, neither thirst any more" (Rev. 17: 16).

9. See Cowie's discussion of the scene's filming and its serendipity, pp. 140. Jof lists them as "The smith and Lisa and the knight and Raval and Jöns and Skat. And Death, the severe master" (*Four Screenplays*, p. 201). See also the analytic script in *The Seventh Seal*, trans. Lars Malström and David Kushner (New York: Simon & Schuster, 1960), "Modern Film Scripts" series.

10. "This is squire Jöns. He grins at Death, mocks the Lord, laughs at himself and leers at the girls. His world is a Jöns-world, believable only to himself, ridiculous to all including himself, meaningless to Heaven and of no interest to Hell," as Jöns describes his drawing of himself to the church painter (*Four Screenplays*, p. 152). See also an early incarnation of the script, *Wood Painting: A Morality Play* (*Trälmålning*, 1954), trans. Randolph Goodman and Leif Sjöberg (reprinted in Birgitta Steene, ed., *Focus on "The Seventh Seal"* [Englewood Cliffs, N.J.: Prentice–Hall, 1972], pp. 159–73); and Melwyn Bragg, *The Seventh Seal* (London: British Film Institute, 1993).

11. And that even Block feels after his encounter with Death in the confessional: "The knight raises his hand and looks at it in the sunlight. . . . 'This is my hand. I can move it, feel the blood pulsing through it. The sun is still high in the sky and I, Antonius Block, am playing chess with Death'" (*Four Screenplays,* p. 151).

12. This is clear in the shooting script, though large parts of the introductory section are not present in the film (and vice versa), which begins with a scene in the present tense before the credits in which Borg speaks of his upcoming ceremony. Following the credits, we see Borg asleep and hear his voice: "In the early morning of Saturday, the first of June [i.e., Sunday, June 2], I *had* a strange and very unpleasant dream" (*Four Screenplays*, p. 216; italics mine).

See also the analytic script in *Wild Strawberries*, trans. Lars Malström and David Kushner (New York: Simon & Schuster, 1960).

13. This is not an honorary degree but occurs normally "on the fiftieth anniversary of the person's graduation from the university" (see Gado, p. 212). This suggests both that the honor is in living that long and, perhaps, that any such life would be naturally worthy.

14. The most recent of "all the evil and frightening dreams which have haunted me these last few years" (*Four Screenplays*, p. 219). Borg's two nightmares in the film flank a series of more gentle dreams about his childhood and youthful romance with his cousin Sara.

15. "Don't try to pull me into your marital problems because I don't give a damn about them. . . . But if you need spiritual masturbation, I can make an appointment for you with some good quack, or perhaps with a minister, it's so popular these days" (*Four Screenplays*, p. 226).

16. In the script – but not the film – as he awakens "in this moment of senseless horror," he sits up and "mutters" these "words of reality against my dream": "My name is Isak Borg. I am still alive. I am seventy-six years old. I really feel quite well" (*Four Screenplays*, 219). This is the same as Albert's reaction when he bursts from his wagon and as the knight's after his confession to Death in the church. Each feels alive again for the first time in years.

17. *Four Screenplays*, p. 273. Gado points out that Marianne sees in the Almans a future picture of herself and Evald, something even more distressing than their example to the children (p. 215).

18. As in *The Seventh Seal*, Bergman replaces Abraham, the suffering prefiguration of Christ, with the mother and her child as the force that fulfills God's promises.

19. "Weren't they married?" "Unfortunately not."

20. The story of Abraham and Isaac haunts Bergman's work. In *Through a Glass Darkly*, Karin feels betrayed and sacrificed to her father's art of writing because he has begun to use her as a source in his journals (this discovery may precipitate her final descent into delusion), and in *Fanny and Alexander* the bishop seeks to transform Alexander into someone fit for his God but by a process that is spiritually murderous. Gado sees this as reflecting Bergman's relationship with his own father. Marianne herself is faced with two kinds of child-murder: abortion or replicating for her own child Evald's childhood.

21. One can look and hear the other without being seen or heard oneself. Touch comes close to being irreducibly reciprocal. This perhaps explains its primacy in *Cries and Whispers* and why it is the familiarity Karin and Maria in that film can least tolerate.

22. This scene has a double temporality. It is a picture both of what occurred in the past and of what is occurring now as Marianne tells it.

23. This "before" "photo" is a picture of a man almost dead, equivalent to the shot of the empty study with which the scene ends. It is the "image in the mirror" that Borg needs to see, and then redraw, if he is to change.

24. Sartre's phrase for this "existential openness" is "we are not what we are and are what we are not." We have a past (truths about us) we cannot escape, yet we also have an open future in which the meaning of those facts (how

they matter to us and the effect they have on our lives) is not determined but open to our choices.

25. In the script, but not the film, there are two other telling references. The twins "tumbled through the door of the bathhouse, two redheaded girls about thirteen years old, as identical as two wild strawberries" (p. 232). And Eva, the pregnant wife at the service station (herself perhaps literally one of Isak's children, delivered when he was a young doctor), "squinted in the sun and beamed like a big strawberry in her red dress" (p. 247). In the script of *Smiles of a Summer Night,* in the final scene Desirée's maid goes off to pick strawberries for breakfast, leaving her to comfort Fredrik and "study for her new role" (p. 123). These are instances, not of romantic/passionate love, but of youthful liveliness, fertility, and love that is older, mature, and wise.

26. *Four Screenplays,* p. 249. This is easily said by Viktor but, for Johan in *Scenes from a Marriage,* very hard to practice.

27. "From the section marked 'The Last Judgment' under the heading 'The Christian Hope Before Death'" (Gado, p. 216). In the treatment for *Cries and Whispers,* the poem is framed on Agnes's wall, but there is no sign of it in the film.

28. Sara's own enamored response, "Aren't they fantastically sweet?" is a youthful version of Isak's reply. The quarrel misses the point (and for Sara, too, it is a love poem, though it doesn't recognize itself as such).

29. Karin, in *The Seventh Seal,* smiles too, a smile that indicates more than just acceptance of her fate and relief that its trials are over. She does not curse the world or doubt the reality of love. She has already forgiven Block and views him more as a lost child returned than as an unfaithful lover (now as much Madonna as wife). The girl, too, has never cursed her existence, wished to be dead, nor closed herself to the wounds and sufferings of others.

30. The hymn Isak quotes ends with: "Be comforted my soul. . . . Your friend waves to you. . . . Soon . . . you shall glide to the shepherd's embrace; like the saved lamb hasten there and find rest" (Gado, pp. 225–6). This is the otherworldly rest found in heaven, in the escape from life. Perhaps Isak's final dream is just the wish for, and acceptance of, death itself. Gado interprets the hymn psychoanalytically as a suppressed reference to Bergman's father and their estrangement.

4. The Great Dance: *Smiles of a Summer Night*

1. Quotations are from the script in *Four Screenplays,* pp. 35–6. Further page references are given in the text.

2. All this to Henrik's impassioned piano in the background. Who is Anne really kissing? Does she know any better than her husband?

3. There are two stages – to reconcile herself with him (to get over the hurt she has suffered) and then to reconcile him to Anne's loss and her as replacement.

4. After Anne has revealed her true feelings and left the dining room, Fredrik stands before a window, caged in by its shadowy bars, looking (and feeling) like Henrik in his clerical suit. It is the same when he sees Henrik and Anne steal away.

5. Carl-Magnus is also in his nightclothes when informed of Charlotte's trickery.
6. What we might now call a "trophy wife."
7. Anne's association with flowers is emphasized throughout – a more symbolic representation of her sexual (and spiritual) virginity, which Petra says shows even in her skin. Fredrik conceals these pictures and views them when no one else is around, as though they (or what he thought and desired) was something illicit or even somehow pornographic, something about which he should be uncomfortable.
8. While "macho" in a way Fredrik is not, Malcolm is as officious and pompous – and about as successful at it. The first thing we learn is that he has been thrown from his horse, no better a rider than Henrik. All three men begin the film by taking a fall, just so they (and we) can have a more realistic idea of who they really are.
9. For Fredrik, it is a moment of abandonment and despair that is given further expression in his seduction by Charlotte and subsequent "death" at Russian roulette. He is now ready for resurrection.
10. As young lovers, Anne and Henrik are foreshadowed by Martin and Märta in *Waiting Women* and Monika and Harry in *Summer with Monika*. In one case the relationship probably survives, in the other it doesn't.
11. Anne and Petra burst into laughter when they imagine being men, while for Petra, Hendrik is "sweet as a little puppy." *Shame*, at least in part, later offers a much harsher version of this in the initial relationship of Jan and Eva.
12. One can understand the plugged cannons along the waterfront at the beginning in the same way – not as signs of impotence but of masculinity qualified, made gentle and more feminine.
13. *Smiles* does end with an image of Desirée mothering Fredrik, both physically and emotionally. Is he still the little boy with the "wife-mother?" This would be too simple, too reductive. *Any* companionship in which partners share a life involves comforting and nourishing, replacing our parents with each other. Later, *Scenes from a Marriage* will end with an essentially similar scene in which positions are reversed and the man comforts the woman. Gender does, for Bergman, account for many of the specifics of our lives, but it does not affect the fundamental categories discussed in Chapter 1. Everyone, man and woman, can be abandoned and must suffer, must face up to their lives and their own deaths, is forever faced with turning toward or away from others, can be humiliated or shamed and moved by a vision of the better. All of this is more basic and central to our being than gender. These are the bones on which gender will always hang. See also Birgitta Steene, "Bergman's Portrait of Women: Sexism or Subjective Metaphor?" *Sexual Strategems: The World of Women in Film*, ed. Patricia Erens (New York: Horizon, 1979), pp. 91–107. For feminist-oriented criticism, see Marilyn Johns Blackwell, *Gender and Representation in the Films of Ingmar Bergman* (Columbia, S.C.: Camden House, 1997); and Molly Haskell, *From Reverence to Rape: The Treatment of Women in the Movies* (New York: Holt Rinehart, 1974), "The Europeans," p. 314 ff.
14. And not just people, but things, cultures, places. There are many hints of this throughout the film: Carl-Magnus's automobile will replace his cavalry,

Madame Armfeldt herself is a relic, a remnant from a past time of king and court, Desirée an independent woman already bespeaking a different future.

15. John Simon, *Ingmar Bergman Directs* (New York: Harcourt Brace Jovanovich, 1972), p. 135.

16. When Anne, still a virgin, supposes that the first time must be disgusting, Petra replies, "It was so much fun, I almost died." And for Anne, too, it must have been special; she is faint and almost deliriously aglow as she boards the carriage to elope with Henrik.

17. As Charlotte is talking to Anne, years of feeling come to the surface: "I hate him, I hate him. Men are beastly! They are silly and vain. . . . He smiles to me, he kisses me, he comes to me at night, he makes me lose my reason, he caresses me, talks kindly to me, gives me flowers, always yellow roses, talks about his horses, his women, his duels, his soldiers, his hunting – talks, talks, talks." And in a whisper, "Love is a disgusting business" (pp. 89–90). How can Malcolm's promise to "be faithful to you in my own way" overcome such deep neglect and misuse?

18. The Masonic trials that Pamina and Tamino undergo in *The Magic Flute* are transformed by Bergman to the purgatory of marriage with its dangers of infidelity and abandonment. In Bergman's version, the two are partners undergoing the trials together, each helping the other (as written, Tamino enters the temple alone).

19. Bergman's final version is Helena and Isak in *Fanny and Alexander,* preceded by the much more resigned and despairing Marianne and Johan in *Scenes from a Marriage.*

20. The final words of the script are these: "She has pulled off her shoes and stockings and walks barefoot through the dewy grass, holding her skirt high above her knees. Frid walks behind her, and the sight of her rounded thighs is so damn beautiful that he begins to sing" (p. 124).

5. A Dream Play: *Shame*

1. In *Port of Call,* Berit refuses to release the name of the abortionist who has caused her friend's death because "the poor need such people to survive," unlike the rich who can always buy their way out of trouble. She finally gives in under the threat of being sent back to reform school by the welfare department. Here there is an oppressive sense of a meddlesome state that does not reemerge until *The Rite* in 1969.

2. The immediately preceding *Hour of the Wolf* is an interior drama, though it does portray the collapse of the artist/art and a corrosive doubt in their worth.

3. Even the specter of a nuclear exchange is present, in the conflict between India and Pakistan over Kashmir or Russian military maneuvers founded on tactical atomic weapons strategy during the Balkans crisis in 1999.

4. Throughout, it is the spiritual struggle that is central and determining. The newly blind Bengt in *Music in Darkness* (1948) can easily enough master Braille and the church organ *if* he can find something or someone to make it worthwhile. Clearly, the world can limit one, and a person must acknowledge and learn to live with those limits, but they are not in themselves defeating.

Only in *Through a Glass Darkly* does this thought begin to emerge with force when Karin must return to the asylum because of the effects of her degenerative disease. (An interesting precursor is the consul's young wife in *Dreams* [1955], who has been confined for twenty years because she thinks her daughter has a wolf's head, but she is not a main character.)

5. In both these films, the soul – one of the senses of the name "Alma" – remains in limbo. The boy in *Persona* is acted by the boy in *The Silence;* his abandonment in *Persona* is thus a kind of continuation of and comment on the last scene in the train, further darkening its limited hope, perhaps even canceling it.

6. This collage includes snippets of political rhetoric from Hitler, Kennedy, Johnson, and others.

7. Jan, perhaps, would like to be the baby Eva so desires and yearns very much for the comfort of being babied, just as Eva desires to give that comfort – to her own child, to the downed paratrooper and the wounded deserter, to the dead child beside the burning farm.

8. Bergman, *"Persona" and "Shame": The Screenplays of Ingmar Bergman,* trans. Keith Bradfield (New York: Grossman Publishers, 1972), p. 108. Further citations are in the text.

9. "They are close together, face to face" (p. 188).

10. Ibid., pp. 188–9, and film dialogue.

11. This is a theme in *The Magician,* for instance, set in 1842.

12. In *The Touch,* David Kovacs has helped find a medieval Madonna with Child that had been immured in an old church. It is infested with the eggs of a black wood beetle ("quite beautiful in their own right") that now hatch. The statue is being eaten away from within and will be destroyed unless it is returned to its ancient chamber and resealed.

13. At the "hour of the wolf," incidentally.

14. The wooden person occurs literally as the masthead figure outside the cottage in *Persona* [see Fig. 19a]; similar figures and images are repeated in *Shame* and in *The Touch,* and finally in Aron's workshop in *Fanny and Alexander.*

15. As does the statue of Orpheus with which both *Cries and Whispers* and *The Magic Flute* begin (as well as the opera curtain inside the theater where *The Magic Flute* is performed). Wooden people cannot dance, and it is this dance (this music of life) that must be recovered.

16. The failure of the modern is reflected in Bergman's use of music. In the 1950s he would have sound tracks with contemporary scores; now, except for ambient sound, he relies almost entirely on Bach and Mozart. ("Bach" is one of the shared words with the unknown language of *The Silence.*)

17. If one did not know that *The Rite* was written some eight years before, one could easily take it as Bergman's account of (and revenge for) his own treatment at the hands of the Swedish tax office.

18. Nine in some six films (ten if you count Viktor, Eva's minister husband in *Autumn Sonata*).

19. *From the Life of the Marionettes,* trans. Alan Blair (New York: Pantheon Books, 1980), p. 16.

20. *The Serpent's Egg*, trans. Alan Blair (New York: Pantheon Books, 1977), p. 118.
21. Figs. 20b,c complete the series of images begun with the silhouetted circus wagons in *The Clowns' Evening*. Life in the full light of modernity has reduced people to a herd of glowering work animals, no different than Alma's bear.
22. Cowie, p. 254; see also Steene, pp. 136–8, and Gado, pp. 357–8. For Gado, "*Shame* is not fundamentally a political film" (p. 358).
23. Sara Lidman in the *Aftonbladet*, c. Oct. 6, 1968; quoted by Cowie, p. 254, and cited from Maria Bergom-Larsson, *Ingmar Bergman and Society* (San Diego: A. S. Barnes, 1978).
24. Bergman himself commented: "I do not know of any party that is for frightened and terrified people who are experiencing the period of dusk and the fact that it has kind of begun and the plane is definitely inclined downwards. I cannot really engage myself in any political activity" (quoted in Cowie, p. 254; from an interview with Nils Petter Sundgren on Swedish TV, February 21, 1968).
25. Admittedly, Bergman provides no detailed analysis, and much of his intent is to capture a widespread mood, whatever its causes may be. But there is more substance to his account than acknowledged by those Swedish critics who charged "that Bergman's vision of war ascribed blame to no one nation or party but presented the conflict as the work of some nameless Destiny, without roots in any divergent socioeconomic ideologies" (Cowie, p. 255). It is clear that for Bergman the cause is not primarily economic; in this regard his view bears comparison to Heidegger's writings on the meaning of technology in the "modern age" (see, e.g., "The Question Concerning Technology" – 1949/1955).
26. "Rosenberg," of course, is also Jan and Eva's surname in *Shame* and thus stands for all the people "frightened and terrified" by their sociopolitical systems, not just Jews. Eva's maiden name (omitted in the film) is Egerman. The island farm is her inheritance from her grandfather, "David Fredrik Egerman, born 25 August 1914. Died 18 July 1968. *God is my strength*" (from his tombstone – p. 122). *Shame* is therefore what came of the promise and smiles of that summer night many years ago at the beginning of this century (and of its modernity, since he is born at the beginning of the First World War). This thread continues in *From the Life of the Marionettes,* where the psychotic killer is an Egermann. (Gado provides a useful list of the repeated names Bergman uses for his characters, pp. 516–20.)
27. Bergman's view is probably closest to that of Camus in *The Plague*. It is also related to Simone de Beauvoir's position in *The Ethics of Ambiguity* where she defends the use of violence in the cause of freedom but holds it must always be attended with guilt recognizing its moral inadequacy and failure (see, e.g., her discussion of violence in the section on "The Antinomies of Action").
28. In the script, Eva's dream concludes with: "And then you came on the other side of the street and I thought that you would be able to tell me about the important thing I had forgotten" (p. 190).

6. The Illiterates: *Cries and Whispers* and *Scenes from a Marriage*

1. In the film, the disease is unspecified. It seems similar to that of Ester in *The Silence* and throughout Agnes coughs up blood. No film script for *Cries and Whispers* has been published. A "short story" treatment is contained in *Four Stories by Ingmar Bergman*, translated by Alain Blair (New York: Doubleday, 1976). There Bergman identifies it as cancer of the womb in which "her belly has swollen up as though she were in an advanced stage of pregnancy" (p. 61). This theme is not carried through in the film. Subsequent quotations are from the film. For feminist responses to *Cries and Whispers,* see Joan Mellen, *Women and Their Sexuality in the New Film* (New York: Horizon Press, 1973), chap. 4, "Bergman and Women: *Cries and Whispers,*" pp. 97–116 (reprinted in Stuart Kaminsky, ed., *Ingmar Bergman: Essays in Criticism* [New York: Oxford University Press, 1975], pp. 297–312); and Constance Penley, "*Cries and Whispers,*" *Women and Film* 1:3–4 (1973), pp. 55–6 (reprinted in Bill Nichols, ed., *Movies and Methods: An Anthology.* [Berkeley: University of California Press, 1976]), pp. 204–8.
2. The Greek meaning of "eucharist" is to give thanks.
3. While all four Gospels place Christ between two thieves, only Luke reports that one is saved: Luke 23:39–43.
4. As children, both Karin and Agnes seem excluded and pushed to the side by their mother; made observers, they have become particularly aware and reflective.
5. Is Karin clumsy, as both she and Fredrik say? Compared to the ease and social grace of Maria, perhaps, but Maria's smoothness is just as Karin says: a facade of "insipid smiles," "idiotic flirtatiousness," "empty caresses," "false laughter and promises." We first see Karin doing intricate needlework as she sits with Agnes. She is not clumsy; rather, she is honest (in spite of herself). She sees the lie in her own and other's behavior, and this gap makes the world an awkward place where she must both be and not be something, must both see the truth and cover it over. Her "ineptitude" with objects and people is thus the outward effect of this deeper knowledge and the fact that, unlike David, she cannot dismiss or suppress it because she still longs for a life that is whole.
6. In this gesture, Ester's two words of "hand" and "face" are brought together, and the "translation" that is needed at the end of *The Silence* is recommended after its failures in *Persona* and *Shame.*
7. Translation by Charles B.Williams, *The New Testament in the Language of the People* (Chicago: Moody Press, 1957); see esp. vv. 2, 4, 7, and 8.
8. Or that Maria's own daughter will herself have a different view of life? The scenes of Maria and her mother and of Maria and her daughter are interchangeable. As for Karin? It is a shock to realize that she is a mother. What is the likelihood that any of these children can grow up to be different than their parents?
9. *From the Life of the Marionettes* uses both color and black-and-white.
10. Sven Nykvist won the Academy Award for Best Cinematography for *Cries and Whispers* in 1974 (and for *Fanny and Alexander* in 1984). Bergman was

nominated as best director for both, as well as for *Face to Face* in 1977, but did not win. See the filmography in the present volume for other awards.

11. See Bergman's "Introduction" to the *Four Screenplays*, pp. 17–18. This idea is specifically mentioned in the treatment for *Cries and Whispers* (see *Four Stories*, pp. 86–7: "So I repeat: This can't be comprehended by the intellect. It's a matter between the imagination and the feelings" [p. 87]).

12. On the manor grounds is a stature of Orpheus, the very first thing one sees after the credits. Is *Cries and Whispers,* too, a quest for Eurydice, the lost joy and meaning of life, which requires confronting and surviving abandonment and overcoming death itself? (In Gluck's *Orfeo e Euridice,* for instance, unlike the myth itself, Orpheus is steadfast, and out of compassion for his suffering the Furies and the god Amor give Eurydice her life again.) This is the same statue with which *The Magic Flute* begins. Indeed, the two films have the same general structure: They open with Orpheus, move about the grounds, then enter the building where the story occurs. Once inside, we never leave, though while within we travel to other times and places. *Cries and Whispers* begins at dawn, *The Magic Flute* begins at sunset; both end in the full light of the sun.

13. *Four Stories*, p. 60. In *The Silence*, Ester speaks of "The blood vessels . . . overflowing, and all the mucous [*sic*]" (*Three Films*, p. 140). Both Ester and Agnes are suffocating, strangling on their own bodily fluids. At one level they are dying because the soul is stifled and cannot breathe. Gado gives a quite different reading, and both he and Cowie cite different passages where Bergman has talked about the film.

14. The clocks are striking 4 A.M., the "hour of the wolf" – "the hour between night and dawn. It is the hour when most people die, when sleep is deepest, when nightmares are most real. It is the hour when the sleepless are haunted by their greatest dread, when ghosts and demons are most powerful. The hour of the wolf is also the hour when most children are born" (*Four Stories*, p. 96). On arising, the very first thing Agnes does is restart her mantle clock, which has stopped, and reset it to 4. (In *Sunday's Children*, Bergman gives his own birth – in the character of Pu – as "the fourteenth of July, 1918. I was born at 3 o'clock in the morning." [Trans. Joan Tate (New York: Arcade Publishing, 1993), p. 44].)

15. Thus, in a way, completing the cycle of nature given in *Smiles of a Summer Night,* adding to its spring and summer, winter and autumn. *Smiles* is not replaced by *Cries and Whispers;* the two must now be taken together.

16. All of these structures place the viewer at a certain distance, as though an observer of a stately pageant or formal dance (or perhaps a pavane – *Four Stories*, p. 74). This effect is continued by the presence of an omniscient but otherwise unnoticed narrator (the film's author?) who introduces Maria's and Karin's insets.

17. During her most acute attack, just before the end of the film, Ester calls out, "Mother, come and help me! I'm so frightened. I'm so frightened. I'm so frightened. I don't want to die" (*Three Films*, p. 141).

18. Can the soul find no modern building for its home? Or is the very idea of a human soul anachronistic, now past belief?

19. It is the same face that tries to look through the screen and touch his mother at the beginning and end of *Persona,* two years later. See note 6.

20. "Two young people, strong, happy, with a constructive attitude toward life in general, but who have never forgotten all the same to give love first place" (from Mrs. Palm's article about them). *Scenes from a Marriage,* trans. Alan Blair (New York: Bantam Books, 1974), p. 14. Further references are in the text.

21. The scenes are titled: "Innocence and Panic," "The Art of Sweeping Under the Rug," "Paula," "The Vale of Tears," "The Illiterates," and "In the Middle of the Night in a Dark House Somewhere in the World."

22. Adapted by Bergman himself in 1981 as part of a trilogy with *A Doll's House* and *Miss Julie,* the three ran concurrently, each performed on a different stage in Munich.

23. This awareness begins in the interview as she is pressed to describe herself and what she thinks.

24. "You can't wear that dress today. It's your Sunday best. You'll never manage that, my dear. Let me help you. Using lipstick, are you? Most unseemly while you're living in our home. Eat up what you have on your plate. You're late again. . . . If you go on like this Grandpa and I will send you to boarding school. . . . I'll do as I like. You're not going to order me around. You're a goddamn stupid bitch. I hate you and I could kill you. . . . Yes, I know you love me. . . . Forgive me. . . . I know I've done wrong. I always do wrong. I will be Grandma's good little girl. . . . I'll be good if only you don't lock me in the closet. . . ." *Face to Face,* trans. Alan Blair (New York: Pantheon Books, 1976), pp. 102–3.

25. Ibid., p. 105.

26. Not even the rape and slaughter of *The Virgin Spring* or the murder of Ka in *From the Life of the Marionettes.* Here, Ester's words of "hand" and "face" are not enough.

27. "It was you who seduced me," Johan asserts, and Marianne agrees (p. 191).

28. Johan and Marianne do what Karin and Maria cannot – actually talk to each other. The symbolic music of their encounter in *Cries and Whispers* gives way to real communication. Throughout *Scenes from a Marriage,* music plays no role. (Johan in the interview remarks that he likes Bach's *St. Matthew Passion* "because it gives me feelings of piety and belonging" [p. 10] – a kind of put-down, comparable to the film's final dismissal of Paul's verses in First Corinthians.)

29. "It would have been carrying things too far to untangle everything." "So we resorted to lying. Sometimes more, sometimes less, as it suited us." "Do you apply these experiences to your new marriage?" "Why of course. I lie all the time." "So do I" (p. 199).

7. The Little World: *Fanny and Alexander*

1. In the script, for instance, there is an older sister, Amanda (Bergman's older brother, Dag?).

2. The theatrical release can stand on its own and is for most viewers deeply

satisfying. But once one sees the original, this edited version becomes incomplete and a reminder of the film it should really be. Bergman's true masterpiece remains virtually unseen outside Sweden (though it is now available in Europe on videotape and on Japanese laser disc). This is a great loss to world cinema.

3. See "Preface."

4. Ingmar Bergman, *Fanny and Alexander*, trans. Alan Blair (New York: Pantheon Books, 1982), p. 208. Further references are in the text.

5. This is the translation of the motto (*Ei Blot Til Lyst*) over Alexander's toy theater in the first shot of the film; at the same time, it is a motto for the film itself, tacked over its top, too.

6. Most clearly articulated in her "farewell" speech when she leaves the theater at the beginning of Act 3 (omitted from the theatrical version) and why she takes nothing from this life when she moves to the bishop's palace. Emilie is like Elisabet Vogler in *Persona*. Her "breakdown" and paralysis is at the same time the refusal to continue *acting,* on- or offstage, and is related to the feeling of not being one's own person in *Scenes from a Marriage* and *Face to Face*.

7. Perhaps Bergman's own minister father – equally mysterious with his violent moods and intransigent, insecure will – is a model. There are eerie echoes when one also reads or views Bergman's three biographical works: *The Best Intentions, Sunday's Children,* and *Private Confessions*.

8. He says to Aron, "If there *is* a God, then he's a shit and piss God and I'd like to kick him in the arse" (p. 195).

9. It is this emotional flatness that most distances viewers: It is hard to know what Vergérus is feeling and thus how to sympathize with him – but this is because he is trying not to feel anything at all.

10. The bishop's religion is also unfavorably contrasted with Judaism. Isak becomes a new father to Alexander, and his apartments are a place of special knowledge, both about religion and art. In addition, Helena is identified in the script as "née Mandelbaum" (pp. 3, 10), and her affair with Isak seems to have been her true love.

11. If the beaten Alexander is associated with Christ on the cross, the bishop is representative of the Old Testament God of anger and rules who is replaced through Christ's sacrifice by the New Testament God of love and compassion. For Bergman, much too much of the Old Testament God still remains. The bishop is also presented as a kind of Christ in his suffering – forsaken by both God and Emilie. This is his (and the Old Testament God's?) realization of spiritual bankruptcy.

12. In fact, there may be only one father, who has here been divided to make the killing easier and more acceptable psychologically.

13. Bergman has always included references to storytelling in his films along with indications that they themselves were as much stories as representations of life, but the difference – and conflict – is explicitly forced on the viewer only in these two places.

14. This essential activity of the audience is the clue to the relationship between Alexander and his sister and to the puzzle of why the film is titled after both of them when the action and viewer's attention seem so much more focused

on him: Fanny is the essential audience who believes in the artist's fictions and without whom they could not have life.

15. See Jesse Kalin, "Philosophy Needs Literature: John Barth and Moral Nihilism," *Philosophy and Literature* 1:2 (Spring 1977), pp. 170–82.

16. It is at this same time that Helena and Isak share their feeling that the present has turned dismal, that everything is getting old, and that nothing matches the stories of their youth and their love "like strawberries."

17. Vergérus is not entirely mistaken. Alexander's motives of striking back and even harming the bishop are like those of a liar or spreader of malicious rumors and gossip – to discredit him.

18. There are hellish spots in the "little world," but it is not hell itself, and anyone can lose his or her bearings. There are thus more possibilities of change open to Carl and Lydia than to the bishop or his sister and mother, though they hardly understand life any better.

19. Viewers sense this from the start, especially in the way Vergérus pats/cuffs Alexander on the head or strokes/grasps him at the neck (as though to draw his head back and cut his throat, like Abraham?).

20. This scene is not in the theatrical version. It is the conclusion of Act 5 and thus of the entire story as framed by the "Prologue" and "Epilogue." The scenes in the theater are among the most omitted in the edited version. (See note 24, which explains why returning to the theater is so important to her.)

21. *Hamlet*, I.v.80–3.

22. In the television version, Fanny and Alexander try to cause the bishop's death by chanting (during a lightning storm): "One, two, three. Die, you bastard! Let's try it again. One, two, three. Die, you bastard!" (p. 125). And, of course, Alexander later "sees" it happen as the product of his own desire.

23. Like Mary rather than Christ, it is Sarah – Abraham's wife – who finally triumphs. And perhaps Hagar also, Abraham's other "wife" and Ishmael's mother. Alexander is empowered to defeat the bishop by the namesakes of Abraham's two sons – Isak and Ismael.

24. In the long version, Oscar does not die at the point where Alexander flees from him in terror. This is followed by a scene with Oscar and Emilie together that is quite tender and moving and in which he passes the responsibility for the theater onto her.

25. A fourth is included in the television version, a story by Isak to help explain his mother to him (and Fanny). Part of it is given in the script (pp. 171–2), and a version of this was given as Bergman's acceptance speech for an award at SMU in 1981 – see William G. Jones, *Talking with Ingmar Bergman* (Dallas: SMU Press, 1983), pp. 71–3. Isak's story is first, and Oscar's advice a commentary on it.

26. When Ismael begins to speak Alexander's deepest thoughts, he/she holds him in poses reminiscent of *Persona* and its themes of fracture and reintegration of identity. Here, it is the congealing of an identity for the first time – Alexander Ekdahl and Ismael Retzinsky made one – and a new Alexander is born with a new name, Alexander Retzinsky. Ismael is those powers and insights of the artist (which Bergman has always found mysterious and a bit dark – darkest in *Hour of the Wolf*) that will now be his own.

27. "For never-ending time leads summer on/ To hideous winter, and confounds him there" (Shakespeare, Sonnet 5).

28. Even at the end, after the family is restored, Gustav warns that the "world is a den of thieves and night is falling. Soon it will be the hour of robbers and murderers. Evil is breaking its chains and goes through the world like a mad dog. The poisoning affects us all. . . . No one escapes" (p. 208).

29. Unfortunately, it is omitted from the theatrical version, leaving Helena's part of the story (and her "rebirth") less developed than it really is. In addition, important connections to *Wild Strawberries* and other films are also lost. The scene is shot with Helena at the end of the room behind a gauze doorway curtain moving in the summer breeze. Her face is uncovered as she begins to smile, as though she were about to step from where she was to someplace new. The image recalls similar shots in *Cries and Whispers* and *Face to Face* where something similar is at issue.

30. "Thou seest we are not all alone unhappy:/ This wide and universal theatre/ Presents more woeful pageants than the scene/ Wherein we play in" (*As You Like It*, II.vii.136–9).

31. *Fanny and Alexander* has been taken as overtly autobiographical, and it is in many respects (see particularly Gado for a good discussion of these aspects). But it is also always much more.

32. Embodied in Isak's house is both story and antistory: In contrast to Isak himself, for Aron, any kind of story, like his God puppet, is just sleight of hand to pull the wool over people's eyes and perhaps make life easier. Bergman's own film might be such a costume drama, set in a remoter, premodern time because it could not be pulled off in the present.

33. All this takes hardly twenty seconds, and it is puzzling that this scene is not included in the theatrical version. In many ways it is the story's most self-aware and telling comment about its own story.

Afterwords

1. Ingmar Bergman, *The Magic Lantern: An Autobiography* (*Laterna magica*), trans. Joan Tate (New York: Viking, 1988), p. 2. See also Cowie and Gado, as well as Hubert I. Cohen, *Ingmar Bergman: The Art of Confession* (New York: Twayne, 1993), for fuller details.

2. *Magic Lantern*, p. 202.

3. Ingmar Bergman, *Sunday's Children*, trans. Joan Tate (New York: Arcade Publishing, 1993), pp. 126–8. There is some disagreement and variation in accounts of these early years. In one famous story, a young Ingmar was punished by being locked in a closet by his father (he says he hid a flashlight there), but his sister reports that it happened only once and was done by their grandmother (see Gado, pp. 8–9).

4. "My brother tried to commit suicide, my sister was forced into an abortion out of consideration for the family, I ran away from home" (*Magic Lantern*, p. 139).

5. Liv Ullmann speaks of Bergman's jealousy of even her friends and family: "My security became living the way he wished. For only then was *he* secure."

This extended even to ordering for both of them at dinner. (Quoted in Cohen, *Bergman: Art of Confession*, pp. 24–5.) See also Liv Ullmann, *Changing* (New York: Knopf, 1977); Ullmann, "Dialogue on Film" *American Film Institute* 2:3 (March 1973), pp. 1–22; and Virginia Wright Wexman, "An Interview with Liv Ullmann," *Cinema Journal* 20:1 (Fall 1980).

6. Bergman has had five wives and eight children: Else Fischer (1943–5: Lena); Ellen Lundström (1945–50: Eva, Jan, and twins Anna and Mats); Gun Grut [Hagberg] (1951–5: Ingmar); Käbi Lareti (1959–66?: Daniel Sebastien); and Ingrid Karlebo [von Rosen] (1971–95). Among others, he had affairs with Harriet Andersson (1952/3), Bibi Andersson (1955), and Liv Ullmann (1965–9: Linn).

7. See Malou von Sivers's interview of Bergman and Erland Josephson for TV4 International, Sweden, 1999; included as *Ingmar Bergman: Reflections on Life, Death, and Love, with Erland Josephson* in the Criterion DVD of *Cries and Whispers* (2001).

8. Kaila's "thesis that man lives strictly according to his needs – negative and positive – was shattering to me, but terribly true. And I built on this ground." See Bergman's "Introduction" to *Four Screenplays*, p. xxi. Bergman met Janov in Los Angeles (probably in 1972) and planned to make a television film based on his material, but the project didn't carry through. See *Magic Lantern*, p. 231.

9. In the summer of 1932, "I read ceaselessly, often without understanding, but I had a sensitive ear for tone: Dostoyevsky, Tolstoy, Balzac, Defoe, Swift, Flaubert, Nietzsche and, of course, Strindberg." *Magic Lantern*, p. 112. For his remarks about reading, see the "Monologue" in *The Fifth Act*, trans. Linda Haverty Rugg and Joan Tate (New York: New Press, 2001 [1994]), pp. 3–4.

10. Maud Webster, quoted by Gado, p. 17: "to comfort himself with the thought of being an Übermensch." This seems to have been a long adolescent occupation, for Bergman describes himself during the summer of 1932 as a boy who was "spotty, dressed wrongly, stammered, laughed loudly and without reason, was hopeless at all sports, dared not dive and liked talking about Nietzsche, a fairly useless social talent on the stony shore where we bathed" (*Magic Lantern*, pp. 111–12).

11. An interpretation now much disputed and largely discredited.

12. "There is nothing which can be called right or wrong. One functions according to one's needs; you can read that in an elementary-school textbook. . . . You have a damned need to live, to exist and create life. . . . My need is to be dead. Absolutely, totally dead." (*Four Screenplays*, p. 272.)

13. See *Bergman on Bergman*, ed. Stig Björkman, Torsten Manns, and Jonas Sima, trans. Paul Britten Austin (New York: Simon & Schuster, 1973), pp. 219 and 181; also 164 and 189.

14. But maybe not. When, in *Private Confessions*, Karin arranges a weekend tryst with her lover far away in Norway at a friend's aunt's house in Molde (in 1925), the friend, a missionary on leave, meets them there at the ferry. As she goes to talk alone with Karin, she gives Tomas a copy of Kierkegaard's *Acts of Love*, recently translated, with a commentary, by Torsten Bohlin. "I'm sure

you haven't read it, Mr. Egerman" (trans. Joan Tate [New York: Arcade Publishing, 1996], p. 103). *Acts of Love* is a profound, if wordy, meditation on Christian/spiritual love, including First Corinthians 13 (ultimately in an opposite direction from Bergman's own readings). Its presence reinforces Tomas's doubts and is probably a cause of his early departure. Did Bergman invent this part? Was it in his mother's diaries? I do not know. "Torsten Bohlin" is the name of Karin's suitor and expected husband sixteen years earlier before she meets Erik Bergman (at least according to *The Best Intentions,* trans. Joan Tate [New York: Arcade Publishing, 1993], p. 21); the real Bohlin would have been nineteen at the time (though in the book he is twenty-four). Is Bergman's point that he, or just someone else, would have been a better match for his mother?

15. See his *The Lutheran Milieu of the Films of Ingmar Bergman* (New York: Arno Press, 1978), p. 16.

16. See *Private Confessions,* "The First Conversation," esp. pp. 27–32; the point is especially strong in Ullmann's film version. (Here Bergman has changed his parent's names to Henrik and Anna.)

17. Cowie reports Bergman as (rhetorically, he says) asking critics "how they could assess his work if they had not even read Luther's shorter catechism" (p. 10). This seems to me to be necessary advice, for all his films.

18. He speaks most admiringly of Georges Bernanos's *Diary of a Country Priest* (1937), Robert Bresson's film version of it (1951), and of Bresson in general (*Bergman on Bergman,* pp. 43–4). There is a religious, spiritual dimension in Bresson lacking in the core existentialists. He also mentions Kafka (p. 27).

19. On Sartre's (ontological) account, there seems to be nothing such "choices of value" could be based on, certainly not the *value* of the value as something independent from the choice. For Bergman, there is only a psychological dependence of values on choice in the sense that they are subject to being recognized and rejected, believed in or not ("we are the makers of our own meaning").

20. One might think of Antonius Block as a loner comparable to Caligula; he, too, is a negative image. Märta is a "hero" because of her persistence (and maybe Tomas, too); Isak Borg not so much a hero as an exemplar. The one character overtly cast as an "existentialist" – Thomas, the young reporter/writer in *Prison* – learns otherwise in the end. And Eva in *Shame* and Agnes in *Cries and Whispers?* Or Marianne and Johan in *Scenes from a Marriage?* None of these is an *existential* "hero."

21. See Arthur Gibson's *The Rite of Redemption in the Films of Ingmar Bergman* (Lewiston, N.Y.: Edwin Mellen Press, 1995) for a discussion of this point.

22. Indeed, sometimes this experience has the opposite effect. In Sartre's "The Wall," Pablo Ibbieta's last-minute reprieve from the firing squad leads him to believe that nothing has value – that all values are hollow because they cannot endure or stand up to an always imminent nonfuture; Pablo's life and political commitments are shattered into nihilism.

23. In the true ontological sense (rather than as a temporary transition to an "afterlife").

24. The greatest influence here was probably the Heidegger of *Being and Time*. See, for instance, the "existential analyses" of psychiatric patients by Ludwig Binswanger; R. D. Laing represents a slightly more Sartrean approach. Though meant as replacements for Freudian analysis, they share its emphasis on choice and intentional structure in understanding our psychic life.
25. E.g., *Bergman on Bergman*, pp. 219–29.
26. "But what does that mean – 'plague'? Just life, no more than that." "They knew now that if there is one thing one can always yearn for and sometimes attain, it is human love. But for those others who aspired beyond and above the human individual toward something they could not even imagine, there had been no answer." ". . . to take, in every predicament, the victim's side." (*The Plague*, trans. Stuart Gilbert [New York: Vintage Books, 1948], pp. 285, 279, 237.) Bergman describes Camus as advancing "a sort of refined existentialism" (compared to Sartre). Around 1960, just before Camus's death, there was correspondence about making a film of *The Fall* (1957). It is hard to imagine how this could be done, particularly how what is essentially an interior dialogue could be turned into a film of relationships. Bergman was not optimistic and said he most of all wanted to meet Camus. (See *Bergman on Bergman*, pp. 12 and 26–7.)
27. Allen's famous response to those questioning his relationship with Soon-Yi.
28. For Allen's response to Bergman, see Woody Allen, "Through a Life Darkly" (review of *The Magic Lantern*), *New York Times Book Review* (1988) (reprinted in Roger W. Oliver, ed. *Ingmar Bergman: An Artist's Journey, On Stage, On Screen, In Print* [New York: Arcade Publishing, 1995], pp. 25–30). See also Bert Cardullo, "Autumn Interiors, or the Ladies Eve: Woody Allen's Ingmar Bergman Complex," *Antioch Review* 58:4 (Fall 2000), pp. 428–40.

Filmography

1. Interview of Liv Ullmann by Sissel Fantoft in the Oslo *Dagbladet*, Nov. 3, 2002; see also Jan Lumholdt, "Ingmar Bergman's *Saraband*," *Film Comment* 39:3 (May/June 2003), pp. 12–14. Starring Ullmann and Erland Josephson, the film examines the lives of Marianne and Johan from *Scenes from a Marriage* thirty years later. Ullmann reports that it is Bergman's final film [www.dagbladet.no/kultur/2002/11/03/352917] Bergman has given his personal papers ("45 packing cases") to the Swedish Film Institute (interview with the curator by Ryan Gibley, Jan. 20, 2003, reprinted from *The Guardian* in the on-line service *The Age* [www.theage.com.au/articles/2003/01/20/1042911324940]).
2. See Bergman, *Images: My Life in Film*, trans. Marianne Ruuth (New York: Arcade Publishing, 1994), p. 439; and see the "Internet Movie Database" (www.imdb.com).
3. See Cowie, p. 93; Bergman, *Images*, p. 439.
4. Bergman also directed, and wrote, plays for Swedish radio. Egil Törnqvist says that, as of 1995, he is "responsible for 39 radio productions, including eight Strindberg, three Hjalmar Bergman and three Ingmar Bergman." See *Between Stage and Screen: Ingmar Bergman Directs* (Amsterdam: Amsterdam University Press, 1995), p. 191.

Selected Bibliography

The most extensive reference source for Bergman is Steene's *Ingmar Bergman: A Guide to References and Resources,* which covers materials through 1984 from North America and Europe, including the press and public reception of each film. There is now a voluminous secondary literature – Steene includes well over a thousand citations. This bibliography should provide a useful guide to research for interested readers. Several collections provide critical overviews and hence good starting points for further investigation (their contents are not usually cited separately). In addition to listing standard sources, I have tried to provide references to areas not discussed in this book, such as feminist criticism on Bergman or his relation to Strindberg.

Books, Scripts, Articles, and Interviews by Bergman

Scripts and Screenplays by Bergman

Autumn Sonata. Trans. Alan Blair. New York: Pantheon Books, 1978.

Face to Face. Trans. Alan Blair. New York: Pantheon Books, 1976.

Fanny and Alexander. Trans. Alan Blair. New York: Pantheon Books, 1982.

Four Screenplays of Ingmar Bergman (*Smiles of a Summer Night, The Seventh Seal, Wild Strawberries, The Magician*). Trans. Lars Malström and David Kushner. New York: Simon & Schuster, 1960.

From the Life of the Marionettes. Trans. Alan Blair. New York: Pantheon Books, 1980.

A Matter of the Soul (radio play, 1990). Trans. Eivor Martinus, in *New Swedish Plays*, ed. Gunilla Anderman. Norwich, England: Norvik Press, 1992, pp. 33–64.

"Persona" and "Shame": The Screenplays of Ingmar Bergman. Trans. Keith Bradfield. New York: Grossman Publishers, 1972.

Scenes from a Marriage. Trans. Alan Blair. New York: Bantam Books, 1974.

The Serpent's Egg. Trans. Alan Blair. New York: Pantheon Books, 1977.

The Seventh Seal. Trans. Lars Malström and David Kushner. New York: Simon & Schuster, 1960. "Modern Film Scripts" series.

Three Films by Ingmar Bergman: Through a Glass Darkly, Winter Light, The Silence. Trans. Paul Britten Austin. New York: Grove Press, 1963, 1967. *Wild Strawberries*. Trans. Lars Malström and David Kushner. New York: Simon & Schuster, 1960. "Modern Film Scripts" series; with a "Discussion on Film-making" and "Tribute to Victor Sjöström" by Bergman.

Books and Articles by Bergman

The Best Intentions (Goda viljian). Trans. Joan Tate. New York: Arcade Publishing, 1993.

"Each Film Is My Last." *The Drama Review* 11:1 (Fall 1996), pp. 94–101. Reprinted in Kaminsky, *Bergman: Essays*, pp. 88–97.

The Fifth Act (Femte akten). Trans. Linda Haverty Rugg and Joan Tate. New York: New Press, 2001. Includes "Monologue," "After the Rehearsal," "The Last Scream: A Slightly Skewed Morality Tale," and "In the Presence of a Clown."

Four Stories by Ingmar Bergman ("The Touch," "Cries and Whispers," "The Hour of the Wolf," "The Passion of Anna"). Trans. Alan Blair. New York: Doubleday, 1976.

Images: My Life in Film (Bilder). Trans. Marianne Ruuth. New York: Arcade Publishing, 1994.

The Magic Lantern: An Autobiography (Laterna magica). Trans. Joan Tate. New York: Viking, 1988.

Private Confessions. Trans. Joan Tate. New York: Arcade Publishing, 1996.

"The Snakeskin." *Film Comment* 6 (Summer 1970), pp. 9–21. Reprinted in *"Persona" and "Shame,"* pp. 9–15.

Sunday's Children (Sondägs barn). Trans. Joan Tate. New York: Arcade Publishing, 1993.

Wood Painting: A Morality Play (Trälmålning, 1954). Trans. Randolph Goodman and Leif Sjöberg. Basis for *The Seventh Seal*. Reprinted in Steene, *Focus on "The Seventh Seal,"* pp. 159–73.

Interviews

Alvarez, A. "A Visit with Ingmar Bergman." *New York Times Magazine* (December 7, 1975), p. 36 ff.

Baldwin, James. "The Precarious Vogue of Ingmar Bergman." *Esquire* 53:4 (April 1960), pp. 128–32. Reprinted as "The Northern Protestant" in *Nobody Knows My Name*. New York: Dial Press, 1961, pp. 163–80. Also reprinted in Oliver, *Bergman: An Artist's Journey*, pp. 79–87.

Bergman, Ingmar. *Bergman on Bergman: Interviews with Ingmar Bergman*. Ed. Stig Björkman, Torsten Manns, and Jonas Sima. Trans. Paul Britten Austin. New York: Simon & Schuster, 1973.

Donner, Jörg. *Ingmar Bergman on Life and Work: A Conversation with Jörg Donner*. Top Story Filmproduction, ARTE, Sveriges Television Drama, 1998; 90 min. On Criterion DVD (1998) of *Wild Strawberries*.

Jacobs, James, M. Sineux, and N.-P. Sundgren. "Ingmar Bergman at Work." *Positif* 204 (March 1978), pp. 18–27. About *The Serpent's Egg*.

Jones, G. William, ed. *Talking with Ingmar Bergman* (Dallas: SMU Press, 1983). Record of four seminar sessions at Southern Methodist University, May 1981.

Kakutani, Michiko. "Ingmar Bergman: Summing Up a Life in Film." *New York Times Magazine* (June 26, 1983), p. 32 ff.

Lahr, John. "Profile: The Demon-Lover – After Six Decades in Film and Theatre, Ingmar Bergman Talks about His Family Secrets and the Invention of Psychological Drama." *New Yorker* 75:13 (May 31, 1999), p. 66 ff.

Sorel, Edith. "Ingmar Bergman: I Confect Dreams and Anguish." *New York Times* (January 22, 1978). (With IB in Munich.)

von Sivers, Malou. *Ingmar Bergman: Reflections on Life, Death, and Love, with Erland Josephson.* Directed by Stefan Brenn, TV4 AB Sweden, 1999; 52 min. On Criterion DVD (2000) of *Cries and Whispers.*

Wolf, William. "Face to Face with Ingmar Bergman." *New York Magazine* (October 27, 1980), pp. 33–8. (With IB on Fårö.)

Books, Articles, and Other Bergman-Related Publications

Collections

Kaminsky, Stuart, ed. *Ingmar Bergman: Essays in Criticism.* New York: Oxford University Press, 1975.

Michaels, Lloyd, ed. *Ingmar Bergman's "Persona."* Cambridge: Cambridge University Press, 1999.

Oliver, Roger W., ed. *Ingmar Bergman: An Artist's Journey, On Stage, On Screen, In Print.* New York: Arcade Publishing, 1995.

Petrić, Vlada, ed. *Film and Dreams: An Approach to Bergman.* South Salem, N.Y.: Redgrave, 1981.

Steene, Birgitta, ed. *Focus on "The Seventh Seal."* Englewood Cliffs, N.J.: Prentice–Hall, 1972.

Books

Bergom-Larsson, Maria. *Ingmar Bergman and Society.* San Diego: A. S. Barnes, 1978.

Blackwell, Marilyn Johns. *Gender and Representation in the Films of Ingmar Bergman.* Columbia, S.C.: Camden House, 1997.

Persona: The Transcendent Image. Urbana: University of Illinois Press, 1986.

Blake, Richard A. *The Lutheran Milieu of the Films of Ingmar Bergman.* New York: Arno Press, 1978.

Bragg, Melwyn. *The Seventh Seal.* London: British Film Institute, 1993. "BFI Film Classics" series.

Cohen, Hubert I. *Ingmar Bergman: The Art of Confession.* New York: Twayne, 1993. Includes an extensive bibliography.

Cowie, Peter. *Ingmar Bergman: A Critical Biography.* New York: Charles Scribner's Sons, 1982.
Scandinavian Cinema. London: Tantivy Press, 1990.
Donner, Jörn. *The Personal Vision of Ingmar Bergman.* Bloomington: University of Indiana Press, 1972.
French, Philip, and Kersti French. *Wild Strawberries.* London: British Film Institute, 1995. "BFI Film Classics" series.
Gado, Frank. *The Passion of Ingmar Bergman.* Durham, N.C.: Duke University Press, 1986.
Gervais, Marc. *Ingmar Bergman: Magician and Prophet.* Toronto: McGill–Queens University Press, 1999.
Gibson, Arthur. *The Rite of Redemption in the Films of Ingmar Bergman.* Lewiston, N.Y.: Edwin Mellen Press, 1995.
The Silence of God: Creative Response to the Films of Ingmar Bergman. New York: Harper & Row, 1969.
Kawin, Bruce. *Mindscreen: Bergman, Godard, and First-Person Film.* Princeton: Princeton University Press, 1978.
Ketcham, Charles B. *The Influence of Existentialism on Ingmar Bergman.* Lewiston, N.Y.: Edwin Mellen Press, 1986.
Lauder, Robert. *God, Death, Art, and Love: The Philosophical Vision of Ingmar Bergman.* New York: Paulist Press, 1989.
Livingston, Paisley. *Ingmar Bergman and the Rituals of Art.* Ithaca: Cornell University Press, 1982. Includes an excellent bibliography.
Long, Robert Emmet. *Ingmar Bergman: Film and Stage.* New York: Abrahams, 1994.
Marker, Lise-Lone, and Frederick J. Marker. *Ingmar Bergman: Four Decades in the Theater.* Cambridge: Cambridge University Press, 1982.
Ingmar Bergman: A Life in the Theater. Cambridge: Cambridge University Press, 1992.
Mosley, Philip. *Ingmar Bergman: The Cinema as Mistress.* Boston: Marion Boyers, 1981.
Simon, John. *Ingmar Bergman Directs.* New York: Harcourt Brace Jovanovich, 1972.
Sjöman, Vilgot. *L136: Diary with Ingmar Bergman.* Trans. Alan Blair. Ann Arbor, Mich.: Karoma Publishers, 1978. A record of the making of *Winter Light.*
Steene, Birgitta. *Ingmar Bergman.* New York: Twayne, 1968.
Ingmar Bergman: A Guide to References and Resources. Boston: G. K. Hall, 1987.
Törnqvist, Egil. *Between Stage and Screen: Ingmar Bergman Directs.* Amsterdam: Amsterdam University Press, 1995.
Ullmann, Liv. *Changing.* New York: Knopf, 1977.
Wood, Robin. *Ingmar Bergman.* New York: Praeger, 1969.

Articles and Book Chapters

Alexander, William. "Devils in the Cathedral: Bergman's Trilogy." *Cinema Journal* 13:2 (Spring 1974), pp. 23–33.

Allen, Woody. "Through a Life Darkly" (review of *The Magic Lantern*). *New York Times Book Review* (1988). Reprinted in Oliver, *Bergman: An Artist's Journey*, pp. 25–30.

Andersson, Bibi. "Dialogue on Film." *American Film* 2:5 (March 1977), pp. 33–48.

Blackwell, Marilyn Johns. "The Chamber Plays and the Trilogy: A Revaluation of the Case of Strindberg and Bergman." In Blackwell, ed., *Structures of Influence: A Comparative Approach to August Strindberg*. Chapel Hill: University of North Carolina Press, 1981, pp. 49–64.

Blake, Richard A. "Sexual Themes in the Films of Ingmar Bergman." *Sexual Behavior* 1:5 (August 1971), pp. 35–43. Reprinted in Kaminsky, *Bergman: Essays*, pp. 29–44.

Borden, Diane M. "Bergman's Style and the Facial Icon." *Quarterly Review of Film Studies* 2 (1977), pp. 42–55.

Buntzen, Lynda. "Bergman's *Fanny and Alexander:* Family Romance or Artistic Allegory?" *Criticism* 29:1 (1987), pp. 89–117.

Buntzen, Lynda, and C. Craig. "*Hour of the Wolf:* The Case of Ingmar Bergman." *Film Quarterly* 30:2 (Winter 1976), pp. 23–34.

Cardullo, Bert. "Autumn Interiors, or the Ladies Eve: Woody Allen's Ingmar Bergman Complex." *Antioch Review* 58:4 (Fall 2000), pp. 428–40.

Davidson, Ann Morrisett. "A Great Man Who Humiliates Women." *Village Voice* (March 29, 1973), pp. 70–80.

Erikson, Erik H. "Reflection's on Dr. Borg's Life Cycle." In *Adulthood*. New York: W. W. Norton, 1978, pp. 1–31.

Fletcher, John. "Bergman and Strindberg." *Journal of Modern Literature* 3 (1973), pp. 173–90.

Gantz, Jeffrey. "Mozart, Hoffmann, and Ingmar Bergman's *Vargtimmen*." *Literature/Film Quarterly* 8 (1980), pp. 104–15.

Gill, Jerry. "On Knowing the Dancer from the Dance." *Journal of Aesthetics and Art Criticism* 34 (1975), pp. 125–35.

Godard, Jean-Luc. "Bergmanorama." *Cahiers du cinéma* (July 1958). Reprinted in *Cahiers du cinéma in English* 85 (January 1966), pp. 56–62, and in Oliver, *Bergman: An Artist's Journey*, pp. 37–41.

Harcourt, Peter. "Bergman's *Passion of Anna:* The Interplay of Forces Large and Small." *Cinema* 6 (Fall 1970), pp. 32–9.

Haskell, Molly. *From Reverence to Rape: The Treatment of Women in the Movies.* New York: Holt Rinehart, 1974, "The Europeans," p. 314 ff.

Hayes, Jarrod. "The Seduction of Alexander Behind the Postmodern Door: Ingmar Bergman and Baudrillard's *De la séduction*." *Literature/Film Quarterly* 25:1 (1997), pp. 40–8.

Holden, D. F. "Three Literary Sources for *Through a Glass Darkly*." *Literature/Film Quarterly* 2:1 (Winter 1974), pp. 22–9.

Holland, Norman. "*The Seventh Seal:* The Film as Iconography." *Hudson Review* 12:2 (1959), pp. 266–70.

Ingelmanson, Birgitta. "The Screenplays of Ingmar Bergman: Personification and Olfactory Detail." *Literature/Film Quarterly* 12:1 (January 1984), pp. 26–33.

Kalin, Jesse. "Ingmar Bergman's Contribution to Moral Philosophy." *International Philosophical Quarterly* 17:1 (March 1977), pp. 170–81.

Kauffmann, Stanley. "The Abduction from the Theater: Mozart Opera on Film." *Yale Review* 81:1 (January 1993), pp. 92–104.

Kennedy, Harlan. "Whatever Happened to Ingmar Bergman?" *Film Comment* 34:4 (July 1998), pp. 64–8.

Kinder, Marsha. "*From the Life of the Marionettes* to *The Devil's Wanton*: Bergman's Creative Transformation of a Recurrent Nightmare." *Film Quarterly* 34 (Spring 1981), pp. 26–36.

Koskinen, Maaret. "The Typically Swedish in Ingmar Bergman." *Chaplin, 25th Anniversary Issue* (1984), pp. 5–11. Reprinted in Oliver, *Bergman: An Artist's Journey*, pp. 126–36.

Librach, Ronald S. "Through the Glass Darkly: *The Serpent's Egg*." *Literature / Film Quarterly* 8:2 (Spring 1980), pp. 92–103.

McBride, Joseph, and Michael Wilmington. "A Long Way from Home" (interview with Max von Sydow and Liv Ullmann). *Sight and Sound* 39 (Winter 1969), pp. 39–43.

McCann, Eleanor. "The Rhetoric of *Wild Strawberries*." *Sight and Sound* 30:3 (Autumn 1961), pp. 44–6.

Madden, David. "*The Virgin Spring*: Anatomy of a Mythic Image." *Film Heritage* 2 (Winter 1966–7), pp. 2–20.

Mellen, Joan. *Women and Their Sexuality in the New Film*. New York: Horizon Press, 1973, chap. 4, "Bergman and Women: *Cries and Whispers*," pp. 97–116. Reprinted in Kaminsky, *Bergman: Essays*, pp. 297–312.

Nykvist, Sven. "Photographing the Films of Ingmar Bergman." *American Cinematographer* 43:10 (October 1962), p. 613 ff.

"Sven Nykvist, ASC, Talks about Filming Bergman's *The Magic Flute*." *American Cinematographer* (August 1975), pp. 894–9, 953–9.

Oliver, Kelly. "Alterity within Bergman's *Persona*: Face to Face with the Other." *Journal of Value Inquiry* 29:4 (1995), pp. 521–32.

Penley, Constance. "*Cries and Whispers*." *Women and Film* 1:3–4 (1973), pp. 55–6. Reprinted in Bill Nichols, ed., *Movies and Methods: An Anthology*. Berkeley: University of California Press, 1976, pp. 204–8.

Phillips, D. Z. *Through a Darkening Glass: Philosophy, Literature and Cultural Change*. Notre Dame, Ind.: University of Notre Dame Press, 1982, chap. 9, "Ingmar Bergman's Reductionism," pp. 133–64.

Rosen, Robert. "Enslaved by the Queen of the Night: The Relationship of Ingmar Bergman to E. T. A. Hoffmann." *Film Comment* 6 (Spring 1970), pp. 26–31.

Rugg, Linda Haverty. "'Carefully I Touched the Faces of My Parents': Bergman's Autobiographical Image." *Biography* 24:1 (2001), pp. 72–84.

Sammern-Frankenegg, Fritz R. "Learning 'A Few Words in the Foreign Language': Ingmar Bergman's 'Secret Message' in the Imagery of Hand and Face." *Scandinavian Studies* 49:3 (Summer 1977), pp. 301–10.

Sandberg, Mark. "Rewriting God's Plot: Ingmar Bergman and Feminine Narrative." *Scandinavian Studies* 63:1 (Winter 1991), pp. 1–29.

"Tracking Out: 'The Bergman Film' in Retrospect." *Scandinavian Studies* 69:3 (Summer 1997), pp. 357–75.

Sarris, Andrew. "*The Seventh Seal.*" *Film Culture* 19 (1959), pp. 51–61. Reprinted in Steene, *Focus on "The Seventh Seal,"* pp. 81–91.

Schillaci, Anthony. "Bergman's Vision of Good and Evil." In *Celluloid and Symbols,* ed. John C. Cooper and Carl Skrade. Philadelphia: Fortress Press, 1970, pp. 75–88.

Scholar, Nancy. "Anaïs Nin's *House of Incest* and Ingmar Bergman's *Persona:* Two Variations on a Theme." *Literature/Film Quarterly* 7:1 (Winter 1979), pp. 47–59.

Scott, James F. "The Achievement of Ingmar Bergman." *Journal of Aesthetics and Art Criticism* 24 (1965), pp. 263–72.

Sitney, P. Adams. "Bergman's *The Silence* and the Primal Scene." *Film Culture* 76 (June 1992), pp. 35–8.

"Color and Myth in *Cries and Whispers.*" *Film Criticism* 13:3 (Spring 1989), pp. 37–41.

Sontag, Susan. "Bergman's *Persona.*" *Sight and Sound* 36:4 (Autumn 1967), pp. 186–91. Reprinted in *Styles of Radical Will.* New York: Farrar, Straus & Giroux, 1967, pp. 123–45, as well as in Kaminsky, *Bergman: Essays,* pp. 253–69, and Michaels, *Ingmar Bergman's "Persona,"* pp. 62–85.

Sprinchorn, Evert. "Fanny and Alexander and Strindberg and Ibsen and...." In *Strindberg, Ibsen and Bergman: Essays on Scandinavian Film and Drama,* ed. Harry Perridon. Maastricht: Shaker Publishing, 1998.

Steene, Birgitta. "Bergman's Portrait of Women: Sexism or Subjective Metaphor?" In *Sexual Strategems: The World of Women in Film,* ed. Patricia Erens. New York: Horizon, 1979, pp. 91–107.

"The Milk and Strawberry Sequence in *The Seventh Seal.*" *Film Heritage* 8:4 (1973), pp. 10–18.

Truffaut, François. "On Ingmar Bergman." From *Cahiers du cinéma,* 1958 and 1973, in Oliver, *Bergman: An Artist's Journey,* pp. 31–6.

Ullmann, Liv. "Dialogue on Film." *American Film Institute* 2:3 (March 1973), pp. 1–22.

Wexman, Virginia Wright. "An Interview with Liv Ullmann." *Cinema Journal* 20:1 (Fall 1980).

Films and Multimedia

Coe, George, and Anthony Lover, directors; Sidney Davis, writer. *De Düva (The Dove).* Liberty Film Studio; bw 15 min., 1968. Parody of *Wild Strawberries* and *The Seventh Seal.* With Madeline Kahn.

Cowie, Peter. Audio commentary (1987) to *The Seventh Seal;* 96 min., on the Criterion DVD (1998).

Audio commentary (2001) to *Wild Strawberries;* 91 min., on the Criterion DVD (2002).

Ingmar Bergman: An Illustrated Filmography. On Criterion DVD (1998) of *The Seventh Seal.*

Nykvist, Carl-Gustav. *Light Keeps Me Company (Ljuset håller mig sällskap).* Documentary on the life and career of Sven Nykvist, by his son; 78 min., bw and color, 2000.

Filmography

Although filmmaking is always a cooperative artistic enterprise, Bergman has also enjoyed an almost unprecedented control over his films and, once established, has always occupied the central position in their creation as both director and writer. Unless noted, in addition to being director Bergman is also responsible for the screenplay. The release date provided (except where indicated) is the Swedish premiere. Fuller details and cast are given for films discussed in the book. Complete details can be found in Cowie's biography, in Gado, or at the "Internet Movie Database" (www.imdb.com). For Bergman's works other than as a film director, see the list of "Additional Credits" at the end of the Filmography.

1946

Crisis (Kris)

From the play *Moderdyret* by Leck Fischer; PH: Gösta Roosling; bw 93 min.; Feb. 25, 1946.

It Rains on Our Love/The Man with an Umbrella (Det regnar på vår kärlek)

With Herbert Grevenius from the play *Bra mennesker* by Oskar Braaten; PH: Göran Strindberg, Hilding Blah; bw 95 min.; Nov. 9, 1946.

1947

A Ship to India/The Land of Desire (Skepp till Indialand)

From the play *Skepp till Indialand* by Martin Söderhjelm; PH: Göran Strindberg; bw 102 min.; Sept. 22, 1947.

1948

Music in Darkness/Night Is My Future (Musik i mörker)

SCR: Dagmar Edqvist from her novel; PH: Göran Strindberg; bw 85 min.; Jan. 17, 1948. (Nominated for a Golden Lion at Venice.)

Port of Call (Hamnstad)
SCR: Olle Ländsberg; PH: Gunnar Fischer; bw 99 min.; Oct. 11, 1948.

1949

Prison (Fängelse) (aka *The Devil's Wanton*)
PH: Göran Strindberg; bw 80 min.; March 19, 1949.

Thirst/Three Strange Loves (Törst)
SCR: Herbert Grevenius from the short stories *Törst* by Birgit Tengroth; PH: Gunnar Fischer; bw 88 min.; Oct. 17, 1949.

1950

To Joy (Till glädje)
PH: Gunnar Fischer; bw 98 min.; Feb. 20, 1950.

This Can't Happen Here/High Tension (Sånt händer inte här [lit. "Such Things Don't Happen Here"])
SCR: Herbert Grevenius from the novel *I løpet av tolv timer* by Waldemar Brøgger; PH: Gunnar Fischer; bw 84 min.; Oct. 18, 1950.

1951

Illicit Interlude/Summer Interlude (Sommarlek [lit. "Summer Play" or "Summer Game"])
With Herbert Grevenius from a story "Marie" by IB; PH: Gunnar Fischer; bw 96 min.; Oct. 1, 1951.

1952

Waiting Women/Secrets of Women (Kvinnors väntan [lit. "Women's Waiting"])
PH: Gunnar Fischer; bw 107 min.; Nov. 3, 1952.

1953

Summer with Monika/Monika (Sommaren med Monika)
With P. A. Fogelström from his novel; PH: Gunnar Fischer; bw 96 min.; Feb. 9, 1953.

Naked Night/Sawdust and Tinsel (Gycklarnas afton [lit. "The Clowns' Evening"])
PH: Hilding Bladh, Göran Strindberg, Sven Nykvist; MUSIC: Karl-Birger Blomdahl; PROD.: Rune Waldekranz; PROD. CO.: Sandrews; bw 92 min.; Sept. 14, 1953.
CAST: Albert Johansson (Åke Grönberg), Anne (Harriet Andersson), Frost

(Anders Ek), Alma (Gudrun Brost), Frans (Hasse Ekman), Mr. Sjuberg, Theater Director (Gunnar Björnstrand), Agda, Albert's wife (Annika Tretow), Jens (Erik Strandmark), Officer (Åke Fridell).

1954

A Lesson in Love (En lektion i kärlek)

PH: Martin Bodin; bw 95 min.; Oct. 4, 1954.

1955

Dreams/Journey into Autumn (Kvinnodröm)

PH: Hilding Bladh; bw 86 min.; Aug. 22, 1955.

Smiles of a Summer Night (Sommarnattens leende)

PH: Gunnar Fischer; MUSIC: Erik Nordgren; PROD. MGR.: Allan Ekelund; ASST. DIR.: Lennart Olsson; PROD. CO.: Svensk Filmindustri; bw 108 min.; Dec. 26, 1955. (Winner for Best Poetic Humor at Cannes.)

CAST: Fredrik Egerman (Gunnar Björnstrand), Anne Egerman, his wife (Ulla Jacobsson), Henrik, his son (Björn Bjelvenstam), Petra, the maid (Harriet Andersson), Desirée Armfeldt (Eva Dahlbeck), Madame Armfeldt (Naima Wifstrand), Frid (Åke Fridell), Count Carl-Magnus Malcolm (Jarl Kulle), Charlotte Malcolm (Margit Carlqvist), Malla, Desirée's maid (Gull Natrop), Desirée's son (Anders Wulff), actresses (Birgitta Valberg, Bibi Andersson), Egerman's cook (Jullan Kindahl).

1957

The Seventh Seal (Det sjunde inseglet)

PH: Gunnar Fischer; MUSIC: Erik Nordgren; PROD. MGR.: Allan Ekelund; ASST. DIR.: Lennart Olsson; PROD. CO.: Svensk Filmindustri; bw 95 min.; Feb. 16, 1957. (Jury Prize at Cannes, tied with Wajda's *Kanal*.)

CAST: Antonius Block (Max von Sydow), Squire Jöns (Gunnar Björnstrand), Death (Bengt Ekerot), girl rescued by Jöns (Gunnel Lindbloom), Jof (Nils Poppe), Mia, his wife (Bibi Andersson), Skat (Erik Strandmark), Plog, the blacksmith (Åke Fridell), Lisa, his wife (Inga Gill), Tyan, the witch-girl (Maud Hansson), Raval (Bertil Anderberg), Karin, the knight's wife (Inga Landgré), flagellant monk (Anders Ek), Albertus, the painter (Gunnar Olsson), tavern owner (Benkt-Åke Benktsson).

Wild Strawberries (Smultronstället)

PH: Gunnar Fischer; MUSIC: Erik Nordgren; PROD. MGR.: Allan Ekelund; ASST. DIR.: Gösta Ekman; PROD. CO.: Svensk Filmindustri; bw 90 min.; Dec. 26, 1957. (Golden Bear at Berlin and Italian Film Critics Award at Venice; special career award for Victor Sjöström at Berlin; Golden Globe, shared, 1960; Academy Award nomination for Best Screenplay, 1960.)

CAST: Prof. Isak Borg (Victor Sjöström), Agda, his housekeeper (Jullan Kindahl), Marianne, his daughter-in-law (Ingrid Thulin), Evald, his son (Gunnar Björnstrand), Sara (Bibi Andersson), Viktor (Björn Bjelvenstam), Anders (Folke Sundqvist), Isak's mother (Naima Wifstrand), Sten Alman (Gunnar Sjöberg), Berit, his wife (Gunnel Broström), Karin, Isak's wife (Gertrud Fridh), her lover (Åke Fridell), Åkerman, gas station owner (Max von Sydow), his wife (Anne-Marie Winman), Uncle Aron (Yngve Nordwall), aunt (Sif Ruud), twins (Lena Bergman, Monica Ehrling), Sigfrid (Per Sjöstrand), Sigbritt (Gio Petré), Charlotte (Gunnel Lindbloom), Angelica (Maud Hansson), Anna (Eva Noreé).

1958

Brink of Life/So Close to Life (*Nära livet*)

With Ulla Isaksson, based on a short story from her book *Dödens faster;* PH: Max Wilén; bw 84 min.; March 31, 1958. (Best Director and Best Actress – Bibi Andersson, Eva Dahlbeck, Barbro Hiort af Ornäs, and Ingrid Thulin – at Cannes.)

The Magician/The Face (*Ansiktet*)

PH: Gunnar Fischer; bw 100 min.; Dec. 26, 1958. (Special Jury Prize at Venice.)

1960

The Virgin Spring (*Jungfrukällan*)

SCR: Ulla Isaksson, based on the fourteenth-century legend *Töres dotter i Wänge;* PH: Sven Nykvist; bw 88 min.; Feb. 8, 1960. (Academy Award and Golden Globe for Best Foreign Language Film, as well as Special Mention at Cannes.)

The Devil's Eye (*Djävulens öga*)

Based on the radio play "Don Juan vender tilbage" by Oluf Bang; PH: Gunnar Fischer; bw 86 min.; Oct. 17, 1960.

1961

Through a Glass Darkly (*Såsom i en spegel* [lit. "As in a Mirror"])

PH: Sven Nykvist; MUSIC: Erik Nordgren, Bach; PROD. MGR.: Allan Ekelund; ASST. DIR.: Lenn Hjortzberg; PROD. CO.: Svensk Filmindustri; bw 89 min.; Oct. 16, 1961. (Academy Award for Best Foreign Language Film; OCIC Award, Berlin.)

CAST: David (Gunnar Björnstrand), Karin, his daughter (Harriet Andersson), Martin, her husband (Max von Sydow), Minus, Karin's brother (Lars Passgård).

1963

Winter Light/The Communicants (*Nattvardsgästerna*)

PH: Sven Nykvist; MUSIC: from *The Swedish Hymnal;* PROD. MGR.: Allan Ekelund; ASST. DIR.: Lenn Hjortzberg, Vilgot Sjöman; PROD. CO.: Svensk Filmindustri; bw 80 min.; Feb. 11, 1963.

CAST: Tomas Ericsson (Gunnar Björnstrand), Märta Lundberg (Ingrid Thulin), Jonas Persson (Max von Sydow), Karin Persson, his wife (Gunnel Lindbloom), Fredrik Blom, organist (Olof Thunberg), Algot Frövik, sexton (Allan Edwall), Knut Aronson, church treasurer (Kolbjörn Knudsen).

The Silence (*Tystnaden*)

PH: Sven Nykvist; MUSIC: Ivan Renliden, R. Mersey, Bach; PROD. MGR.: Allan Ekelund; ASST. DIR.: Lars-Erik Liedholm, Lenn Hjortzberg; PROD. CO.: Svensk Filmindustri; bw 95 min.; Sept. 23, 1963.

CAST: Ester (Ingrid Thulin), Anna, her sister (Gunnel Lindblom), Johan, Anna's son (Jörgen Lindström).

1964

All These Women/Now about These Women (*För att inte tala om alla dessa kvinnor* [lit. "Not to Mention All These Women!"])

Under pseudonym "Buntel Eriksson," with Erland Josephson; PH: Sven Nykvist; color 80 min.; June 15, 1964.

1966

Persona

PH: Sven Nykvist; MUSIC: Lars Johan Werle, Bach; PROD. MGR.: Lars-Owe Carlberg; PROD. CO.: Svensk Filmindustri; bw 84 min.; Oct. 18, 1966. (National Society of Film Critics, USA, for Best Director.)

CAST: Elisabet Vogler (Liv Ullmann), nurse Alma (Bibi Andersson), psychiatrist (Margaretha Krook), Mr. Vogler (Gunnar Björnstrand), Elisabet's son (Jörgen Lindström).

1967

"Daniel"

One of eight episodes in the complilation film *Stimulantia*, featuring his son Daniel Sebastien Bergman and the boy's mother, Käbi Laretei; PH: Bergman; color 16mm; March 28, 1967.

1968

Hour of the Wolf (*Vargtimmen*)

PH: Sven Nykvist; bw 89 min.; Feb. 19, 1968. (National Society of Film Critics, USA, for Best Director.)

Shame/The Shame (Skammen)

PH: Sven Nykvist; PROD. MGR.: Lars-Owe Carlberg; ASST. DIR.: Raymond Lundberg; PROD. CO.: Svensk Filmindustri/Cinematograph (Bergman's own production company); bw 102 min.; Sept. 29, 1968. (National Society of Film Critics, USA, for Best Film, Best Director, and Best Actress – Liv Ullmann.)

CAST: Eva Rosenberg (Liv Ullmann), Jan Rosenberg (Max von Sydow), Jacobi (Gunnar Björnstrand), Mrs. Jacobi (Birgitta Valberg), Filip (Sigge Fürst), Lobelius (Hans Alfredson), interrogator (Frank Sundström), doctor (Ulf Johansson), interviewer (Vilgot Sjöman).

1969

The Rite/The Ritual (Riten)

PH: Sven Nykvist; bw 74 min.; March 25, 1969 (on Swedish television).

The Passion of Anna/A Passion (En passion)

PH: Sven Nykvist; color 101 min.; Nov. 10, 1969. (National Society of Film Critics, USA, for Best Director.)

1970

Fårö-Dokument

PH: Sven Nykvist; narration IB; bw, color 78 min.; Jan 1, 1970 (on Swedish television).

1971

The Touch (Beröringen)

PH: Sven Nykvist (title sequence, Gunnar Fischer); American–Swedish co-production, in English; color 113 min.; Aug. 30, 1971.

1973

Cries and Whispers (Viskningar och rop [lit. "Whispers and Cries"])

PH: Sven Nykvist; MUSIC: Bach, Chopin; PROD. MGR.: Lars-Owe Carlberg; PROD. CO.: Cinematograph, with Svensk Filmindustri; color 91 min.; March 5, 1973. (Five Academy Award nominations, including for Best Picture, with an award to Sven Nykvist for Best Cinematography; National Society of Film Critics, USA, for Best Screenplay and Best Cinematography; New York Film Critics Circle Award for Best Director, Best Screenplay, Best Film, and Best Actress – Liv Ullmann; Technical Grand Prize at Cannes.)

CAST: Agnes (Harriet Andersson), Maria/mother (Liv Ullmann), Karin (Ingrid Thulin), Anna (Kari Sylwan), doctor (Erland Josephson), Joakim, Maria's husband (Henning Moritzen), Fredrik, Karin's husband (Georg Åhlin), Pastor Isak (Anders Ek), Maria's daughter (Linn Ullmann), Maria as child (Lena Bergman), Agnes as child (Rosanna Mariano), Karin as child (Monika Priede).

Scenes from a Marriage (*Scener ur ett äktenskap*)

PH: Sven Nykvist; PROD. MGR./EXEC.: PROD.: Lars-Owe Carlberg; PROD. CO.: Cinematograph; color 16mm 168 min. (theatrical version); in six weekly parts on Swedish television, April 11 through May 16, 1973. (Golden Globe for Best Foreign Language Film; National Society of Film Critics for Best Film, Best Screenplay, Best Actress – Liv Ullmann, and Best Supporting Actress – Bibi Andersson; New York Film Critics Circle Award for Best Screenplay and Best Actress.)

CAST: Marianne (Liv Ullmann), Johan (Erland Josephson), interviewer (Anita Wall), Katarina (Bibi Andersson), Peter (Jan Malmsjö), Eva (Gunnel Lindbloom), Mrs. Jacobi (Barbro Hiort af Ornäs).

1975

The Magic Flute (*Trollflöjten*)

IB screenplay based on Mozart–Schikaneder; PH: Sven Nykvist; color 135 min.; Jan. 1, 1975 (on Swedish television). (National Society of Film Critics, USA, Special Award "for demonstrating how pleasurable opera can be on film.")

1976

Face to Face (*Ansikte mot ansikte*)

PH: Sven Nykvist; color 136 min.; in four weekly parts on Swedish television, April 28 to May 19, 1976.

1977

The Serpent's Egg (*Das Schlangenei /Ormens ägg*)

PH: Sven Nykvist; German–American coproduction, in English; color 119 min.; premiered Germany and Sweden, Oct. 28, 1977.

1978

Autumn Sonata (*Herbstsonat /Höstsonaten*)

PH: Sven Nykvist; color 92 min.; Oct. 8, 1978.

1979

Fårö-Dokument 1979

PH: Arne Carlsson; color 16mm 104 min.; Dec. 24, 1979 (on Swedish television).

1980

From the Life of the Marionettes (*Aus dem Leben der Marionetten*)

PH: Sven Nykvist; bw and color 104 min.; premiered Paris, Oct. 8, 1980; Swedish release Jan. 24, 1981.

1982

Fanny and Alexander (Fanny och Alexander)

PH: Sven Nykvist; MUSIC: Daniel Bell, Bach; EXEC.: PROD.: Jörn Donner; PROD. CO.: Svenska Filminstitutet/Sveriges TV/Personafilm (Munich – Bergman's own company)/Gaumont (Paris); color; theatrical version 199 min., Dec. 17, 1982; television version in four parts 312 min. (Academy Awards for Best Foreign Language Film, Best Cinematography – Nykvist, Best Costume Design, and Best Art/Set Direction; Golden Globe for Best Foreign Language Film; Venice, Film Critics Award, to Bergman; New York Film Critics Circle Award for Best Foreign Language Film and Best Director.)

CAST: *Ekdahl House:* Helena Ekdahl (Gunn Wållgren), Oscar Ekdahl (Allan Edwall), Emilie, his wife (Ewa Fröling), Alexander (Bertil Guve), Fanny (Pernilla Allwin), Carl Ekdahl (Börje Ahlstedt), Lydia, his wife (Christina Schollin), Gustav Adolf Ekdahl (Jarl Kulle), Alma, his wife (Mona Malm), Petra (Maria Granlund), Jenny (Emelie Werkö), Putte (Kristian Almgren), Maj (Pernilla Wallgren August), Aunt Anna (Käbi Laretei), Miss Vega, cook (Majlis Granlund), Miss Ester, parlor maid (Svea Holst-Widén); *Theater:* Mr. Philip Landahl, director (Gunnar Björnstrand), Miss Hanna Schwartz (Anna Bergman); *Bishop's Palace:* Bishop Edvard Vergérus (Jan Malmsjö), Henrietta Vergérus, his sister (Kerstin Tedelius), Mrs. Blenda Vergérus, his mother (Marianne Aminoff), Elsa Bergius, his invalid aunt (?), Malla Tander, cook (Marrit Olsson), Justina, maid (Harriet Andersson), Pauline and Esmeralda, ghost daughters of the bishop (Linda Krüger and Pernilla Wahlgren); *Isak's Shop:* Isak Jacobi (Erland Josephson), Aron and Ismael, his nephews (Mats Bergman and Stina Ekblad), young man (Peter Stormare).

1984

After the Rehearsal (Efter repetitionen)

PH: Sven Nykvist; color 72 min.; April 9, 1984 (on Swedish television).

1986

The Blessed Ones (De två saliga)

SCR: Ulla Isaksson from her novel; PH: Per Norén; color 81 min.; Feb. 19, 1986 (on Swedish television).

The Making of Fanny and Alexander (Dokument Fanny och Alexander)

PH: Arne Carlsson; color 110 min.; Aug. 18, 1986 (on Swedish television).

Karin's Face (Karins ansikte)

PH: Arne Carlsson; color 14 min.; Sept. 29, 1986 (on Swedish television).

1995

The Last Gasp (Sista skriket)

bw 60 min.; Jan. 6, 1995 (on Swedish television).

1997

In the Presence of a Clown (Larmar och gör sig till)

PH: Tony Forsberg, Irene Wiklund; color 119 min.; Nov. 1, 1997 (on Swedish television).

2003

Sarabande

Color 120 min.; scheduled for Fall 2003 (on Swedish television).[1]

Availability

Aside from his first three films and the early *This Can't Happen Here,* the Fårö films, "Daniel," and the films following *After the Rehearsal,* all of Bergman's films are or have been available on videotape, as well as on laser disc and DVD. The one exception is *Face to Face.*

Additional Credits

Awards

Bergman was given an Academy Irving G. Thalberg Award in 1971, a career Venice Golden Lion in 1971, and two awards at Cannes – the Palm of the Palms in 1997 and the Prize of the Ecumenical Jury in 1998 for his films as a body of work.

Theater

Bergman has been active in the theater throughout his career. A list of his major productions, including his own plays, is given in Cowie's biography and in Steene's guide, and both Cowie and Gado include some discussion of his theatrical career in their books. Lise-Lone Marker and Frederick J. Marker provide the most detailed account of Bergman's theater practice, especially with respect to Strindberg, in their *Ingmar Bergman: Four Decades in the Theater* (New York: Cambridge University Press, 1982).

Theater for Television

As well as continuing throughout his career to direct for the theater (and opera), Bergman from time to time made television productions of theater plays. *Sleeman's Coming* (*Herr Sleeman kommer*) by Hjalmar Bergman (April 18, 1957); *The Venetian* (*Venetianskan*) adapted from Giacomo Oreglia (Aug. 21, 1958); *Rabies* by Olle Hedberg (Nov. 7, 1958); *Storm Weather* (*Oväder*) by Strindberg (Jan. 22, 1960); *A Dream Play* (*Ett drömspel*) by Strindberg (Feb. 5, 1963); *The Misanthrope* (*Misantropen*) by Molière (Denmark, May 10, 1974); *School for Wives* (*Hustruskolan*) by Molière (Dec. 25, 1983); *Madame de Sade* (*Markisinnan de Sade*) by Yukio Mishima (April 17, 1992); *Backanterna* (April 9, 1993), based on Euripides' *Bacchae;* and *The Image Makers* (*Bildmakarna*) by Per Olov Enquist (Nov. 15, 2000) [lit. "The Picture Makers"].[2]

Commercials

In 1951, during a studio shutdown to protest excessive state taxes, Bergman wrote and directed nine deodorant soap commercials.[3]

Other Film Scripts

Some of Bergman's scripts have been produced and directed by others, most notably *Torment/Frenzy* (*Hets*) directed by Alf Sjöberg in 1944 (awarded the Grand Prize at Cannes in 1946) and recently *The Best Intentions* (*Den goda viljan* – 1991, dir. Bille August, winning the Golden Palm at Cannes and Best Actress for Pernilla August), *Sunday's Children* (*Söndagsbarn* – 1992, dir. Daniel Bergman), and *Private Confessions* (*Enskilda samtal* [lit. "Private Conversations"] – 1996, dir. Liv Ullmann), Bergman's reflections about his parents' troubled marriage and his early childhood, as well as the most recent *Faithless* (*Trolösa* – 2000, dir. Liv Ullmann). Other films that Bergman wrote but did not direct are *Woman without a Face* (*Kvinna utan ansikte,* 1947), *Eva* (1948), and *Divorced* (*Frånskild,* 1951), all directed by Gustav Molander; *While the City Sleeps* (*Medan staden sover,* 1950, dir. Lars-Eric Kjellgren), *Last Couple Out* (*Sista paret ut,* 1956, dir. Alf Sjöberg), *Night Light* (*Nattens ljus,* uncredited; 1957, dir. Kjellgren), *The Pleasure Garden* (*Lustgården,* with Erland Josephson; 1961, dir. Alf Kjellin), *The Reservation* (*Reservatet,* for Swedish television; 1970, dir. Jan Malander), *The Lie* (BBC "Play for Today"; 1970, dir. Alan Bridges).[4]

Index

249